The Jewish Cultural Tapestry

OXFORD UNIVERSITY PRESS ✦ NEW YORK ✦ 2000

The Jewish Cultural Tapestry

International Jewish Folk Traditions

STEVEN M. LOWENSTEIN

Oxford University Press

Oxford   New York

Athens   Auckland   Bangkok   Bogatá   Buenos Aires   Calcutta
Cape Town   Chennai   Dar es Salaam   Delhi   Florence   Hong Kong   Istanbul
Karachi   Kuala Lumpur   Madrid   Melbourne   Mexico City   Mumbai
Nairobi   Paris   São Paulo   Shanghai   Singapore   Taipei   Tokyo   Toronto   Warsaw

and associated companies in

Berlin   Ibadan

Published by Oxford University Press, Inc.
198 Madison Avenue, New York, New York 10016

Oxford is a registered trademark of Oxford University Press

Book design by Carla Bolte; maps by Carto-Graphics

Library of Congress Cataloging-in-Publication Data

Lowenstein, Steven M., 1945–
    The Jewish cultural tapestry : international Jewish folk traditions / Steven M. Lowenstein.
        p.   cm.
    Includes bibliographical references.
    ISBN 0–19–513425–7
    1. Jews—Social life and customs.   2. Judaism—Customs and practices.   3. Judaism—Social aspects.
    4. Cookery, Jewish.   5. Jews—Music.   I. Title.

DS112.L76 2000
305.892'4—dc21
                                                                                        99–088194

1   3   5   7   9   8   6   4   2

Printed in the United States of America
on acid-free paper

To my family with love

Contents

✦ FOLK TRADITIONS ✦

What Are They and Why Do They
Vary Geographically?

✦ REGIONAL CULTURES ✦

From Jerusalem to Spain, Poland, and Morocco:
The Influence of Jewish Migrations

Acknowledgments

THIS PROJECT, MORE THAN ANY THAT I HAVE UNDERTAKEN, IS THE PRODUCT OF the efforts of a large number of people. Some of the ideas, which eventually were incorporated in this book, go back to the training I received as an interviewer and researcher for the Language and Culture Atlas of Ashkenazic Jewry in the 1960s. The director of the Atlas, Uriel Weinreich and his assistant director at that time, Marvin Herzog, went out of their way to train me and give me the rudiments of linguistic theory as well as practical knowledge of the Yiddish language. They spent countless hours explaining their ideas to me and were willing to devote a great deal of effort to me, although I was only 20 years old at the time. Mordkhe Schechter, one of my colleagues at the Atlas, devoted much effort and zeal to get me to learn the Yiddish language. I owe many of the insights, which led to this book to fascinating courses I audited at the Max Weinreich Center for Advanced Jewish Studies at the YIVO Institute for Jewish Research in New York. Especially influential were two memorable courses, one on Jewish vernacular languages given by Haim Blanc, and the other on Jewish folklore given by Barbara Kirshenblatt-Gimblett. I picked up first hand knowledge of a non-Ashkenazic Jewish culture during the year (1969) I spent in Montpellier, France, working on my dissertation in French history. I attended a North African synagogue, was invited for Sabbath and holiday dinners by community members and was treated with great hospitality. The Elkyess and Kalfa families were especially hospitable and we have remained in contact. In the mid 1970s our family belonged to a congregation of Sephardic Jews from Greece in Highland Park, New Jersey and we were exposed to new melodies, languages, and customs.

The students of my class "Jewish Folk Traditions around the World," who used an early version of this book, gave me valuable feedback which helped me improve it. I owe a special debt of gratitude to David Greenfield, formerly my student and now resource center media coordinator at the Skirball Cultural Center in Los Angeles. David's computer graphic skills helped me get many of my ideas into usable charts and maps at an early stage of this project. Someday I hope we will be able to realize our joint dream of creating an interactive, multimedia method of presenting our ideas on Jewish folk traditions around the world.

My friend and colleague Prof. David Ellenson of Hebrew Union College, Los Angeles, read the entire first draft of this book and gave me much valuable advice and encouragement. My colleagues at the University of Judaism, Professors Susan Kapitanoff, Ziony Zevit, and Aryeh Cohen, read sections of this book and gave me valuable help. I am thankful to my friend Leonard Korobkin for the good advice he gave me on some of the business aspects connected with this book.

A number of persons at Oxford University Press played an important role in making the appearance of this book possible. Nancy Lane, with whom I had my initial contact, gave me encouragement and advice during the early stages of proposing this project. Thomas Le Bien did a large part of the work, which enabled me to go from a vague project to a completed manuscript. It was a pleasure consulting with him and working out the details about how the book would be constructed and what kinds of illustrative material would go into it. Susan Ferber, my editor during the final phases of publication, helped guide it to a successful conclusion and smoothed over many problems which came up. Liz Szaluta, who was in charge of production, patiently answered my many questions, and rapidly and patiently replied to my many messages.

I wish to thank all the archives which supplied me with photo reproductions and other materials for this book, as well as the institutions and individuals who generously gave their permission to use their photographs and collections. A list of these individuals and institutions appears in the credits section of this book. Among those with whom I was in contact, I would like to give special thanks to a few individuals who went beyond the call of duty to be helpful. These include Zippi Rosenne of the Visual Documentation Center of the Diaspora Museum in Tel Aviv, and Susanne Kester of the Skirball Cultural Center in Los Angeles. Adaire Klein of the Simon Wiesenthal Center Library in Los Angeles gave both advice and practical aid. Emily Rose, whose fascinating family history, *Portraits of Our Past: Jews of the German Countryside* will be published this year by the Jewish Publication Society, helped me in a number of ways. I hope that I will be forgiven if I omitted any of the names of those who helped me. I am grateful to all of them.

My special thanks goes to the personnel of the mail room at the University of Judaism who endured my frequent rush mailings and helped smooth delivery of my voluminous correspondence concerning the illustrations and publications rights for this book. Their unfailing efficiency and cooperation is much appreciated.

Finally, my greatest thanks go to my wife Marilynn, whose patience and encouragement made this book possible. I hope her fondest wishes for the success of this book are fulfilled beyond her expectations.

Introduction

WORKING ON THIS BOOK HAS BEEN A DEPARTURE BOTH FROM MY OWN USUAL scholarly pursuits and from previous approaches to this subject. My own writing up to now has been focused on the close analysis of the process of modernization of German Jewry. It has dealt with carefully delimited topics and been addressed mainly to an audience of scholars and specialists. This volume, on the other hand, is a study of a very wide field—Jewish folk tradition—covering the entire world settled by Jews before the nineteenth century and all of Jewish history; it is addressed to the educated lay reader. There was no way for anyone to know all the subjects I cover in the detail that a scholarly specialist would know. Yet I felt that a general overview of the entire subject was the only way to achieve my goals. I wanted to present the overall structure of Jewish culture, to compare and contrast Jewish folk traditions in various parts of the world, seeking similarities and differences among them. I was looking for patterns that applied widely rather than details of a single narrow aspect. Only a comparative study of a large number of regions and a large number of aspects of folk life would enable me to discover the overall patterns I sought to describe.

This book makes no claims to represent the latest in scholarship on the Jews of Yemen or India or China. It is written for the general reader who, I hope, shares my interest in a broad, general overview. In most cases I have not undertaken original research in the many fields covered by this book (the exceptions are in

Ashkenazic linguistic and musical traditions). I have endeavored to be as accurate as possible. I have read very widely in the abundant secondary literature available on Jewish traditions, which allowed me to benefit from the scholarly discoveries of others and to apply the techniques of scholarly research in order to choose among rival claims made in the various sources. I did not want to fall into the trap, characterizing many books on "exotic" Jewish communities, of making very vague claims, presenting flawed information, or going way beyond my sources in reconstructing the past. My goal was a popular book, but one true to the standards of scholarly excellence.

What makes this book popular rather than scholarly, besides its reliance on secondary sources, is its style. I have tried to write in a conversational tone using the kind of language I would use when giving a talk to a general audience or teaching a class. Unless absolutely necessary, I have not used technical terms and, when it was necessary, I have tried to give clear explanations of the terms. From time to time I have even tried to inject some humor into the narrative (successfully, I hope). I have also left out all footnotes and almost all source references in the text. For those interested in further reading and in the main sources of the ideas presented in this book, I have provided a bibliography of the major works in the field.

Jewish folk traditions have long fascinated me, even though they have not been the focus of my scholarly work until now. One stimulus for this interest comes from my own background. I grew up in Washington Heights, a traditional German Jewish community in New York City, where many Western Ashkenazic folk traditions in music, cuisine, and synagogue liturgy were still practiced. By the time I was a teenager, I had already noticed how different these traditions were from the Eastern Ashkenazic traditions, which predominated outside our little community, and discussed them with others (probably to their annoyance). By a series of coincidences in college, I was selected as an interviewer of German Jews for the *Language and Culture Atlas of Ashkenazic Jewry* at Columbia University. There I was introduced to the concepts of linguistic geography and to the idea, which horrified most of the members of the German Jewish community, that what we considered German contained many remnants of the now extinct Western Yiddish dialects.

After college, these interests became dormant until 1979, when I was asked to teach courses in the Continuing Education program at the University of Judaism, in addition to my regular academic courses. I began to develop a "repertoire" of courses on genealogy, Jewish folk traditions, and Jewish languages. The students of these courses, mostly adults, some of them with direct knowledge of Jewish folk traditions in their own families, always expressed great enthusiasm about the subject, asking me to recommend a book for further reading. I always had to tell them that there was no single book covering all the subjects I discussed, but rather a large number of works on specific aspects. Eventually I came to the conclusion that I should try to write the book that wasn't available elsewhere. That was the genesis of this volume. In the spring of 1998, I taught this subject for the first time as a regular undergraduate course using an early draft of this book. Again there was a great deal of enthusiasm. I owe many thanks to the students of History 290—"Jewish Folk Traditions around the World"—for their suggestions and feedback.

In this study, I have emphasized precisely those aspects of the Jewish tradition that have received the least emphasis (and certainly the least systematic treatment). Most Jewish religious education introduces students to the sacred texts and the general history of the Jews, but it rarely addresses the largely unwritten folk traditions that once loomed so large in Jewish life. The contemporary member of the Jewish community who has received some formal Jewish education is faced with a strange gap. What do the biblical or talmudic texts composed in the Middle East thousands of years ago have to do with the recent traditions of his or her family that stem from Eastern Europe, North Africa, or Yemen? One of the goals of this book is to bridge this gap by showing the interrelationship between these two aspects of Jewish life—the ancient written tradition and more recent local traditions.

Many books about Jewish traditions in various parts of the world emphasize the picturesque, exotic, and "primitive." Much more has been written about the customs of the far-off Jews of Yemen, Ethiopia, and Kurdistan than about the more familiar Ashkenazic Jews of Northern Europe. The tone of many of the descriptions of these "Jews of the East" is in the style, that Edward Said has called

"Orientalism," emphasizing the strangeness of the "mysterious East." In this book I have consciously avoided this Orientalist style. I have tried to make no distinction between the way I describe the customs and folkways of European, Asian, and African Jews. The emphasis has been on comparison, not on exoticism.

This book is intended as an introduction to a very broad and complex field. I could cover only a tiny percentage of the many aspects of Jewish traditional culture that are available for study. My intention is to give food for thought and to whet the appetite of the readers so that they will wish to explore this exciting subject further. I hope you will find this book to be as enjoyable, entertaining, and enlightening as it was to write.

The Jewish Cultural Tapestry

$\mathcal{F}$olk $\mathcal{T}$raditions

What Are They and Why Do They Vary Geographically?

WHAT IS IT THAT HAS MADE THE JEWISH PEOPLE, SCATTERED ALL OVER THE WORLD for over 2000 years, one people despite the lack of a homeland for most of that time? The answer, in the words of the Broadway musical *Fiddler on the Roof*, is "tradition." At least until the beginning of modern times, Jews shared a common devotion to the Torah. Torah meant both a set of books (the Five Books of Moses) and a common set of religious norms, laws, and practices that they could carry with them wherever they went. The Torah and its tradition taught Jews that they were descendants of the same ancestors, had been slaves in Egypt, had entered the Holy Land, and then had been expelled because of their sins. Study

of the Torah and the other sacred texts, as well as prayers, were conducted in Hebrew, the shared ancestral language of the Israelites.

The Great Tradition and the Little Tradition

Even though Jews felt such strong ties to a common book, a common tradition, and a common ancestry, they differed from each other tremendously. This wasn't only evidence of the truth of the proverb "two Jews, three opinions," it was a result of the fact that the same tradition that held the Jews of the world together also separated them.

Actually it wasn't the same tradition. Jewish culture, like all other major traditions, really consists of two parts: the official culture and the folk culture, or, as anthropologists like to put it, the "great tradition" and the "little tradition." The great tradition, written in books and enshrined in the laws of the Jewish religion, was the uniting factor. It stretched back to ancient times and described the very beginning of the Jewish people. It spoke of their heroic common ancestors—Abraham, Isaac, and Jacob; Sarah, Rebecca, Rachel, and Leah. The great tradition had an advantage that was particularly important for the Jews—it was portable. Wherever Jews went, they could take their books with them. Because all Jewish scholars and many Jewish laymen (but not most Jewish women) were literate in the common Hebrew-Aramaic language, they could read what Jews in other lands wrote with little difficulty. If scholars wrote new works, the manuscripts could make their way to other countries to be copied or printed there. Jews of Yemen studied the Bible and Talmud commentaries of Rashi born in eleventh century France, just as Jews in Poland could study the works of Maimonides, born in twelfth century Spain. Neither time nor place made much difference. Once something was written down and codified, it was made permanent.

But Jewish communities never enshrined all of their culture in books. No book, even the most holy or the most comprehensive, could include every detail of life. There was always room for filling in the details not codified in the great tradition through the creation and practice of Jewish folk tradition (the little tradition). Folk traditions, which were intended to make the pages of the written tradition come to life, had completely different characteristics from the great tradition. Since they were not written down, they could not be passed down at a distance. They depended on example, word of mouth, and local conditions. They could be learned only from people with whom one came into personal contact.

The little tradition learned through the family and the community did not have the ancient pedigree of the Bible and the Talmud. It did not require formal education to acquire the little tradition, as it did to learn the texts of the great tradition. But for the unlearned, probably always the majority, it was the little tradition to which they had the greatest emotional attachment. The melodies of family and synagogue rituals, holiday foods, spoken language, proverbs, and lifestyle were what gave flavor to Judaism. The holy texts might be venerated, respected, and even obeyed, but they seemed more distant from daily life. The common people knew the great tradition of Jewish religion mainly via the little tradition of the life of their own communities.

When you look at the great and little traditions from the outside, the tremendous gap between the two becomes apparent. The world of the Bible and of ancient Judaism seems very distant from the world of the Eastern European small town (*shtetl*) or North African ghetto (*mellah*). Whatever Moses looked like, he certainly did not look like a nineteenth century Polish Hasid. Whatever Jews of the biblical and talmudic period ate, it was not gefilte fish or falafel. The little tradition seems much more recent, more folksy, less exalted, more down to earth. You can see the difference even in language—between Hebrew, the language of text, and the various spoken languages of the Jews. This is expressed in Yiddish by the way in which both languages are labeled. Hebrew is *loshn koydesh*, or the Holy Language, but Yiddish is *mame loshn*, or the mother tongue.

Sometimes it is hard to see the connection between the two types of tradition. How does the religion and ethos of the Bible turn into the religion and the ethos of the nineteenth century Diaspora? In this book I will trace some of the historic stages that led from the earliest periods of Jewish history to the very different recent patterns. I will look at how Jews moved from their homeland to the various lands in which they settled. I will compare the various local traditions and look at how they fit together in similar structures despite their differences. But in the end, there will be many aspects of the folk tradition whose relationship to ancient Jewish roots cannot be documented. A telling example of the tenuous connection between modern Jewishness and the Jewishness of the Bible is furnished by genealogy. It is a firm part of the faith of most Jews that they are the descendants of Abraham, Isaac, and Jacob. In the blessings for Chanukah, for instance, all recite the words "who has done miracles *for our ancestors* in those days at this season." Yet, it is virtually impossible for any Jew researching a family tree to go back further than a few hundred years. Almost all Jews except recent converts can connect themselves directly to a specific little tradition, whether Yemenite, Eastern European, or Persian, but almost no one can prove that their ancestors really were biblical Israelites. Their descent has to be taken on faith.

But it is not origin alone that makes a person or a cultural trait Jewish. Even a cultural practice whose origin is demonstrably not Jewish can be Jewish to the core because it performs a Jewish function. When one culture borrows an element from another culture, it can do so in one of two ways: It can assimilate to the outside culture by taking on characteristics of the other culture in order to become a part of its society; alternatively, it can incorporate a feature of an outside culture into its own culture and make it its own. Traditional Judaism was highly adept at the second process—borrowing and "Judaizing" traits belonging to the people among whom the Jews lived. Considering only their origins, Yiddish is primarily a Germanic language, borsht is a Russian food, some Hasidic tunes are Ukrainian shepherds' songs, and the hora is a Romanian dance. But when a culture adopts a practice from another culture, it gives the practice a function within its own culture that changes its meaning. If Jews take a Polish or Moroccan Berber food and associate it with a particular Jewish holiday observance, the food becomes a Jewish food. When a Hasid today wears a fur hat that may be the same as hats worn by Polish noblemen of the seventeenth century, he is not wearing a Polish hat; he is wearing a Hasidic costume. In adopting foreign traits, Jews have changed the meaning (a shepherd's melody becomes a religious tune), the form (a German, Polish, or Arab food has its recipe changed to make it kosher; an Arabic amulet acquires a Hebrew inscription), or the function (a Mardi Gras food becomes a Purim food). Very often a practice that the Jews originally borrowed from their neighbors becomes Jewish because non-Jews stop practicing it, or Jews migrate to a new country where no one but Jews practice it.

Often cultural traits that have different origins and different appearances are tied together by a common function. A good example is the Jewish Sabbath lunch food in various parts of the world. The names differ, the basic ingredients differ, and therefore the tastes differ greatly. But these dishes share the common characteristic that they can simmer slowly for many hours overnight. They therefore fulfill the common function of obeying the Jewish tradition requiring warm food on the Sabbath but forbidding cooking (except where the process began before sundown on Friday). Accordingly, these foods are functionally the same, even though their outward characteristics are different. Something similar can be said about the relationship between the Ashkenazic Jewish name Katz and the Italian Jewish name Sacerdote, which don't sound alike but both mean Cohen or Jewish priest. These examples can be multiplied by the hundreds. It could be predicted that any local Jewish culture will have certain items—a Sabbath food, a way of covering the Torah, a method of Torah cantillation, a melody or chant for Kol Nidre—but how that item will taste, look, or sound, remains unpredictable.

Because the little tradition was not written down but had to be learned by word of mouth, it varied from place to place. Members of Jewish communities only knew the folk traditions that they themselves had seen. They incorrectly assumed that the way things were done in their town was the way things were done throughout the Jewish world. But in other parts of the world with which they had no personal contact, different local traditions developed from the same written great tradition. As long as the bearers of local traditions did not encounter each other in person, they could not influence each other.

The more stationary a population, the more isolated its local traditions. But the Jews as a group were less sedentary than their neighbors, who were mostly farmers. Many of them were merchants who traveled large distances on business and came into contact with people from other regions. Therefore Jewish local traditions never developed in total isolation; although each community had its own nuances, local traditions generally resembled those of communities in nearby towns. Jewish little traditions often stretched over large areas. This was especially true because the Jewish population also migrated, sometimes over large distances, taking traditions born in one region to new areas where conditions were totally different.

The result of Jewish migrations and Jewish business travel was neither total uniformity of Jewish customs around the world nor extreme local variation. Instead Jewish little traditions were regional, often covering large areas but still remaining markedly different from one cultural region to another. In later chapters, about a dozen Jewish cultural regions will be described, each of which can be broken down into subregions with more subtle differences among them.

Cultural Boundaries

Students of linguistics and ethnography (the studies of languages and culture) have developed the idea of the cultural boundary, which scholars refer to as "isoglosses" or "isopleths." They generally theorize that sharp cultural boundaries or bundles of isoglosses are evidence of communications barriers. So, if a mountain range separates two groups of people, their dialects differ because the range greatly restricted personal contact between people on either side of the mountains. Instead, the people near the mountains are in closer contact with the valleys on their side of the range. Other communications barriers might be oceans, rivers, forests or political boundaries.

The various Jewish cultures are an interesting check on the theory of communications barriers. Because Jews were almost always in the minority in their places of residence, they shared the same territory with another culture and sometimes with more than one culture. If a mountain range or river was a communications barrier, it would be expected to perform the same function for both Jews and non-Jews. If, as is frequently the case, the geographical patterns within Jewish culture are not the same as those of the non-Jews living in the same area, an important question about communications barriers is raised. It is not that such barriers had no effect on Jewish culture, but rather that different factors were communications barriers for Jews than for non-Jews.

A political boundary might have had no effect on non-Jewish cultural communications, but it could have been a barrier to Jews who were not allowed to cross the frontier. A river that served as a barrier to non-Jewish communications might be no barrier at all to itinerant Jewish merchants who crossed the river frequently. Differences in settlement history might also create different patterns. A certain area might have been settled very late by the Jewish population (or alternatively, the Jews from the area could have been expelled). Because of this, when Jews did settle in the area, they came from both sides of the previously "uninhabited areas" and the isoglosses all crossed the "new territory." This is the reason, for instance, that the main cultural boundaries among Jews in Germany before World War II divided the east from the west. By contrast, the main cultural boundaries among German non-Jews divided the north from the south.

It is the nature of the development of tradition that oral culture can become fixed once it is written down. In the course of Jewish history the codified practices constantly grew in number and importance. Many a practice that began as a folk practice could end up as a part of the written law, such as the bar mitzvah, or the Ashkenazic prohibition on eating beans on Passover. Once something became a part of the written tradition, available in books, it was much less likely to disappear than were practices that were merely part of the oral little tradition. Such written practices were probably more likely to spread than those that no one thought worthy of writing down.

Reasons for Local Variations

Although more and more practices were codified as written laws, it was impossible for all practices to be written down. Without a system of Western notation,

Jewish liturgical music could not be put into a fixed written form. Its performance would always depend on traditions passed down orally. Patterns of dress were also not easily recorded in writing. One might prohibit a particular item (perhaps luxurious clothes that were considered improper or that showed too much of the human body to outsiders) and require another article of clothing (for instance, a hair covering for married women), but it was impossible to codify every detail of dress. Color, cut, type of material, style of embroidery or sewing, and types of ornaments were too complicated to prescribe in a law code. Even if they were prescribed, it was almost impossible to enforce so many details. The same pattern is true of Jewish food customs. Certain items or combinations could be forbidden or required, but it was impossible to prescribe an exact recipe. Even if an item of clothing or a festive food had the same name in two different places, it was not necessarily the same.

Other local variations in the tradition resulted from the conditions prevailing in different lands. The foods eaten by a particular cultural group depended largely on the availability of various staples. In premodern times, the group was generally restricted to foodstuffs grown in the immediate surroundings. The foods of Jews in a cold climate would necessarily differ from those living in a subtropical area. Jews, like all other inhabitants, would be affected by whether the main grain of their region was rye, wheat, or rice and by what fruits or vegetables were available on the market. The languages that Jews spoke among themselves were largely influenced by the languages their neighbors spoke. Sometimes they picked up a version of their neighbors' language and sometimes they brought a spoken language, such as Yiddish or Ladino, from a previous migration. But even in the latter case, they adopted all sorts of words, phrases, and grammatical forms from the languages spoken around them.

This book will concentrate on those aspects of Jewish tradition and culture not found in the Holy Books. It will deal specifically with the little traditions. This exploration does not intend merely to list variations demonstrating that there was much diversity within Judaism. That seems obvious. Instead, this book attempts to look at the geographic differences in Jewish tradition in a comparative way. Exploring common functions and different forms in music, costume, language, religious rites, and names, this book will trace the stages of migration that have created the various Jewish folk traditions and will look at the cultures that have influenced these traditions. Although this book will contain a great deal of description of specific items of food, clothing, and ritual, I will link them to the basic analytic themes of this study:

1. The great tradition as outline and the little tradition as content
2. The interplay between common function and different origins
3. Similarities and differences between Jews and their neighbors
4. The relationship between outside cultural and natural forces (like climate) and internal belief systems

All of these subthemes will help to answer the basic question raised by the material to be explored: Why are Jews in different countries so similar to and so different from one another, and why are they so similar to and so different from their non-Jewish neighbors?

Regional Cultures

From Jerusalem to Spain, Poland, and Morocco:

The Influence of Jewish Migrations

Introduction: The Chief Regional Jewish Cultures

For over 2500 years, Jewish life has been marked by the coexistence of a Jewish national homeland in the Land of Israel and a Diaspora (the Greek word for "dispersion") outside the homeland. For most of these centuries, the Jewish population of the dispersion far outnumbered those in the "center," and they often had greater influence on world Jewish life than did Israel. Sometimes Jewish life in the Jewish homeland was virtually nonexistent—for instance, after the Crusaders captured Jerusalem in 1099. The Jews were dispersed to many lands and came into contact with many different peoples, climates, languages, and ways of life.

Jews were not the only dispersed people in the world. Others included the Armenians, the Parsees (Zoroastrians in India), the overseas Chinese, and the Gypsies. Except perhaps for the Gypsies, none were quite as dispersed as the Jews. Like other migrants, Jews moved from one place to another for one of two reasons. They were attracted (pulled) to a new land by economic opportunity, adventure, and a chance to start anew, or they were escaping (pushed) from an old country because of religious persecution, financial hardship, warfare, or general chaos. Sometimes push and pull combined to motivate Jews to change location.

To understand how Jews got from Jerusalem to such distant places as Krakow, Poland, Kaifeng, China, and Gondar, Ethiopia, we have to look both at the history of the Jews and at the history and cultures of the peoples among whom they ended up living. In the early part of the story, military conquests and invasions play an important role. In later times, persecutions and economic opportunity are often more important. Throughout the story, long periods of stability alternated with periods of rapid change. Sometimes Jews were very open to the new cultures they came into contact with and rapidly learned their languages, customs, and habits. At other times they seemed to hang on tenaciously to the culture of the Old Country (whatever the Old Country happened to be) and avoided becoming like the peoples among whom they lived.

At the end of over 2000 years of wandering, Jews found themselves scattered over a wide area with many different local cultures, but the range of their dispersion was not unlimited. Jews did not go everywhere (at least not until very recently), nor were they influenced by all the cultures of the world. There were no Jews before the nineteenth century in central and southern Africa, Japan, Indochina, Siberia, Ireland, Australia, or Scandinavia (except for Denmark). Only a tiny number settled in the Americas before 1800.

Before beginning a historical outline of how the Jews got to where they ended up living, a quick survey of the main geographic and cultural areas in which Jews lived is in order. Often people speak of Ashkenazic (northern European) and Sephardic (Mediterranean) Jews, but this distinction is much too simple to explain all the various Jewish traditions.

We can draw a kind of "family tree" of the various descendants of ancient Judaism (Table 2.1). Some of these descendants, like Christianity of course, have ceased to be part of Judaism and will not be dealt with in this book. Others, which will be addressed, branched off from the rabbinic Judaism that became the normative Jewish tradition. Some of these nonrabbinic Jews, like the Samaritans, were already a separate group during the time of the Second Temple (Time Line), but others, like the Karaites, separated in the Middle Ages over 1000 years later. The Samaritans and Karaites continued to use the Bible and other holy books in Hebrew, but two other nonrabbinic Jewish groups, the Bene Israel of India and the Beta Israel of Ethiopia, forgot (or never learned) the Hebrew language.

The distinction between rabbinic and nonrabbinic Jews is the most basic subdivision of the Jewish people in premodern times. By comparison with the groups just mentioned, the rabbinic Jews shared many things: the Hebrew language, the basic structure of the prayer book, the same holidays, and the same structure of Jewish religious law. Still there was plenty of room for local and regional differences. There are alternative ways of classifying the major subdivisions of the rabbinic Jews. They can be divided by (1) traditions of Hebrew pronunciation, prayer book liturgy, and liturgical music; (2) spoken traditional Jewish language; or (3) settlement history. These classifications overlap to some extent but also show important differences. The most profound divisions based on our first criterion are three: Ashkenazic, Sephardic-Oriental, and Yemenite (Map 2.1). These three cultural groups and their major traits will be explained in the following chapter. There are many subgroups within the three divisions, some of them fairly substantial. As will be shown later, the Jews of Italy form a kind of transitional group between the Ashkenazic and Sephardic-Oriental groups.

When it comes to grouping by traditional vernacular language, the divisions are more complicated than a three-way split. In order to follow the complicated divisions and subdivisions, it will be helpful to look at Map 2.2. No fewer than nine main groups of Jewish languages spoken by rabbinic Jews survived into modern times (and a few more became extinct before then). Most of these

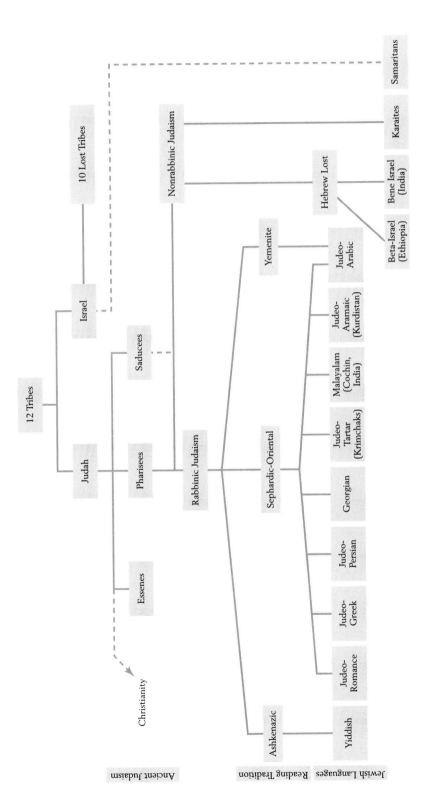

Table 2.1a Genealogy of Chief Jewish Cultural Groups

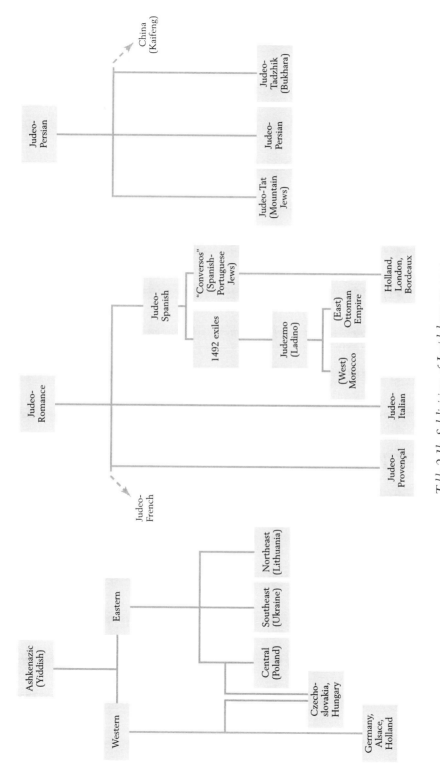

Table 2.1b Subdivisions of Jewish language groups

	Political History	Migration History
1800		
	1772–1795 Partitions of Poland	
1700		
1600		
	1569 Union of Lublin between Poland and Lithuania	1450–1550 Main period of Ashkenazic migration to Eastern Europe
1500	1492 Expulsion of Jews from Spain	
1400		
1300		
1200		
1100		
1000		First Ashkenazic Jews
900		
800		Conversion of Khazars to Judaism
700	711 Muslim conquest of Spain	Beginning of Karaite movement
600	Founding of Islam	
500	476 Fall of Roman Empire	
400		
300	312 Christianization of Roman Empire	
200		
100 CE		
	70 Destruction of Second Temple	Beginning of Christianity
0		
100 BCE	63 Roman conquest of Judea	Beginning of Jewish settlement in Roman Empire
	168–165 Maccabee revolt against the Greeks	146 Beginning of Roman conquest of Greek lands
200		
300	333 Alexander the Great conquers the Persians	Beginning of Jewish contact with Greek culture (Hellenism)
400		Samaritans separate from Jews
500	515 Second Temple building completed	Beginning of Iranian Jewry
	538 Babylonians conquered by Persians	Beginning of Iraqi Jewry
600	587 Jerusalem conquered by Babylonians	
700		"Ten Lost Tribes"
	721 Northern Kingdom of Israel conquered by Assyrians	
800		

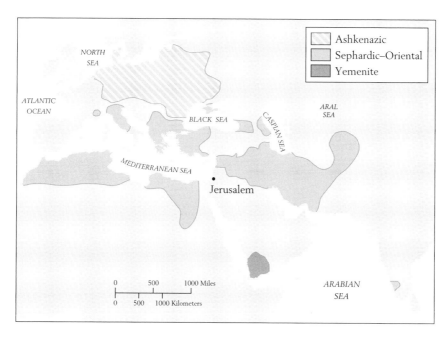

Map 2.1 Main traditions of Hebrew pronunciation

groups have further subdivisions. The approximate order of size, from largest to smallest, during the nineteenth century was:

1. Ashkenazic Jews in Central and Eastern Europe, whose traditional language, Yiddish, was mainly Germanic in origin. Around 1900 they numbered over 10 million.
2. Approximately 470,000 Jews speaking various types of Judeo-Arabic. One subgroup, the Jews of Yemen, had traditions that differed greatly from those of the others. Other Arabic-speaking Jews were to be found in almost every Arabic-speaking country (Iraq, Syria, Lebanon, Egypt, Libya, Tunisia, Algeria, and Morocco) except Sudan, Jordan, and Saudi Arabia.
3. Jews speaking languages of Romance origin. The best-known group among these were the approximately 400,000 Sephardim who spoke a language of mainly Spanish origin. After their expulsion from Spain, Jews carried this Judeo-Spanish language (which was also known as Djudezmo or Ladino) to the Turkish Empire (what is now Greece, Turkey, Bulgaria, Romania, Bosnia,

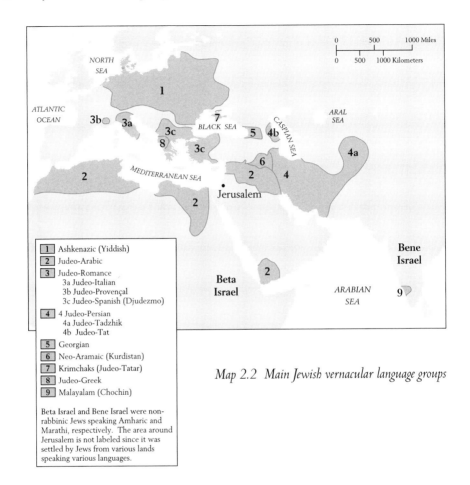

Map 2.2 Main Jewish vernacular language groups

Macedonia, and Serbia). Others settled in Morocco. Later, former Conversos, that is, Jews who had converted to Christianity at least outwardly, escaped from Spain and Portugal and settled in Amsterdam, London, Hamburg, Bordeaux, and other Western European ports.

A less well known group was the ancient Jewish community of Italy, numbering some 45,000, which has survived to this day. The Judeo-French-speaking community disappeared after the medieval expulsions of Jews from France, but a small group of Jews speaking Judeo-Provençal survived in the area around the southern French town of Avignon up to the early twentieth century.

4. Approximately 90,000 Jews speaking languages of Persian origin. Besides the Jews of Iran, these included the Bukharan Jews, the "Mountain Jews" in the Caucasus Mountains in parts of the former Soviet Union, and the Jews of Afghanistan. The now-extinct Jewish community of medieval China was also descended from this group.
5. About 20,000 Georgian-speaking Jews in the former Soviet Republic of Georgia.
6. The 10,000–15,000 Aramaic-speaking Jews of Kurdistan in northern Iraq.
7. The 3500 or so Krimchaks, rabbinic Jews living on the now Ukrainian peninsula of Crimea, who spoke a Tatar language.
8. From 3000 to 5000 Jews in the Yanina region (Epirus) of northern Greece who spoke a Jewish dialect of Greek, unlike the other Greek Jews, who spoke Judeo-Spanish (see group 3).
9. From 1500 to 2000 Jews of Cochin in southern India, who spoke an Indian language (Malayalam).

As will become clear in the following chapter, Jews sometimes spoke their own version of the language of their non-Jewish neighbors and sometimes spoke a language totally different from (and incomprehensible to) the non-Jews.

Migration History

Migrations played a large role in creating the subdivisions outlined above. In most cases, the migration history helps to explain the linguistic patterns of the various Jewish groups, but sometimes groups of Jews changed languages even when they did not migrate. Because so many migrations happened over so long a period of time, this summary will be very rapid (covering about 200 years or more per page in places). Again the narrative is accompanied by maps and time lines. First, we will refer mainly to the map of Asia (Map 2.3).

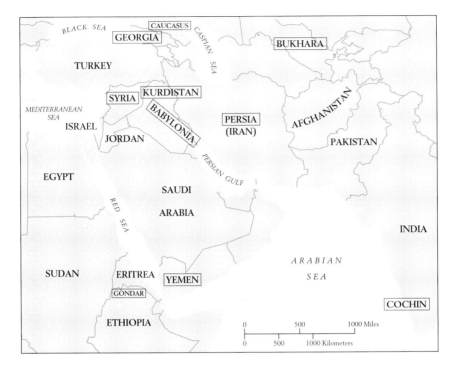

Map 2.3 Jewish settlement areas in Asia

The story of the Jewish Diaspora begins in the year 587 BCE, when the Judean kingdom was conquered by the Babylonians, who destroyed the Temple in Jerusalem. A large proportion of the Jewish population of Judea was exiled from the land and taken by force to Babylonia (what is now the southern part of Iraq). Jewish settlement in Iraq continued uninterruptedly from the time of this first exile until the years immediately following the creation of the State of Israel in 1948, when most of the Iraqi Jews emigrated to Israel.

There were Jews in Iraq long before it was an Arab country or a Muslim one. The ancient Babylonians spoke an ancient Semitic language called Akkadian (and later Chaldean); their religion was polytheistic. Later the Aramaic language (originally the language of Syria) became the official language of Babylonia and the entire eastern Mediterranean. It wasn't until the Arab conquest of the seventh century (1200 years after the arrival of the first Jews) that the population of Iraq learned Arabic and adopted the Muslim religion.

Actually the Babylonian exile was not the first exile of the Israelites. First there was the Israelite slavery in Egypt mentioned in the Bible. Later the Israelite kingdom of David and Solomon was divided between the north (Israel, with its capital in Samaria) and south (Judah, with its capital in Jerusalem). The northern kingdom was conquered by the Assyrians of northern Iraq in 721 BCE and its population deported. What became of the deportees of the northern kingdom, no one knows. Referred to as the Ten Lost Tribes, they have been the subject of countless legends, but no real ascertainable facts.

The Assyrian exile also created a second subgroup of Israelites. It was Assyrian policy to deport residents of various provinces they conquered and mix them together with the old native populations in order to make it more difficult for the conquered nations to rebel. When the Ten Lost Tribes were deported to Assyria, some of the populations of other areas in the Assyrian Empire were brought to the conquered area around Samaria. Later known as the Samaritans, these people eventually converted to a form of Judaism but were not accepted by the main body of Jews who returned to build the Second Temple in Jerusalem (see below). Among their differences from other Israelites were their rejection of Jerusalem as the site of the Holy Temple and their use of a different Hebrew alphabet and a different calendar. While they consider themselves descendants of the ancient Israelites, they are called Cuthim in the Talmud, implying that they are non-Jews from Cutha in southern Iraq. Once there were many thousand Samaritans, but today only a few hundred survive—in Nablus on the West Bank and in Holon, a suburb of Tel Aviv.

Returning to the fate of the Judean exiles in Babylonia, tradition says that their exile lasted only 70 years. But even before the 70 years were up, the Babylonian Empire was conquered by the Persians under King Cyrus (538 BCE). The Persian Empire was much larger than the Babylonian Empire had ever been; as the Book of Esther says, it ruled "from [the border of] India to [the border of] Ethiopia." It controlled the whole of what is now the east coast of the Mediterranean, including much of today's Turkey, as well as Iraq, today's Iran, areas of what was Soviet Central Asia, and even Egypt (Map 2.4). In the western part of their empire the Persians used Aramaic as their official language, and in the eastern part they used Persian (a non-Semitic Indo-European language).

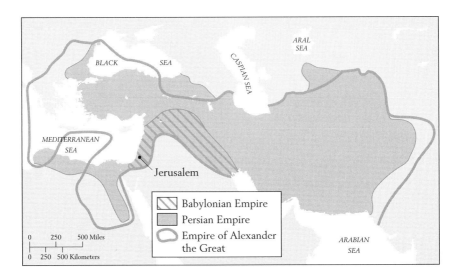

Map 2.4 Boundaries of ancient empires

Cyrus permitted the Jews to return to their homeland and rebuild the Temple in Jerusalem and, over the next century and a half, waves of Jewish migrants returned. But the majority of the Jews remained in their new homes in Babylonia and in other parts of the Persian Empire. The Persian-speaking Jews of Iran, like the Jews of Iraq, could look back on 2500 years of uninterrupted Jewish settlement.

The Aramaic language, which was the official language of the western half of the Persian Empire, had a tremendous influence on the Jews. The Jewish prayer book contains a number of prayers in Aramaic, most notably the Kaddish. Some of the most important religious works of rabbinic Judaism, including the Talmud, were written in the Aramaic language.

The next major change in Jewish migrations again resulted from the conquest of the empire in which the Jews lived. In 333 BCE, Alexander the Great of Macedonia overthrew the Persian Empire and established a Greek-dominated empire of his own. Though, shortly after his death, the empire splintered into a number of warring kingdoms, the Greek influence, known as Hellenism, became dominant throughout the areas which Alexander had conquered. As in earlier

The influence of various offshoots of the Persian language were not limited to the areas that are part of Iran today. To the northwest of today's Iran, in what is now the Russian region of Daghestan and in the northern part of formerly Soviet Azerbaijan, lived the "Mountain Jews." Living in the foothills of the Caucasus Mountains, they were unusual among world Jewry because, like their Christian and Muslim neighbors, they were armed and wore shirts with bandoleers containing ammunition (Illustration 2.1). Jews seem to have arrived in the region in the fifth and sixth Christian eras from Persia. Their language, Judeo-Tat, was related to the dialects of non-Jewish Tats living in the same region, but not necessarily in the same towns, as them.

2.1. Group of armed mountain Jews from the Caucasus, with pockets for cartridges on their chests.

To the northeast of Iran lived the Bukharan Jews. In the Middle Ages these Jews were concentrated in the city of Bukhara, which was the capital of an emirate of the same name. In the nineteenth century they spread to many of the major cities of Uzbekistan, including Samarkand and Tashkent, and neighboring areas. A language closely related to Persian, called Tadzhik, was spoken by many Muslims in Central Asia, especially in what is now known as Tadzhikistan in the former Soviet Union. The Bukharan Jews spoke a version of the Tadzhik language even though they lived mainly among Muslims who spoke Uzbek, a language related to Turkish but not to Persian. In present-day Afghanistan there were also Jews who spoke Judeo-Persian. Finally, sometime in the Middle Ages, a group of Persian-speaking Jews migrated to Kaifeng in central China. We know this because the instructions in their prayer books were in Judeo-Persian. Even though, by the fifteenth century, they were physically indistinguishable from the Chinese, their language and liturgy show that they were an offshoot of Iranian-speaking Jewry.

*A*mong the Jews in the Persian Empire whom we know spoke Aramaic were a strange colony of Jews at Elephantine in Upper Egypt. At the time of the Babylonian conquest of Jerusalem some Jews fled to Egypt, taking the biblical prophet Jeremiah with them against his will. About 150 to 200 years later (at the end of the fifth century BCE), a colony of Jewish soldiers in the Persian army wrote a series of documents and letters in Aramaic that have been preserved. These texts show that they had a temple with sacrifices at Elephantine (despite the biblical prohibition of temples outside of Jerusalem), celebrated Passover, and, it seems, honored several Canaanite goddesses along with the Jewish God.

conquests, the Jews reacted to the conquest by learning a new language and by spreading throughout the conquering empire.

The influence of the Greek culture on the Jews was at least as great as the influence of Aramaic culture. Hellenistic culture was different from other conquering cultures in the ancient Near East because it claimed to be universal and therefore open to (and right for) everyone. This brought Hellenism—in its most extreme form—into conflict with Judaism, the only other national culture in the area with claims of universalism, as can be seen in the famous Chanukah story. When Jewish Hellenists imposed Greek religious rituals on the Temple in Jerusalem and the "Syrian Greek" ruler, part of the Seleucid dynasty, one of the successors of Alexander the Great, forbade many Jewish rites, the Jews, led by Judah Maccabee, revolted against the Greeks in 167 BCE. Not only did they recapture the Temple and cleanse it of Hellenistic influences, but they eventually reestablished Jewish independence. The independent Jewish kingdom, ruled by the descendants of the Maccabee family (the Hasmonean dynasty), remained in existence for about 80 years, from c. 140 to 63 BCE.

Hellenism and Judaism were not merely in conflict; they also influenced each other tremendously. Jews, living in cities dominated by Greek culture scattered throughout the eastern Mediterranean, organized themselves in self-governing communities within the Greek city-states. There they came into contact with many competing philosophies and religions. In this competition the Jews stood out as different for several reasons. Their gathering places, *synagogues* (a Greek word), had neither images of the gods nor animal sacrifices. Their ancient holy book, the Bible, was soon translated into Greek as the Septuagint and became available to educated non-Jews as well as Jews. Because the Bible was available in Greek, large Jewish communities developed whose main, perhaps only, language was Greek and who may not have known Hebrew. The translation of the Bible also resulted in large numbers of non-Jews becoming interested in Judaism, some of whom converted to Judaism and others of whom remained sympathizing "God fearers." In this Diaspora environment, an interpretation of Judaism arose that tried to reconcile it with the dominant culture of the Greeks. Out of this mixed culture emerged not only much of today's Judaism but also early Christianity.

The Greek cultural influence remained dominant over much of the Mediterranean area for centuries, but Greek political influence did not last nearly as long. Within 200 years of Alexander's conquest, the Greek world fell under the military and political domination of the Romans. At first the Jews, who had regained their independence, welcomed the Romans as allies against the Greeks. But after the Greeks were conquered, the Romans turned to Judea and occupied it in 63 BCE. One hundred thirty years later, in 70 CE, the Romans destroyed the Second Temple, and in the ensuing centuries the Jewish population of what the Romans called Palestine declined steadily.

Jews who were displaced by force or who voluntarily left their homeland joined Jews already in the Greek cities to settle within the rest of the Roman Empire. Jews have lived in the city of Rome uninterruptedly since the time of Julius Caesar, over 100 years before the destruction of the Second Temple. Many Romans of good families converted to Judaism, and by one estimate (probably exaggerated), one of every ten inhabitants of the Roman Empire was a Jew. Jews were found all over the Empire: in what are now Syria, Egypt, Greece, Turkey, Libya, Morocco, Spain, Italy, the former Yugoslavia, Hungary, France, and even far-off Germany. The Jewish catacombs, or underground cemeteries, which were discovered in Rome and other places, show that many Jews were assimilated into non-Jewish culture. Their tombstones were usually in Greek (the language of the

Old Country before Rome) rather than in Hebrew (some Jewish inscriptions were also in Latin), though they often had Jewish symbols or the Hebrew word *shalom* in a corner (Illustration 2.2).

The Roman Empire continued to dominate the Mediterranean world for centuries, maintaining order, establishing trade, and uniting much of the Western world. But the Empire began to change and then to decline. The Christians, formerly a despised Jewish sect, became the dominant religion among the urban population and, around 312 CE, the Roman emperor Constantine converted to Christianity. Meanwhile, Rome had an increasingly difficult time fighting off the Hun, Germanic, and other barbaric tribes pressing in on its north. At the end of the fifth century CE, the Germanic Goths, Vandals, Franks, and others conquered the Empire and divided its western half into various tribal kingdoms. The eastern half remained a Greek-speaking "Roman" empire with its capital in Byzantium (later called Constantinople, now Istanbul) until the fifteenth century.

2.2 *Tombstone from Jewish catacombs in Rome in Greek and Latin. Note the Jewish symbols and the Hebrew word "shalom" at the bottom.*

After the destruction of the Roman Empire, we can summarize the geographic spread of the Jewish people more or less as follows. The Jews of northern Europe (Germany, northern France, and Hungary) disappear from sight. It is not known whether they fled, were killed, or continued to live there without leaving any records. In the parts of the former Roman Empire nearest the Mediterranean, Jewish communities survived in today's North Africa, Spain, southern France, and Italy, as well as in the Byzantine (Eastern Roman) areas of Egypt, Syria, Greece, and Turkey, where Greek influence remained strong. Outside the former Roman Empire there were many Jews in today's Iraq and Iran, and some were scattered in other parts of Western and Central Asia.

In the seventh century, another worldwide force came into existence and conquered a large part of the Western world—the Muslims. The Islamic religion began in Arabia when Mohammed came into contact with Jews and Christians living in the area. This monotheistic religion, whose teachings are preserved in the Koran, taught the faithful that it was their duty to spread the Muslim religion throughout the world, by the sword if necessary. At the time of Muhammed's death in 632 CE, Islam was still confined mainly to the area of the Arabian Peninsula. But less than 80 years later, it had conquered most of the lands of the Byzantine Empire (Palestine, Syria, Egypt), taken over the former Persian Empire, swept across North Africa, and captured nearly all of Spain.

The Muslim conquest divided the Western world into two parts. The areas north and west of the Mediterranean remained mostly Christian, and the areas to the south and east became mostly Muslim. In almost all of the Muslim world west of Iran, the Arabic language slowly replaced the former native languages Aramaic, Greek, and Coptic (ancient Egyptian). A huge Arab-speaking area with a common language and culture, many trade opportunities, and an advanced culture brought all populations under its rule into contact with each other (Map 2.5)

Jewish life and settlement patterns were profoundly affected by the Muslim conquest. In what is now Saudi Arabia, the spread of Islam meant the expulsion of the Jewish population. The only Jews left in the Arabian Peninsula were in the south (the Arabic word for south is Yemen). The Yemenite Jews who had arrived on the peninsula centuries before (no one knows exactly when) now found themselves hundreds of miles from their nearest Jewish neighbors (in Egypt, Iraq, or Syria), which probably explains why their traditions were distinctively different from those of other rabbinic Jews. In other parts of the Muslim world, Jews were permitted to live as "protected people" or "people of the book" with second-class status. Indeed, in some areas, such as Spain, where Jews had been persecuted under Christian (Visigoth) rule, the Arab conquest meant a new chance at religious freedom. Throughout the Arab world, Jews traded with each other, migrated from region to region, and remained in contact by correspondence and by reading each other's works. Slowly over the centuries, the Jews of

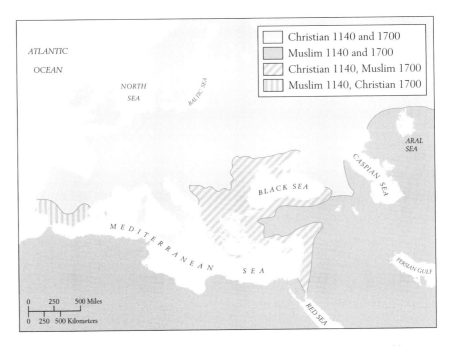

Map 2.5 The changing boundary between the Christian and Mulsim world

these countries, like their Christian and Muslim neighbors, began to use the Arabic language as their regular means of communication. Even works of Jewish religious philosophy like Maimonides' *Guide for the Perplexed* were written in Arabic (though in Hebrew letters).

There was one important exception to the victory of Arabic over the former spoken languages. In northern Iraq is the region called Kurdistan. The majority of the Muslims there spoke (and continue to speak) Kurdish, a language related to Persian. But some of the Christians and most of the Jews in that region stayed with a version of the old spoken Aramaic language of the region. (The Jewish version is usually called Targumic or Neo-Aramaic, and the Christian version is called Assyrian or Chaldaic.)

Before turning back to the Jews of Europe, we should discuss the origins of the remaining Jewish groups in Asia and Africa, which we have not yet referred to.

Already mentioned are the Mountain Jews living in the northern and eastern foothills of the Caucasus Mountains and speaking the Tat Iranian language. Across the mountains on the southern and western sides was the ancient Christian kingdom of Georgia (Gruzia). Jews have lived among the Georgians for hundreds, perhaps thousands, of years. Although not far away from the Mountain Jews in terms of miles, they were totally separated from them by the high mountains (at least until the nineteenth century). In their traditions and language they were quite different from the Tat-speaking Mountain Jews. Like their Christian neighbors these Jews spoke Georgian, a language related neither to Persian nor to Arabic nor to any Indo-European or Semitic language.

To the north and west of Georgia, at the northern end of the Black Sea, lies the Crimean peninsula. This area has gone through many conquests and changes of culture during its history. Its native peoples were first colonized by the ancient Greeks, who were followed by the Goths, the Khazars, and the Turkic-speaking Tatars. Since the Muslim Tatars were expelled after World War II, the area is now inhabited mainly by Ukrainians and Russians. Jewish settlement

*I*t was in the Muslim world that a major sect broke away from rabbinic Judaism in the eighth century. Founded by Anan ben David, a member of a distinguished Iraqi Jewish family, this sect came to be known as the Karaites, a name derived from a Hebrew word that referred to the written Bible. The Karaites rejected the Talmud and the oral tradition and developed their own practices, which differed in many ways from those of the rabbinic Jews. The Karaites later spread east to Persia and west to other Muslim-controlled areas such as Palestine and Egypt. In the Middle Ages the Karaite centers shifted into what is today's Turkey, and in early modern times new Karaite centers developed in the Crimea and in scattered parts of Eastern Europe. In the Crimea and Eastern Europe the Karaites spoke a Tatar language, while in Egypt they spoke Arabic. The Karaites of Eastern Europe and the Crimea have now generally assimilated. The bulk of the Karaites of Egypt migrated to Israel, where they form the main surviving Karaite community of about 7000.

in the Crimea seems to have gone through the same cultural changes as the general population. The first Jews probably came with the Greeks almost 2000 years ago and were part of Jewish-Hellenistic culture. During the Khazar period, many Jews fleeing persecution in the Byzantine Empire seem to have come to the Crimea; there were also later Jewish settlers from Italy and Spain. The rabbinic Jewish population of the Crimea in the nineteenth century were known as the Krimchaks. They spoke a Tatar language that had some resemblances to the language of the Karaites, who also lived in the Crimea in large numbers. The Nazis persecuted the Krimchaks as Jews while leaving the Karaites alone.

Just as the Crimea had two separate Jewish populations, Karaites and Krimchaks, the far-off subcontinent of India also had two (and later three) distinct Jewish populations. Though there were tens of thousands of Jews in India, they were invisible among the hundreds of millions of Indians. Unlike virtually all other traditional Jewish settlements (China being the other exception), those in India were not located mainly among Muslims or Christians. Perhaps because of the small numbers of Jews and their lack of connection to the native religions of India, there was little or no anti-Jewish feeling in India. The two oldest Jewish groups in India were the Bene Israel, residing mainly in the area around Bombay, and the Cochin Jews, living chiefly in the city of the same name in the southern Indian state of Kerala.

The origin of the Bene Israel is shrouded in mystery. Their traditions speak of a shipwreck of Jews on the Indian coast, of their progressive forgetting of their traditions and of their reattachment to Jewish tradition through the teaching of David Rahabi in ancient times. (Historians now think Rahabi lived in the eighteenth century rather than hundreds of years earlier, as the Bene Israel believed.) The Bene Israel knew only the Marathi language and virtually no Hebrew; their residual Jewish practices seem to have included the Sabbath and some dietary laws. The practice of the Sabbath and their predominant occupation caused their neighbors to call them "Saturday oil pressers." In the past 200 years, the Bene Israel have become reacquainted with Jewish traditions, acquired the Hebrew language, founded synagogues, and adopted Jewish holiday practices and prayers.

Though they do not follow all rabbinic traditions, their practices are now much closer to standard Jewish tradition than they were earlier.

The Jews of Cochin, unlike the Bene Israel, have always been rabbinic Jews. Nevertheless, they have adopted certain Indian practices, most striking of which is the Indian caste system, which divides the Jews into "White Jews" and "Black Jews." Jews are known to have lived in southern India for almost 1000 years, though there is little documentation of their early origins. Connections between their musical and liturgical traditions and those of Jews in Iraq (including Kurdistan) and Yemen have been identified. A look at Map 2.3 shows that these are likely places from which people could have sailed to India. There is also reason to believe that many of the White Jews are descended from Spanish and Portuguese Jews fleeing after the Expulsion and that the Black Jews are closer to the native Indian population. Some at least seem to be freed Indian slaves (known by the Hebrew term *meshuchrarim*).

The third group of Jews came to India in the nineteenth century from Iraq. Generally known as the Baghdadi Jews, some of them became very wealthy. In general the three groups of Jews in India did not mix. The Iraqi Jews looked down on the "native" Jews, and neither the Cochin Jews nor the Iraqis considered the Bene Israel (the largest group) to be real Jews. Nevertheless the bulk of all three groups migrated to Israel after 1948.

Another far-off land where a considerable Jewish population lived was Ethiopia. The connection between the Jews and Ethiopia is an ancient one. Some Ethiopian languages belong to the Semitic language family, and the former royal family of the country considered themselves the descendants of King Solomon and the Queen of Sheba. The majority Christian religion of the country shows considerable influence from Judaism. So clearly there was early contact between Ethiopia and the Jewish religion. But the origin of the Jewish minority (known as Beta Israel) is less clear. They were certainly not Christians, though they did have such seemingly Christian practices as monasticism. There are three chief theories about the origin of the Ethiopian Jews. One theory is that the Jews traveled up the Nile River from Egypt; the second argues that the Jews came from southern Arabia (what is now Yemen) across the narrow Red Sea; and the third sees Beta

Israel as composed either of native Ethiopians converted to a form of Judaism or as a Judaizing sect of the Ethiopian church that broke away to become a separate Jewish group. The chief centers of the Ethiopian Jews were the mountainous northern provinces of Gondar and Tigre. At one time Beta Israel, whom the Christians called Falashas, meaning "foreigner" or "landless exile," were a serious military threat to the ruling dynasties, but in recent times they were a relatively small minority living under varying degrees of discrimination. Since 1905, when the European Jewish scholar Jacques Faitlovitch founded his "pro-Falasha Committee," Beta Israel has been (re)acquainted with the Hebrew language and some rabbinic traditions, though to a lesser extent than the Bene Israel of India. Today most of them reside in Israel, where many still preserve their ancient religious traditions.

At the same time that Jewish life was developing in Asia and Africa, the minority of Jews in Europe under Christian rule were also going through important changes (Map 2.6). Beginning in the ninth, tenth, and eleventh centuries, Jews again began to migrate into Northern Europe from the Mediterranean area. Jews from southern France moved into northern France, and Jews from France and Italy (and perhaps the Byzantine Empire) began to settle in southern and western Germany. From France some Jews migrated to England.

For reasons we can only guess at, the Jews of medieval Western Europe called their countries of residence by biblical names that originally applied to areas in the Middle East. Perhaps this was a way for them to feel at home in areas so far from their homeland. (After all, one of the greatest Spanish Jewish poets wrote a poem that begins "My heart is in the East but I am in the far, far West.") Whatever the reason, the Jews of northern France called their country Tsarefath, originally the name of a town in northern Israel. (Southern France was not called Tsarefath in Hebrew, but was referred to by the nonbiblical term Provensa, meaning "Provence.") The Jews of Spain applied the biblical name Sefarad (probably originally the city of Sardis in what is now Turkey) to their country. The Jews of Germany began to use the name Ashkenaz (one of the nations listed in Genesis, chapter 10, possibly applying to the Scythians, who lived near today's Crimea on the Black Sea). They referred to the Slavic countries (especially Bohemia) and

Map 2.6 Jewish migration patterns in Europe

their inhabitants as Canaan. This was based on an association of the biblical story that Canaan was to be "a servant of servants" and the relationship of the words "Slav" and "slave" (Map 2.7).

Since Jews under Christian rule and those under Muslim rule had few contacts with each other, their Jewish cultures also became differentiated. But, over time, the boundaries between Muslim and Christian lands changed. Muslim Spain was reconquered by the Christians in a slow process, from about the year 1000 to 1492. On the other side of Europe, the Byzantine Empire was conquered by the Muslim Turks, who also gained control over most of Southeastern Europe

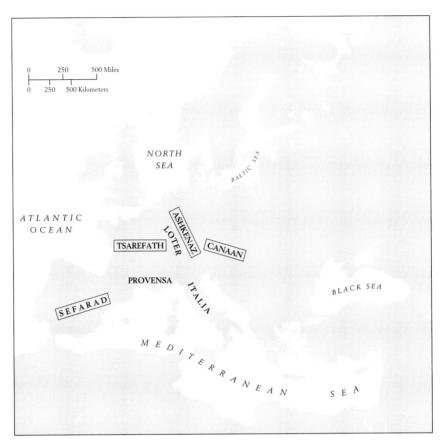

Map 2.7 Medieval Jewish geographic names

(today's Greece, Serbia, Bosnia, Albania, Bulgaria, Romania and part of Hungary) (Map 2.5).

During the Late Middle Ages the Jews became more and more estranged culturally from their non-Jewish neighbors. Until then, Jews coming to a new country usually learned the local language and culture, though often retaining a strong Jewish nuance. This pattern changed during the two most momentous Jewish migrations, those of German (Ashkenazic) Jewry and Spanish (Sephardic) Jewry to different parts of Eastern Europe.

The story of the Sephardic migration is complicated but less confusing than that of the Ashkenazic one. The migration was clearly rooted in persecution. Jewish conditions began to decline in 1391, when anti-Jewish riots spread through-out the Iberian Peninsula, causing the forced conversion of a large percentage of Spanish Jewry. The final blow came in 1492, when the newly united Spanish kingdom of Ferdinand and Isabella gave the Jews a choice: convert or leave the country within three months. Large numbers of Jews left Spain, some for nearby Portugal or Morocco, others for Italy; the bulk of them eventually arrived in the Ottoman Turkish Empire, where they were welcomed. Great new Sephardic Jewish communities arose in cities like Salonika, Constantinople, Smyrna (Izmir), Sarajevo, Safed in the Holy Land, and other Ottoman cities (Map 2.8).

The Jews who left Spain in 1492 took with them their Spanish Jewish cul-

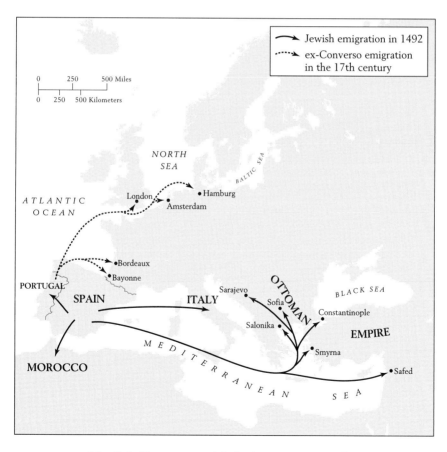

Map 2.8 Various waves of Sephardic emigration from Spain

ture and language. When they settled in established Jewish communities, they did not merge with the older Jewish population. Nor did they adopt the language of their new land. In North Africa, Jews of Spanish origin refused to intermarry with Arabic-speaking Jews for centuries. In the Turkish Empire, the newly arrived Sephardim soon outnumbered the Greek-speaking native Jewish population. In most places (except the area of Yanina mentioned earlier), they converted the native Jews into speakers of Judeo-Spanish (Djudezmo) and imposed their Sephardic customs on them.

A second type of Sephardic migration occurred after 1492 and was very different from the migration to Morocco or Turkey. This migration consisted of Jews who had either chosen to convert to Christianity rather than leave Spain or who had been caught in Portugal in 1497, when the Jews there were told to convert or leave without their children. Some of the converts (Conversos) sincerely became Christians, while others retained at least some of their Jewish practices and beliefs. Under the constant threat of exposure and punishment by the Inquisition, the Conversos had little alternative but to deny their Jewishness until the 1570s, when the former Spanish possessions in the Netherlands revolted, became independent, and provided a refuge for them. In the 100 years that followed, many Conversos (known officially as the "Portuguese nation") settled in Holland and in western seaports like Hamburg, London, and Bordeaux. With Christian family names like Nunez, Castro, and Rodriguez, these Spanish and Portuguese Jews had lived like Christians, married and baptized their children in church, spoke unaccented Portuguese or Spanish, and knew little about Judaism except the Bible. Often they had difficulty reintegrating themselves into Judaism, but some became pioneers of Jewish modernity in the West, since they were the first to combine outwardly non-Jewish culture and manners with an adherence to Judaism. These former Conversos differed from the "Eastern Sephardim" in the Ottoman Empire in their dress, names, and spoken language (Portuguese instead of Djudezmo) and in the degree of their adherence to rabbinic Judaism.

Like the Sephardic Jews who went to the Ottoman Empire, the Ashkenazic Jews who left Germany to go to Eastern Europe brought the culture of the Old Country with them. The migration from Germany to Poland, the main country here is an alternative explanation of the origins of Eastern European Jewry that most scholars reject but that has had considerable popular vogue. The "Khazar theory" was publicized by Arthur Koestler in his book *The Thirteenth Tribe* and has been picked up not only by some Jews, but also by many anti-Semitic writers (who use it as evidence that the Jews are not the true descendants of biblical Israel). The Khazars were a nomadic tribe speaking a Turkic language who created a large kingdom centered at the mouth of the Volga River and extending over parts of what is now the Ukraine and southern Russia. In the eighth century the king of the Khazars and an unspecified proportion of his subjects converted to Judaism. No one knows exactly what happened to these Jewish Khazars after the downfall of the Khazar kingdom in the tenth century. The theory claims that they migrated westward and became the core of the later Eastern European Jewish community.

There are a number of reasons, historical, cultural, and especially linguistic, for rejecting the Khazar theory. Perhaps the strongest is that the language of the Ashkenazic Jews, Yiddish, is structurally Germanic and the majority of its vocabulary is of German origin, not Turkic. In fact, Yiddish contains virtually no words of Turkish or Tatar origin.

On the other hand, two Jewish populations in Eastern Europe, the Krimchaks and the Karaites, did speak languages in the Turkish linguistic family. Some Karaite communities could be found in the same towns as Ashkenazic Jewish communities, although they had few close ties to each other. It is more likely that descendants of the Khazars are to be found among the Krimchaks and East European Karaites than among Ashkenazic Jews.

of Jewish settlement in the East, was a less abrupt process than the migration of the Sephardim in 1492. The process began slowly, partly as a result of increasing persecution in Germany in the twelfth and thirteenth centuries. It grew in intensity with the terrible massacres at the time of the Black Death of 1348–1350 and probably reached its peak between 1450 and 1550. About 90 percent of the Ashkenazic Jews ended up in the Polish Commonwealth, with the rest remaining in German-speaking Central Europe. Besides the push of the massacres and expulsions from parts of Germany (and from France and England), there was also the pull of economic opportunity in Poland. The Polish Commonwealth was a huge frontier land of opportunity for the Jews, with only a small native middle class to compete with them. Since the discriminatory laws of the West were rarely enforced in medieval Poland, the country was called by some "the Paradise of the Jews."

There is a remarkable parallel between the way the German Jews arriving in Poland acted and the way the Spanish Jews acted when they arrived in Turkey. The German Jews also found a native Jewish population, but like the Sephardim in Southeastern Europe, they did not adopt the language of their new country but rather imposed their own language on the older Jewish population. So, after 500 years in Poland, most Jews spoke Yiddish and knew little or no Polish, just as Sephardic Jews in the Turkish Empire spoke Djudezmo rather than Greek or Turkish.

Jews arriving in Poland found conditions very different from those in their land of origin. Medieval Poland was one of the largest countries in Europe (second only to Russia in size), covering not only today's Poland but also the former Soviet and now independent republics of Lithuania, Latvia, Ukraine, and Belarus (Map 2.9). Poland was not only a huge country, it was also a weak one, controlled by a dispersed but powerful nobility rather than by the king. By the seventeenth century the king was largely a figurehead elected by an assembly of nobles; the candidate who made the most concessions to the nobility usually won. By the eighteenth century the central government had become so destabilized that a single noble member of the *sejm* (Parliament) could veto any law. The weakness of the Polish government was both good and bad for the Jews. On the one hand, the weak government gave the Jews leeway to govern themselves; on the other hand, it was often too weak to protect them.

The Polish Commonwealth came into existence through the 1386 marriage of Grand Duke Jagiello of Lithuania and Queen Jadwiga of Poland. This union loosely tied together two separate entities—the Kingdom of Poland, which was Catholic and mainly Polish speaking, and the Grand Duchy of Lithuania, which was originally pagan and later became mainly Eastern Orthodox and was popu-

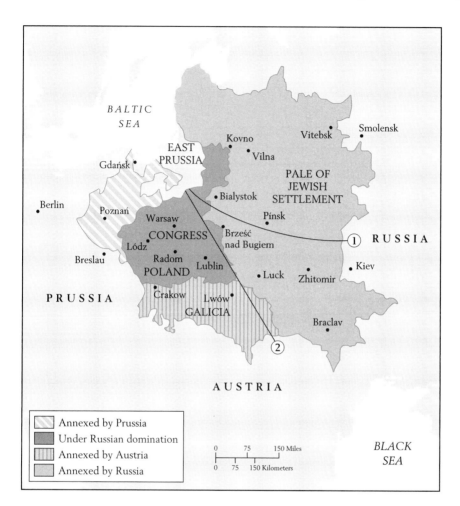

Map 2.9 Jewish cultural divisions of medieval Poland and the fate of Polish territories after partition

lated by many nationalities, especially Lithuanians, Byelorussians, and Ukrainians. In 1569 the two areas were more closely linked by the Union of Lublin, which also changed the internal boundaries of Poland. The southeastern area (Ukraine) was taken from Lithuania and placed under the direct rule of the Kingdom of Poland. Only the area north of line 1 remained part of Lithuania (Map 2.9).

The details of shifting Polish boundaries in the sixteenth century are crucial to the story of the Ashkenazim because these became the chief cultural boundaries of East European Jewry. The divisions between the major dialects of Yiddish follow both the pre-1569 (line 2) and the post-1569 boundaries (line 1) be-tween Lithuania and Poland. No later boundary changes have had nearly the same influence. These boundaries also demarcate important cultural distinctions. For instance, the Hasidim were largely restricted to the south of line 1. Jews liv-ing west of line 2 people ate gefilte fish sweetened with sugar, to the horror of those east of the line, who spiced it with pepper and salt. Why these borders were so vital to Ashkenazic cultural life is hard to say.

Because Poland was so weak, had few natural boundaries, and was sur-rounded by strong countries, it could not keep its independence for long. Be-tween 1772 and 1795, Poland was partitioned among Russia, Austria, and Prussia (later part of Germany). After a brief interlude when Napoleon conquered East-ern Europe, the division was made permanent in 1815, with the lion's share of Old Poland going to czarist Russia. The former Jews of Poland now found them-selves under four different jurisdictions (Map 2.9). In the western province called Posen (and West Prussia) that went to Prussia, the forces of Germanization be-came strong. Jews there learned German, supported the dominant German mi-nority against the Polish majority, and eventually became part of German Jewry. Most of them emigrated to German cities like Berlin and Breslau. The second area, Galicia, became part of the multiethnic Austrian Empire. Although at first the Galician Jews were treated harshly, they were eventually given full citizen-ship in 1867, when Austria was converted into the Austro-Hungarian Empire. Because there was no single majority nationality in Austria, the Galician Jews re-tained their Yiddish-speaking culture and in the main remained Hasidic and poor. The third area was made into a Polish kingdom at the 1815 Congress of Vienna and was generally called Congress Poland. Since the king of this new state was also the czar of Russia, the semi-independence of this area soon disappeared and the area was treated virtually the same as the rest of the Russian Empire. The fourth and largest part of Poland was simply incorporated into Russia, with no pretense of Polish autonomy. Most of its inhabitants were not ethnically Polish, unlike those of Congress Poland.

Before the partitioning of Poland, Russia's policy regarding Jews was sim-ple—they were forbidden to live in the country. Following the partitions, Em-press Catherine the Great found herself ruling over the largest Jewish population in the world. After much hesitation the Russian government decided on a compromise: the Jews would not be expelled from the newly acquired areas, including parts of southern Russia recently conquered from the Turks, but they would not be allowed to settle in other parts of the empire. The provinces in western Russia where Jews were permitted to live have come to be known as the Pale of Settlement. One of the Pale's effects was to ensure that Jews did not live among many ethnic Russians, but rather among other minority nationalities, like Ukrainians, Latvians, Lithuanians, and Poles, and thus had relatively little incentive to assimilate to Russian culture.

These divisions remained in effect until World War I, when the map of Eastern Europe was completely revamped. In 1917 the Pale of Settlement in Russia was finally abolished by the Russian Revolution. The three great empires of Russia, Austria-Hungary, and Germany were either dissolved or sharply reduced in territory. Instead a host of new, or in some cases revived, countries were created based on the principle of national self-determination. The boundaries of the new Poland, Lithuania, Latvia, Estonia, Czechoslovakia, Hungary, Romania, and Yugoslavia were determined (at least in part) by the majority ethnic population distribution.

These new boundaries broke up the old cultural connections and created new ones. Often the cultural divisions among the Jews did not fit the new political situation at all. What had once been a fairly uniform Hungarian Jewish population (most of which had adopted the Hungarian language) now found itself split among a reduced Hungary and Czechoslovakia, Romania, and Yugoslavia. The Jews of western Romania (Transylvania and Maramures) and of southern Slovakia and Carpatho-Russia (in Czechoslovakia) still considered themselves Hungarian Jews (Map 2.10). The end of World War I created a greatly increased Romanian kingdom. Besides the areas of old Romania (Moldavia and Wallachia), there were the areas in the northwest taken from Hungary (see above), areas in the north taken from Austria (Bukovina), and areas in the northeast taken from Russia (Bessarabia) (Map 2.11). Romanian Jewry between the two world wars consisted of culturally disparate Jewish communities with different customs, Yid-

Map 2.10

Map 2.11

dish dialects, and religious and political attitudes. Unlike the other Jews in the Romanian state, the former Hungarian Jews spoke a different Yiddish dialect (more like the Yiddish of Galicia), often spoke Hungarian as well, and were heavily influenced by Hungarian culture.

"Jewish Geography"

Jews and their non-Jewish neighbors shared the same topography, climate, and rulers, but often Jewish geographic vision differed from that of the non-Jews. The Jews' connection to the Holy Land might be purely religious, but images of Jerusalem and the other holy cities often appeared in paintings on synagogue walls or in illustrated popular books and thus often played a great role in their imagination. As traders and craftsmen, Jews often traveled more than their agricultural neighbors and therefore had a wider geographical vista. They were more likely to have traveled to the local market town or even the nearest big city and more likely to correspond with relatives in faraway places. In some cases, Jewish networks of business connections, relatives, and correspondents were less tied to the political boundaries than were the networks of the non-Jews, though sometimes the reverse was true. Their historical memory went back to different ancestors and different places of origin than did the historical memory of their neighbors. After 1000 years, Ashkenazic Jews in northern and Eastern Europe still prayed for the welfare of a no longer existing exilarch and academy leaders in Babylonia. On the walls of the synagogue in Mohilev, deep in eastern Belarus, was an imaginative depiction of Worms, one of the first Ashkenazic settlements on the Rhine. In the imaginations of traditional Jews, centers of Jewish life in towns like ancient Alexandria, Sura, medieval Fez, Rotenburg, or Troyes and the small modern towns of Volozhin, Lubavitch, Radin, and Sadagura loomed large. For non-Jews the associations were different—Rome, Byzantium, Mecca, and Moscow.

Jews also drew the boundaries of regions differently from non-Jews. "Ashkenaz" is a concept that has had at least three quite separate meanings in Jewish culture. In the Bible it referred to some area near the Black Sea. In the Middle Ages, Jews applied the term to Germany. Finally, after German Jews migrated to Eastern Europe, Ashkenaz and Ashkenazic Jewry were widened geographically to include all of Europe from Holland to Belarus, Romania to Latvia. The term "Sepharad" was similarly expanded. Originally it applied to a specific place in Asia Minor; then it was applied to mean Spain, and after the expulsion of Jews from Spain it was expanded include all of the lands where the exiles settled (the Ottoman Empire, Holland, and parts of North Africa). The term "Sephardic" has expanded even more than "Ashkenazic," since it is often loosely applied to all Jews who are not Ashkenazic. The Jewish conception of Lithuania was over six times as large as the modern Lithuanian Republic. In popular Israeli parlance today, "Kurdish" refers not to the Kurdish language and people, but to the Aramaic language and ethnicity of Jews from the Kurdish regions. The Jews of Central Asia are still known as "Bukharans" after the former Khanate of Bukhara, whether they live in what is now Uzbekistan, Tadzhikistan, or Turkmenistan.

Not only is the terminology applied to Jewish groups often different from that of the non-Jews, but so are the geographic patterns. In Germany the most profound linguistic and ethnographic differences are between the northern and southern parts of the country, whereas in the culture of the Jews of Germany, the main cultural divide was between the areas east and west of the Elbe River. Similarly, the major cultural differences within Eastern European Jewry follow administrative boundaries of the eighteenth century and earlier, with later boundaries having a much less profound effect. The cultural boundaries within Slavic culture often run in very different directions than those within Jewish culture.

Overall Patterns of Jewish Settlement

As we can see, the migration history of the Jewish people is long and complex and does not lend itself to simple generalization, but there seem to be a few overall patterns worth recognizing. First, traditional Jewish settlement was more or less confined to those parts of the world where Christianity and Islam became the dominant religions. Although Jews sometimes settled in areas whose inhabitants were pagans, this situation does not seem to have lasted long in the Middle Ages and thereafter. Either the pagans were Christianized, as in Lithuania, or Islamicized, or the Jewish community tended to assimilate and disappear, as in China. Even the seeming exception of India, where the main religion was not one of the "daughter religions" of Judaism, is not really an exception. The longest-lasting settlement of rabbinic Jews, in Cochin, was in the province of India (Kerala), where Christian influence was strongest.

In Asia, with few exceptions, there is a remarkable congruence between the eastern boundaries of the great empires of the Persians and Alexander the Great and the eastern boundaries of Jewish settlement before the nineteenth century. Only in Yemen and India did important Jewish communities arise in areas that had not been part of these two empires. Even far-off Bukhara had been part of the Persian and Hellenistic empires in ancient times. In Africa, too, premodern Jewish settlement was largely confined to areas that had been in territories of the Roman Empire. The one exception, Ethiopia, was an unusual community, and, even there, the Jews lived in a culture dominated by Christianity. Only in Europe were there important Jewish communities far to the north and east of the ancient empires. The Ashkenazic Jews, the Yemenites, and, to a lesser extent, the Sephardic Jews were the main Jewish groups outside the ancient empires. The push and pull of internal and external forces scattered traditional Jews over a large, but still delimited, area in Asia, North Africa, and Europe. Although the pattern changed over time, in most places the overall picture remained stable for centuries.

When we compare the ages and sizes of the various Jewish cultural groups, we are faced with an interesting and unexplained paradox. The largest Jewish group by far, the Ashkenazim, is also one of the most recent to come into existence. Ashkenazic settlement itself was most highly concentrated precisely in those areas of Eastern Europe where it was most recent. Although 500 years of mass settlement in Eastern Europe is certainly not a short time, it is not terribly old by the standards of ancient Jewish communities like those of Iraq and Iran.

When the Ashkenazic community began to emerge about 1000 years ago in the valley of the Rhine, it was a small group. Many historians number medieval Ashkenazic Jewry at only some 10,000 to 20,000 individuals. The vast majority of Jews in the Middle Ages lived in Muslim countries, and Judeo-Arabic was probably the spoken language of most Jews. In more recent centuries, however, Ashkenazic Jewry underwent explosive growth, while other Jewish communities remained stagnant. By 1650 the majority of world Jewry was Ashkenazic, and by 1900 the figure was well over 80 percent, mostly concentrated in what had been the medieval kingdom of Poland.

The huge population growth of Ashkenazic Jewry is especially puzzling because they lived in Christian Europe, the typical locale of persecution of the Jews. Despite the much higher rate of massacres among Ashkenazim than among Jews in the Muslim world, it was the Ashkenazim who kept growing. Not only do we not know the precise reasons for these demographic changes, very few scholars have even considered the phenomenon worthy of exploration. Did the Ashkenazim increase mainly from migration from other parts of the world, because of explosive birth rates, or, as is most likely, as a result of the increased prosperity and lowered death rates of the Western countries in modern times?

Our discussion of the migration history of the Jews has been restricted mainly to an enumeration of the various cultural areas, with some information on the chronology of the early settlement of each area. What we have not done, mainly because it is virtually impossible to reconstruct, is trace the precise routes by which Jews moved from one country to another. Even the few dates of origin that have been supplied may give an impression of precision, which is in fact misleading. In almost every area, the first settlements are undocumented. Often there are wildly differing oral traditions, legends, and documents about the first Jews in a particular region.

Also characteristic of Jewish settlement patterns is their discontinuity. This was especially evident in Europe, but it can be seen in parts of Asia and Africa as well. Jewish settlement was often interrupted by persecutions and expulsions, and many a Jewish community had to be refounded four or five times. Sometimes the later community had a different origin than the first. A simple example is Vienna. Jews first settled there in the thirteenth century, were expelled in 1421, and returned in the sixteenth century, only to be expelled "definitively" in 1670. Even after this expulsion, small numbers of privileged Jews remained in the city. The Jewish population of Vienna stayed small until the middle of the nineteenth century, but between 1857 and 1910 it increased from 6200 to 175,000. Another example is Jewish settlement in Spain. Jews first arrived there in Roman times but were persecuted by the Christianized Visigoths in the sixth and seventh centuries. Jewish settlement resumed after the Muslim conquest in 711. Were the Jews of Muslim Spain the descendants of secret Jews who survived from Roman times, or were they new immigrants coming with the Arabs, and if so, from what Arab countries? Similar stories and questions can be repeated for hundreds of European communities.

Directions of migration sometimes reversed over time. In the early Middle Ages, Jews traveled from Southern Europe, especially Italy, to Northern Europe, especially France, England, and Germany. Expulsions of the thirteenth, fourteenth, and fifteenth centuries forced Jews to move east into Poland. By the eighteenth and nineteenth centuries migration reversed, and Jews from Galicia and the Russian Empire moved west to Germany, France, and England. In the latter two countries they made up the majority of the Jewish population. Similarly, Ashkenazic Jews settled in northern Italy in the late Middle Ages and the Renaissance, reversing the direction of migration that occurred years earlier. There were two-way migrations between Poland and Italy. As a result, some Eastern European Jews had names like Padwa and some Italian Jews were named Polacco. If we were to draw a precise map of all Jewish migrations, it would be so filled with overlapping arrows, reversed directions, and mixtures between immigrant waves coming from different directions that it would be impossible to read. The actual history of each Jewish community is more complicated than any summary view can delineate. No community of any size is uniform. Some Sephardic Jews migrated to Poland, and some Ashkenazic Jews came to Turkey even if they were a minority there. Descendants of various waves of migration lived in the same communities, intermarried with each other, and eventually merged into a single community. Similar patterns of migration and mixtures of cultural groups continue up to our own day, but on a much larger scale than ever before.

Beginning in the late nineteenth century and continuing until the present, the traditional geographic pattern of the Diaspora outlined in this chapter changed totally. These changes were caused by economic opportunity, improved transportation, the horrors of the Holocaust, and the remarkable rebirth of the State of Israel. The areas that had the largest Jewish populations 150 years ago, now generally have very small or no Jewish communities. The largest Jewish communities today are located in areas where there was little or no Jewish population in 1850: the United States, Israel, the Russian Republic, France, England, and Argentina. Even in Russia, seemingly an exception, the areas of Jewish settlement today center in Moscow and St. Petersburg, both areas outside the Pale of Settlement, which lasted until 1917. While the traditional pattern of Jewish settlement coincided with traditional patterns of culture, expressed through language, food and costume, the overwhelming majority of Jews in the new population centers no longer follow most of these traditional patterns or retain only a few symbolic remnants of them. Although Jewish life continues, the old Diaspora communities have mostly come to an end.

Jewish Languages

Similarities and Differences

WHAT IS A JEWISH LANGUAGE? THIS IS A SIMPLE QUESTION WITH A COMPLICATED answer. A language doesn't become Jewish just because some Jews speak it. Otherwise English would be the most widespread Jewish language today. Throughout most of their dispersion, Jews have been multilingual. It was not merely that they spoke their Jewish language among themselves and another language to their non-Jewish neighbors. Rather, the Jews were internally bilingual. In most places they communicated in two different "Jewish" languages. One of these languages, Hebrew, was the language of prayer, holy texts, and scholarship; the other was the Jewish vernacular used in daily life. Using the categorization of the first chapter, Hebrew represents the great tradition and the vernacular the little tradi-

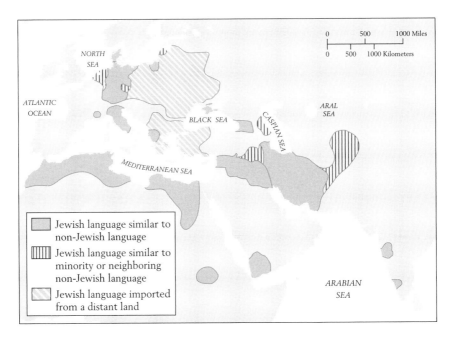

Map 3.1 Similarity and dissimilarity of Jewish and non-Jewish languages

tion. Hebrew was what Jews in most, but not all, cultures had in common, while the vernaculars differed from country to country and were not mutually intelligible.

What made a Jewish vernacular Jewish? In most cases, the vernacular languages of traditional Jewish communities had several characteristics in common. First, they were languages that Jews had learned by contact with non-Jewish neighbors at some point in their migrations. They were thus not of Jewish origin, although they often had Jewish characteristics (like the Hebrew alphabet) and performed Jewish functions (such as describing details of Jewish ritual). Second, they were generally learned not in formal schooling but by listening to native speakers. Since the languages were learned orally and based on colloquial usage, Jews generally wrote them down in their own Hebrew alphabet. The main exception to this is ancient Greek, which Jews did write in the Greek alphabet. Third, Jewish languages generally had a larger or smaller admixture of words of Hebrew origin (more precisely, of Hebrew and Aramaic origin). Fourth, Jewish languages often had elements of languages spoken at an earlier stage in Jewish migrations. Finally, Jewish languages were often different in nuance, pronunciation, intonation, and grammar from the speech of the non-Jewish population among whom Jews lived.

Usually the Jewish languages began by resembling those of the Jews' neighbors. Sometimes, however, as the result of migrations, Jews and non-Jews spoke totally different languages, and the speech of the Jews resembled that of non-Jews in another part of the world (Map 3.1).

Variations in Hebrew

Though I began by referring to Hebrew as a unifying factor among the Jews of the world, this statement requires a number of qualifications. First, as noted in Chapter 2, certain Jewish groups, like the Beta Israel of Ethiopia, did not use Hebrew at all. But even among the majority of Jews who did use Hebrew, the unifying nature of the common language was limited. Except for rabbis and scholars (and even sometimes among these groups), most Jews could barely write, much less speak, Hebrew as an independent language. They could recite their prayers in Hebrew, read it by rote, and perhaps translate some passages from the Bible or Talmud into the vernacular. Hebrew functioned as a holy language, not as a living, spoken one. The unifying force of Hebrew was restricted to its written aspect. What Jews around the world shared were Hebrew or Aramaic *texts*, including the Bible, prayer book, Talmud, and Passover Hagada. But because they shared only the written form of these texts, they were unable to hear how the Hebrew of their fellow Jews *sounded*. As a result, the same words could be read by Jews in different lands, but they would be read according to different reading traditions.

Without getting too technical, it will be helpful to look at some examples of the differences in reading tradition. Among rabbinic Jews, as mentioned in Chapter 2, there were three main reading traditions—Ashkenazic, Sephardic-Oriental, and Yemenite. Nonrabbinic groups such as the Samaritans had a very different reading tradition. Consider the well-known Hebrew word שַׁבָּת (Sabbath). You can notice that this word has two different vowel marks under the letters even if you cannot read Hebrew. Hebrew is read from right to left. The first vowel (below the letter on the right) is called *patach* and the second is called *kamatz*. You will also notice that the final letter ת (*tav*) has no dot (*dagesh*) inside it. In the Ashkenazic tradition the word is pronounced *sha'bos*, differentiating the two vowels and placing the accent on the first syllable. The last letter is pronounced *s* since the final tav does not have a dot. If it had a dot, it would be pronounced *t*. In the Sephardic-Oriental tradition, which is the basis of modern Israeli Hebrew, the word is pronounced *shaba't*, with the accent on the second syllable and no distinction between the first and second vowel or between tav with or without a dot (both are pronounced *t*). Thus Ashkenazic Hebrew preserves several distinctions not found in Sephardic-Oriental Hebrew. Yemenite Hebrew differs from both systems. It pronounces the word *shabo'th*. Like Ashkenazic Hebrew it distinguishes between the two vowels and between tav with or without a dot, but unlike Ashkenazic Hebrew, it pronounces the final letter *th* (as in "teeth") and puts the accent on the final syllable. Italian Jewry, which was transitional between the Sephardic and Ashkenazic traditions, had an intermediary pronunciation. In Italy the word is pronounced *shaba'd*, with the Sephardic-Oriental accentuation and loss of vowel distinctions but with the Ashkenazic distinction between tav with or without a dagesh (though pronounced *d* rather than *s*).

Which tradition is the original one? Probably none of them. We can assume that the three reading traditions diverged from a common ancestor, but we cannot know how that common ancestor sounded. We know that the divergences were caused mainly by communications barriers created by distance. People only heard the Hebrew pronounced in their area; they never heard the alternate types. Presumably each tradition preserves some element from the common ancestor missing in the other traditions. Samaritan Hebrew, which diverged from the other traditions at a very early date, is much poorer in distinctions than any rabbinic Hebrew reading tradition. Perhaps it derived from a totally different source than the three rabbinic traditions (Table 3.1).

Distinction between letters with or without dot (dagesh): + = distinct - = both same		Samaritans	Yemenite	Other Judeo-Arabic	Judeo-Persian	Sephardi	Italian	Georgian	Ashkenazi
ב beth	b/v	-	+	-	+	+	+	+	+
ג gimel	g/gh(r)	-	+	+	+	-	-	-	-
ד daleth	d/dh	-	+	-	-	-	-	-	-
כ kaf	k/kh	-	+	+	+	+	+	+	+
פ pe	p/f	-	+	+	+	+	+	-	+
ת tav	t/th, t/d or t/s	-	+	- (+ in Iraq)	-	-	+	-	+
pronunciation of ayin + = guttural - = silent ng = as in sing q = guttural k		-	+	+	-	-	ng	q	-

There are many other systematic divergences between the three main traditions, and there are also divergences within each tradition. Without going into too much detail, I will outline some of them. Going back to the dagesh, Hebrew distinguishes up to six letters with or without a dot: *beth, gimel, dalet, kaf, pe* and *tav*. Samaritan Hebrew has none of the distinctions and pronounces these letters, respectively as *b, g, d, k, p,* and *t* in all cases. Yemenite Hebrew and some Oriental traditions (for example, that of Iraq) distinguish all six. Yemenite Hebrew, for example, pronounces beth as *b* and *v*, gimel as *j* (as in "jam") and *r* (in the back of the throat), dalet as *d* and *dh*, kaf as *k* and *kh* (like *ch* in German *ach*), pe as *p* and *f*, and tav as *t* and *th* depending on whether or not they have a dagesh. Ashkenazic and Italian Jews distinguish between letters with and without a dot in only four cases. Most other Sephardic-Oriental traditions distinguish three, though some have two, four, or five distinctions (Table 3.1). Ashkenazic Jews pronounce *alef* and *ayin* as silent letters, while most Jews in the Arab world pronounce them as two separate guttural consonants. (You have to hear them to understand the difference; English has no equivalents.) They also distinguish between *khaf* and *ḥet* and often between *kaf* and *quf*. All these are distinctions completely lost to Ashkenazic Jews and to many Sephardic-Oriental Jews outside the Arab countries.

Modern Israeli Hebrew is said to follow the Sephardic tradition. This is true only in part. Israeli Hebrew was created by secularized Ashkenazic Jews who wished to break with their *galut* "Diaspora" past. They rejected their native tradition and copied the pronunciation of the Sephardim. But they did so with an "Ashkenazic ear." They were unable to pick up the guttural ayin, the rough-breathing het, or the back-of-the-throat quf. So modern Hebrew is generally pronounced the way Ashkenazic Jews thought Sephardic Hebrew sounded. Since Ashkenazic Jews generally make up the bulk of the wealthier and most prestigious population in Israel, many Jews from the Arab countries have become ashamed of their native pronunciation and have dropped their Middle Eastern gutturals. So modern Hebrew is a homogenized version of the former multiplicity of reading traditions and the result of the different traditions coming together in one country.

Jewish Vernaculars

Great as the differences in Hebrew reading traditions were, they were relatively minor compared to the differences in vernaculars. If a traditional Jew from one country entered the synagogue of a different tradition where modern Israeli Hebrew was not used, he would probably recognize that the language of prayer was Hebrew but would have difficulty following the prayer. But with regard to the vernaculars, the various Jewish traditions did not even share texts they could all read. Even the Hebrew elements, which all the languages had in greater or lesser number, were often quite divergent. Ashkenazic Jews would wish *mazel tov* (congratulations, literally, "a good constellation"), while Oriental Jews would say *besi-*

man tov (literally, "with a good sign"). Ashkenazic Jews in Eastern Europe would pray from a daily or weekly *sidur*, while Ashkenazic Jews in Germany and many Sephardic Jews used the word *tfila* (literally, "prayer") for prayer book. Ashkenazic and Sephardic Jews prayed from a *machzor* on the holidays, while Yemenite Jews used a *tiklal*. These examples can be multiplied by the hundreds.

But most of the words in the Jewish vernaculars were not of Hebrew origin at all. Sometimes this applied even to words referring to religious matters like "to pray," "to read the Torah," "warm Sabbath food," "skullcap," or "synagogue." Were we to map these expressions, we would find that the boundaries fall in different places for different words. For instance, the Jewish vernacular word for synagogue in many Christian countries originally meant "school" (*shul* among Ashkenazic Jews, *scola* among Italian Jews, *ecole* among Jews in medieval France). One explanation of this term is that government restrictions were placed on building new synagogues, and so, in order to evade the official Christian rules, the Jews said they were building schools rather than synagogues. In other countries Jews used versions of the Greek *synagogos* (literally, "place of assembly"). Among Spanish-language Sephardim a synagogue was called *esnoga*, pronounced by Jews in parts of the Arab speaking world *snugha* (with *gh* pronounced like a throaty *r*). Jews in other Arabic countries used the Arabic word *sla* (literally, "prayer"), while in Iran and among Karaites in the Crimea the word *kenisa* was used.

The best way to try to understand the nature of Jewish vernaculars is to look at the examples of a few specific Jewish languages, to see how they developed and how they differed from each other. To begin with, we will look at the language best known in the West and the one that had the largest number of speakers—Yiddish.

Though the basic structure of Yiddish is Germanic, the language (as spoken in Eastern Europe) had at least three other major linguistic elements: Hebrew-Aramaic, Romance, and Slavic. This is a reflection of the migration history of the Ashkenazic Jews. The Romance element, which today consists only of a small number of words but was once larger, tells us much about the origin of the Ashkenazic Jews. It supports the idea, based on historical documents and Jewish names, that the first Jews in Germany came mainly from France and Italy. Many words relating to religious life came from this Romance element. The word for "to bless," *benshn*, is one such word, coming from the Latin root *benedicere*, probably via Italian. One theory is that Jews coming into medieval Germany avoided the German word for to "bless," *segenen*, because it originally meant "to make the sign of the cross." Another religiously bound word is the word for "to read," especially "to read the Torah." The Ashkenazic word for this, *leyenen*, comes from the Old French *leier*. It is a good example of a word that came from an earlier "stop" in Jewish migrations. This point is further illustrated by a curious peculiarity. If Ashkenazic Jews used the Romance word *leier*, one would expect Jews speaking vernaculars based on Romance languages also to use that word. But they don't. Instead they use a word from an even earlier stage of their migration: the Greek *meletare*. So, in Djudezmo the word is *meldar*, in Judeo-Italian *meletare*, and in now extinct Judeo-French *miauder*. German Jews preserved some Romance words lost by their fellow Ashkenazim who migrated to Eastern Europe. Among these are *oren*, meaning "to pray" (from Latin *orare*), *prayen* for "to ask, invite" (from Old French *preier*), and *piltsl* for "maid" (from Old French *pulcelle*).

One very interesting example of the Romance element in Yiddish is the word referring to the Sabbath dish cooked overnight and kept warm until the next day, which enabled Jews to enjoy a warm meal without violating the prohibition on cooking on the Sabbath. Such foods are found in all rabbinic Jewish communities, though the recipes differ widely, as will be seen in Chapter 6. The Talmud refers to such foods as *hamin* (literally, "warmed"). Ashkenazic Jews used the Old French word for "warming up," *chalent* (the same root as the English word "nonchalant," literally "not all heated up"). This is the origin of the Yiddish *cholent* (in Germany called *shalet*).

Other Romance elements are found in Ashkenazic Jewish personal names. Generally the "funny-sounding" names are the ones with Romance origins, for instance *Vitl* (from Latin *vita*, "life"), *Shprintza* (from Italian *speranza*, "hope"), *Bunem* (from Old French *bon homme*, "good man" or *bon nom* "good name"), *Feitel* (from Italian *vitale*, "alive"), or *Feivush* (from Old French *vives* or Latin *vivus*, "living"). My favorite is *Yente*, which began as a woman's name, derived from Old French or Italian *Gentil* or *Gentile*, "the gentle one." Now it is generally applied to a gossip or someone who talks too much. It's a long way from "the gentle one" to a yente.

When speakers of Judeo-French and Judeo-Italian arrived in the Rhineland some 1000 years ago, they came into contact with various dialects of spoken German. Modern Yiddish contains elements of several German dialects, especially those of southern and central Germany. The dialects of northern Germany, which are closer to English than to modern German, have had almost no influence on Yiddish. (In northern Germany, local dialects said *up*, *planten*, *wat*, *dat*, and *tid*, whereas southern German dialects had *auf*, *pflanzen*, *was*, *das*, and *zeit*. Modern standard Yiddish has *af*, *flantsn*, *vos*, *dos*, and *tsayt*.) Despite the fact that the first Ashkenazic Jews came into contact with western German dialects, modern Eastern European Yiddish is based mainly on the Bavarian and Saxon dialects, which belong to the eastern group of dialects. Although Jews began speaking Germanic dialects at least 1000 years ago, their speech separated into a distinctive Yiddish only slowly. Yiddish shared most of the changes of medieval German until about 1500 or so, and diverged greatly only after that time, when the bulk of Ashkenazic Jews migrated to Poland. The Yiddish dialects among Jews who remained behind in Germany were closer to the speech of their neighbors than to the Yiddish of Eastern Europe, but they were still noticeably different. In a manner analogous to Black English dialects in the United States, which whites could generally understand but considered improper English, German Gentiles could understand most of what their Jewish neighbors said but thought they spoke corrupt German. When the bulk of Ashkenazic Jews migrated to Eastern Europe, they lost contact with German speakers and therefore their language diverged more and more from modern German. Still, even today, modern Yiddish is closer to German than are such other Germanic languages as Dutch, English, and Danish.

The Hebrew element in Yiddish was important from the start and still plays an important part in modern Yiddish, even though words of Hebrew origin are greatly outnumbered by words of German origin. Hebrew words are incorporated into Yiddish in a number of ways. First, there are individual words incorporated into Yiddish sentences. Generally these are pronounced more like Yiddish than they are when read in the prayer book. So the word read *sha'bos* in Ashkenazic Hebrew is pronounced *sha'bes* in the vernacular. *Ba'al habayis* (house-holder) becomes *balebo's* and *yoym toyv* (holiday) becomes *yo'ntef*. Hebrew words in Yiddish are conjugated and declined like Germanic words. Hebrew-origin nouns are also combined with German articles, as in *der shabes, di mikve*, and *dos sefer*, and non-Hebrew words sometimes acquire Hebrew plural endings, as in *doktoyrim*. Sometimes one word is made up of elements from several different language families: *Rebetsin* (rabbi's wife) includes a Hebrew origin root *rabi* and Romance and Germanic feminine endings (respectively, *-etse-* and *-in*).

Finally, there is the Slavic element in Yiddish, which comes from many different Slavic languages. The oldest are Czech-origin words like *nebekh* ("poor thing") or *pareve* ("neither meat nor milk"). Most common are words of Polish origin. These are often pronounced as they were in older stages of Polish. In addition, Yiddish, unlike Polish, reduces unaccented syllables to *e* (*shwa*) and lacks the Slavic noun case endings. It sometimes simplifies the complicated Polish consonant groups. (So the Polish town of Mszczonow [pronounced like *mshtsho'noov* in modern Polish] was pronounced A'mshenev by the Jews.) Sometimes words mean something different in Yiddish than in Polish. The most extreme example is Polish *modny* (in style), which becomes Yiddish *mo'dne* (strange). There are variations in accent that differ from modern Polish (for instance, *po'dlege* [floor] in Polish Yiddish as against *podlo'ga* in Polish. Curiously, outside Polish-speaking areas, the Yiddish word is pronounced *podlo'ge*, much as in modern Polish). Polish-origin words are found even in areas where Polish was not spoken, like the Ukraine or Lithuania, while some Ukrainian words have penetrated the Yiddish of Polish-speaking areas.

These various elements in Yiddish have fused together in such a way that words of different origin are generally treated the same way grammatically. This is similar to the way words of Anglo-Saxon, French, and Latin origins have merged together in modern English to form a single language.

In Eastern Europe, Yiddish played a very different role than it did in Germany. Whatever their neighbors thought of the Jews and their language, they couldn't consider it merely a corrupted form of the local language. They had to think of it as a separate "language of the Jews." This is reflected in the name Yiddish itself, which literally means "Jewish." Its status was perhaps more closely comparable to the status of Spanish in the United States, perhaps resented but still recognized as a language in its own right, unlike the status of Yiddish in Germany as improper Jewish German.

The vernacular of the Sephardic Jews expelled from Spain has many parallels to Yiddish, but also considerable differences. It contains fewer words of Hebrew origin than Yiddish and adopted fewer new elements in Greece and Turkey than Yiddish did in Poland. Still, it had the same status as an imported and foreign language not understood by the non-Jewish population. Having been cut off from contact with living Spanish since the end of the fifteenth century, the language of the Sephardic Jews developed in a somewhat different direction. The language had two separate styles. The style used for translations of the Bible and other Hebrew works, called Ladino, followed Hebrew word order and style. The more folksy vernacular style used in ordinary speech was called Djudezmo, which like Yiddish is literally translated as "Jewish."

A few examples will show the special nature of Djudezmo. Its vocabulary avoids certain words that have a strongly Christian connotation. While "Sunday" in Spanish is *Domingo* (literally, "the Lord's day"), Djudezmo used the more neutral Arabic *alhad* (literally, "the first day"). Saturday was not Sabado but *shaba't*, and Friday night was *noche de shaba't*. Similarly, Spanish *Dios* ("God") sounded like a plural to the Jews, who instead spoke of *el Dio* (literally, "*the* God").

Everyone knows that in modern Spanish *j* is pronounced like an *h*, as in José, which is pronounced *hosay*. But when the Jews left Spain, this *j* was still pronounced either like English *j* or like *z* in "azure." So in Djudezmo, one says *muzher'* for "woman," *i'zho* for "son," and *Djidio'* for "Jew." The distinction between *s* and *z*, which is lost in Latin American Spanish (in Spain the latter is pronounced like the English *th*), is still retained in Djudezmo. So Jews can distinguish between *caza* (house) and *cassa* (box). Modern Djudezmo incorporated some Turkish, Greek, and Slavic expressions, for instance *Ke habe'r* ("What's new?"), as well as Hebrew ones, such as *aboltar de cazal, aboltar de mazal* ("Change your house and change your luck") and *kheynozo* meaning "charming," with a Hebrew root and a Spanish ending.

Students of Spanish language and literature have shown great interest in the language of the Sephardim of the former Turkish Empire. Sephardic Jews have preserved much medieval Spanish epic and lyric poetry (*Romansas*) often lost in Spain. Unlike most modern Yiddish songs, these songs are rich in motifs both about chivalry and adventure and about love and desire. The language of the Sephardim also preserves grammatical, phonetic, and vocabulary forms no longer found in modern Spanish. Some scholars of Spanish enthusiastically (probably wrongly so) refer to the Jews as still speaking the classic language of Cervantes.

Judeo-Arabic has a longer history than either Yiddish or Djudezmo. Many of the greatest works of medieval Jewish philosophy were written in this language. Judeo-Arabic shares a number of the peculiarities of the Arabic language as a whole. The spoken language differs tremendously from the modern written language and from classical Arabic. Used over a large geographic area, the spoken Arabic of the various Arab countries differs so much that the various dialects are not mutually understandable. There are especially great differences between the Arabic of North Africa (Morocco, Algeria, and Tunisia) and that of other countries.

In general, the Arabic speech of the Jews in a particular country was a variant of local Arabic. It was usually closer to (but not the same as) the speech of local Muslims than it was to Jewish speech in other parts of the Arabic world. Besides using some Hebrew words (sometimes in Arabic grammatical form), Jews often used different vocabulary and sometimes different pronunciation than their non-Jewish neighbors. In North Africa, Jews often pronounced their sibilants differently than everyone else. In some places they said "sh" where non-Jews said "s," and in other place it was the other way around, with Jews "hissing" instead of "hushing." In Baghdad, Jews and Christians spoke more like each other than either spoke like the Muslims, whose dialect was called *badawi* (Bedouin), implying that it was imported from the desert. In the Muslim East, the Muslims were often the newcomers and the Jews were the old native population—the opposite of the situation in Europe.

Jews wrote Arabic in the Hebrew alphabet, and there is much literature in this form, including religious works and even newspapers. The written form of

Map 3.2 Main regions of Italy

Judeo-Arabic, unlike Muslim Arabic, is less conservative and less influenced by the classical Arabic of the Koran.

Many people are unaware of the fact that a Judeo-Italian language ever existed. A much smaller number of Jews spoke Judeo-Italian than spoke Judeo-Arabic, though Judeo-Italian also has a long history. The earliest texts in Judeo-Italian date back to the Middle Ages. Like the other Jewish languages, Judeo-Italian was written in the Hebrew alphabet, contains quite a few Hebrew words, and reflects the unique history of the Italian Jews. Like Arabic, Italian has regional dialects, which differ widely from each other. At one time, a large percentage of the Jews of Italy lived in the southern areas of Naples and Sicily. However, these areas of Italy came under the control of Spain, which expelled the Jews from the southern half of Italy between 1493 and 1510. As a result, Jews in Italy often spoke with the accents of areas farther south than those of the non-Jews. Roman Jews sounded more like Neapolitans and Florentine Jews sounded more like Romans. Only in the far northern area of Piedmont did the Jews speak dialects with few southern features (Map 3.2).

Internal Variation in Jewish Vernaculars

As we have already seen, Jewish languages varied internally from place to place. Sometimes this seems to reflect mainly the variation in speech of the non-Jewish population. In the case of Yiddish, however, the geographic patterns are quite independent of the non-Jewish languages. This raises some questions about the usual explanation that dialect boundaries are caused by communications barriers. If the boundaries for Jews run in a different direction from those for non-Jews, then maybe a mountain range or river or provincial boundary was not so much a physical boundary as a cultural one. For one group it might act as a barrier, while for the other, it might not impede communication at all. From this we can see that Jews not only had their own spoken languages but also their own geography.

One example of this difference in geographic concept is the diverging definition of Lithuania. Usually Lithuania in twentieth century Europe is associated with the speakers of the Lithuanian language and with the small Baltic republic that has recently regained its independence. This republic covers a fairly small area and has a relatively small population (about 3 million). Jewish Lithuania is much larger than the Lithuanian republic (Map 3.3). For Jews a "Litvak" (Lithuanian Jew) is someone who comes from anywhere in the eighteenth century Grand Duchy of Lithuania (see Chapter 2). This covers an area five or six times that of modern Lithuania, with a population of some 15 million people. Litvaks can come not only from today's Lithuania but also from Belarus, Latvia, and the northeastern part of Poland (the area around Bialystok, for instance).

The Lithuanian dialect of Yiddish follows the boundaries of eighteenth century Lithuania and is quite distinctive from the other dialects. A Litvak would wear *a por heyzen* (a pair of pants), study the *Teyre* (Torah), and eat *kugl* (a Sabbath pudding) and *fleysh* (meat). He or she would not be able to pronounce the difference between a long or short vowel and in some cases would mix up "s" and "sh" (and say *gut sa'bes*). To the south and west, a Polish Jew would wear *a puur*

Map 3.3 Jewish Lithuania in comparison to modern independent Lithuania

hoyzen, study the *Toyre*, eat *kigl* and *flaysh*, and would distinguish the long *a* in *haant* (today) from the short *a* in *hant* (hand). In most of Eastern Europe outside Litvak territory, the Hasidic movement was dominant. In Jewish Lithuania the Hasidim were a minority, often a despised minority, especially in the western part of Lithuania (outside Belarus).

Before the eighteenth century, Yiddish was spoken not only in Eastern Europe but in Germany as well, where it was later replaced by High German. The former Yiddish dialects of Germany were even more different from what was spoken in Eastern Europe than Lithuanian Yiddish was from Polish Yiddish. Using our test words, a Jew in Frankfurt would wear *e paar hauzen*, study *Taure*, and eat *kugl* and *flaash*. He would also get his *ds* and *ts*, *bs* and *ps*, and *ks* and *gs* mixed up. So he would say *Daure* instead of *Taure*. He would also use a lot of vocabulary unknown to Jews in Eastern Europe. He would eat *datsher* or *berches* instead of *challe* (Sabbath bread) and go to the synagogue for *oren* instead of *davenen* (prayer). Despite these differences though, 18th century Jews in Frankfurt often read the same Yiddish books as Jews in Poland or Lithuania and were thought by their Christian neighbors to speak in a peculiar Jewish manner.

The Functions of Jewish Vernaculars

Jewish vernacular languages were not really purely vernacular. Most of them had a written form (in Hebrew script), and several of them developed complex and sophisticated literatures. This is especially true of Yiddish, Djudezmo (Judeo-Spanish), Judeo-Persian, and Judeo-Arabic. Judeo-Arabic was the chief vehicle for Jewish philosophical writing in the Middle Ages, and a number of epic poems on biblical themes were composed in Judeo-Persian.

Although Hebrew was the official language of the Jewish liturgy, folk tradition often introduced bits of the vernacular into the liturgy as well. This was probably least true among Ashkenazic Jews, among whom hardly a word of Yiddish was heard in the synagogue service. At most, we can cite the introduction to the grace after meals, "*Rabosai mir veln benshn*" ("Gentlemen, let us say grace") and the women's prayers at the beginning and end of the Sabbath—all of them more likely to be recited at home than in the synagogue. Among other Jewish groups, the use of the vernacular in prayer was slightly greater, but nowhere did it predominate. Sephardic Jews sang "*Bendicho su nombre de el senyor de el mundo*" ("Blessed be the name of the Lord of the universe") in Ladino when they took out the Torah, and alternated Hebrew and Ladino in singing En Kelohenu ("*Non como muestro Dio*" ["There is none like our God"). Their grace after meals ended with the Ladino words "*Siempre mezhor, nunca peor, nunca mos manke la meza del Criador*" ("Always may it be better and never worse; may we never be lacking the Creator's table"). Speakers of Judeo-Arabic also used the vernacular but less frequently. On the feast of Shavuot, North African Jews recited the Arabic commentary of Saadia Gaon on the Ten Commandments for hours during the service. Algerian Jews told me that Muslims would come to the synagogue on that day to listen to the classical Arabic of the prayer.

In most Jewish cultures the ceremony at which the vernacular was most used was the Passover Seder. This fit with the familial, folksy, and home-centered nature of the Passover ritual. Not only did the celebrants often translate the Hebrew Hagada into the spoken language, but they sometimes sang the various Seder songs in the vernacular as well. Alongside the almost universal Aramaic Had Gadya, one could hear the Judeo Italian "*Un caporetto que ho compro mio Padre*" ("A Goat That My Father Bought"), the Ladino "*Un cavretico que lo merco' mi padre,*" the Judeo-German "*Ein Zickelein, ein Zickelein,*" and the Judeo-Arabic "*Wahad al dj'di.*"

In recent times, the Jewish vernaculars have also acquired more modern and secular functions. Newspapers appeared in Judeo-Arabic, Djudezmo, and Yiddish. In the Soviet Union, periodicals were published in several other Jewish languages including Judeo-Tat and Judeo-Tadzhik. Some Yiddish periodicals in Poland had circulations of over 100,000. There were literary magazines, theaters, advertisements, and sometimes even official documents (for instance, birth and marriage certificates) issued in the Jewish languages. Yiddish became the language of a whole network of modern schools in Eastern Europe, and textbooks for many subjects were published in the language in the 1920s and 1930s.

The Fading of the Jewish Vernaculars

With modernization, the Jewish languages encountered severe pressure. As Jews were granted political rights and required to acquire a secular education, the national languages of the majority began to supplant the Jewish vernaculars. Many countries began to refuse to accept documents or even signatures in the Hebrew alphabet. Educated Jews aspired to learn French and German rather than Yiddish or Djudezmo. Speaking in a Jewish dialect rather than in the "proper" language taught in school came to be seen as a sign of backwardness. The schools set up all over the Middle East by the Alliance Israelite Universelle (a French Jewish organization) used French as the language of instruction and tried to spread French culture among Jews in Persia, North Africa, and the Ottoman Empire.

In Turkey in the 1920s, all languages had to be written in the Latin alphabet; thereafter, Djudezmo newspapers used Latin letters. Similar attempts were made in the Soviet Union, where writers of Judeo-Tat and Judeo-Tadzhik were forced to use first the Latin and then the Russian alphabet in place of Hebrew script. As traditional religious instruction and practices declined in many countries, fewer and fewer Jews could read the alphabet in which the Jewish vernaculars were written.

There was one other, totally unexpected, development, which probably sealed the fate of the declining Jewish spoken languages—the revival of Hebrew. Throughout much of the history of the Diaspora, Hebrew was the language of scholars, and the vernacular Yiddish, Djudezmo, or Judeo-Arabic was the daily language of the Jewish masses. With the return of more and more Jews to their ancient homeland in the early twentieth century, attempts were made to make Hebrew the everyday spoken language of the modern Jewish settlement. The cause of Hebrew was fostered by the fact that it was the only language the Jews, coming from a host of different countries, had in common. The vernaculars served to divide the new settlers in Israel. Hebrew served to unite them.

Ironically, Hebrew has now become a living language spoken by virtually all Israeli Jews and taught as a living language in the Diaspora. Yiddish and the other Jewish vernaculars are spoken by fewer and fewer people outside extreme Orthodox circles. The vernaculars are now esoteric subjects, more likely to be studied by scholars than by the masses. Most Jews in the world today speak either the same language as their non-Jewish neighbors or Hebrew. The old pattern of Jewish speech in the Diaspora has almost completely disappeared.

$\mathcal{N}$ames

What They Mean and How They Developed

JUST AS JEWS IN DIFFERENT PARTS OF THE WORLD HAD THEIR OWN LANGUAGES, which were distinguished from the speech of the non-Jews but incomprehensible to each other, they also had names that the local non-Jews thought of as Jewish, even though Jews elsewhere might not have recognized them. Many of the same patterns of name formation can be found in widely separated and unrelated cultures, though there are a few that are distinctively Jewish. To further complicate matters, sometimes a name that was seen as typically Jewish in one area might be considered a non-Jewish name elsewhere.

Originally, in almost every society, a name had a specific meaning known to those giving the name. So, in the Bible there are many passages of the type "And his hand was grasping the heel ['akev] of his brother, so they called his name Jacob [Ya'akov]." This pattern is familiar to us from Native American names that we customarily translate into English, such as Sitting Bull and Crazy Horse, but it was originally virtually universal. This contrasts with the way names are derived in many Western societies today, where they are frequently borrowed from foreign languages. In our society the name is just a series of sounds, and it is unusual for George or John, Mary or Alice to know the original meaning of their names.

In small communities where everyone knows everyone else and where government record keeping plays no role, people generally can get by with only a single "given" name. In more complex or larger societies they often have to add a surname (literally, "over name") in order to be distinguished from other people with the same given name. These surnames do not have to be fixed or hereditary family names, but could instead be nicknames that change from generation to generation. Throughout much of the history of the Jewish people, fixed family names simply did not exist.

In the Bible, individuals are generally identified by a single name that has a clear meaning in the Hebrew language: Yitzhak ("he will laugh"), Rachel ("ewe"), David ("beloved"), Yonatan ("God has given"), Naomi ("pleasantness"), and so on. If more identification is needed, this is usually provided by giving a father's name: Moses son of Amram (Moshe ben Amram), Joshua son of Nun (Yehoshua ben Nun), or David son of Jesse (David ben Yishai). Occasionally the Bible gives a whole genealogy as an identification: Bezalel ben Uri ben Hur or Mordechai ben Yair ben Shime'i ben Kish. Sometimes the tribal affiliation or the hometown is added. But nowhere is there a family name.

The lack of family names continued throughout the talmudic period and well into the Middle Ages. Great leaders, sages, and public figures continued to be described by their occupations, fathers' names, or residences but never by a family name. Such leading lights of the early rabbinic period as Rabbi Akiva, Hillel, Shim'on ben Yochai, and Yochanan HaSandlar (the sandal maker) all did without family names. Rashi, the great medieval commentator in northern France (d. 1105), was really named Rabbi Shlomo the son of Yitzhak, and Rashi was just the abbreviation of those names. The "Maimonides" in Moses Maimonides (1135–

1204) was not a family name either, merely Greek for "son of Maimon." Among Jews in the Muslim countries as well as in Italy, family names began to appear in the later Middle Ages, as shown by the names of such great rabbis as Joseph Caro (1488–1575), Itzhak Abravanel (1437–1508), and Ovadia Sforno (c.1470–c.1550). Among Ashkenazic Jews, family names were still largely absent in the eighteenth century. Take the examples of three famous religious and intellectual leaders of eighteenth century Ashkenazic Jewry: the Ba'al Shem Tov (d. 1760), founder of the Hasidic movement; the Vilna Ga'on (d. 1797), a great talmudic scholar and the chief opponent of the Hasidim; and Moses Mendelssohn (1729–1786), the first important Jewish Enlightenment philosopher in Germany. None of them had a family name. Even the seeming exception, Mendelssohn, was the son of Mendel Sofer (Mendel the scribe). Whenever he signed his name in Hebrew, it was as Moshe Dessau (Moses of Dessau), never as Mendelssohn.

Most modern societies, however, sooner or later, have had to require their inhabitants to take permanent hereditary family names for bureaucratic purposes. In some countries the taking of family names was relatively recent. In a few, such as present-day Iceland, family names are still not used. Instead all Icelanders have surnames ending in *-son* or *-dottir*, which are preceded by their father's given name. Among Europeans, the Ashkenazic Jews were one of the last groups to take fixed family names, in most cases between 1781 and 1835.

In their selection of given or first names, Jews could choose names of either Hebrew or vernacular origin. Even when they chose names of Hebrew origin, these often differed from region to region. Such Hebrew male given names as Hai, Rahamim, Saadia, Ovadia, and Nissim and female names like Mazaltov and Simha (the latter a male name among Ashkenazim) are typical of Jews of Muslim countries but are virtually unknown among Ashkenazic Jews. The names Shraga, Yerachmiel, Shifra, and Basya seem more typically Ashkenazic and are rare in Muslim countries. Even when Jews took vernacular names like those of non-Jews, they traditionally avoided names that had non-Jewish religious connotations (e.g., Christopher, Mary, and John in Christian countries or Ali, Aysha, and Muhammed in Muslim ones).

The choice of Hebrew or vernacular first names often differed by gender. Men were much more likely to have names of biblical and Hebrew origin, while women more frequently had vernacular names. There are various reasons for this. First of all, more male names are mentioned in the Bible and in rabbinic literature than female names, as women in ancient Jewish texts were often anonymous, referred to merely as Noah's wife or Lot's wife and daughters. Second, in traditional Jewish society, only men were called to the Torah, where they needed to use a "sacred" Hebrew name. Third, women were more likely to be given "pet names" whose meaning in the vernacular was well known (gold, rose, flower, queen). For these reasons, men's given names varied less around the Jewish world than did women's.

Patterns of Family Name Formation

The development of surnames, which turned into family names, tends to follow similar patterns in many countries. The four types of derivation that are most international in distribution are based on (1) the parent's name (patronymics and matronymics), (2) occupation, (3) nicknames (personal characteristics), and (4) place names. In the English language, for instance, we can find the following examples from each category: (1) Williams, Johnson, (2) Carpenter, Farmer, Smith, (3) Shorter, Black, White, and (4) Lincoln, Scott, Flanders.

These four basic categories are also to be found among Jews, though the distributions and specific examples differ widely. In the early stages, surnames were not yet hereditary. So if Jacob had a son named Abraham, that son would be called Abraham Jacobson, but if Abraham had a son named Moses, he would be called Moses Abramson. Later on the family name became hereditary, with the strange result that women can have family names like Jacobson or Ben Chaim (son of Chaim).

The patronymic, or father's name, is a very common form of Jewish family name in many parts of the world, but its specific form depends on the local language(s) spoken in the area. Returning to the example of Abraham son of Jacob mentioned above, in Hebrew this would be Abraham ben Ya'akov. But most Jewish surnames were vernacular rather than Hebrew. Among Ashkenazic Jews who spoke Yiddish, the surname would become Jacobs or Jacobson. In Eastern Europe, where most Ashkenazic Jews lived, governments often used Slavic translations of the Yiddish surnames, so Jacobson would be written in Polish records as Jakubowicz and pronounced "Yakubo'vitch." The -*owicz* ending would have varied spellings in other Eastern European languages, including -*ovič* (Czech), -*ovics* (Hungarian), and -*ovici* (Romanian), but would still be pronounced "ovitch." German scribes might transcribe the name in the form -*owitz*. Russian officials used the Cyrillic alphabet; when Jews came from Russia to the United States, they sometimes spelled their last names phonetically in English with -*ovitch*. Some Jews in the Caucasus, Bukhara, and the Crimea were given surnames with the Russian endings -*ovitch* and -*ov* when the Russians conquered their homelands in the nineteenth century.

The name Jacobson could take many other forms as well. In Iran "son" was expressed in names with the endings -*zadeh* or -*ian*. In Georgia it was -*eshvili*; in Arabic, as in Hebrew, it was *ben* (or *ibn*) and preceded rather than followed the name. Italian Jews often used the ending -*i*, as in Abrami or Israeli. Some Moroccan Jews have names based on the Berber patronymic prefix O-(for instance, Ohana, son of Hanna), almost like the Irish prefix in O'Donnell and O'Malley.

Complicating the situation still further was the fact that many Jewish vernaculars (especially Yiddish) loved to give vernacular translations or nicknames for Hebrew names from the Bible and Talmud. Among Ashkenazic Jews the nicknames for Jacob were Yankel and Koppel, from which arose such family names as Yankelovich and Koppelson. Sometimes biblical names were associated with specific symbols or nicknames. Yehuda (Judah), for instance, was associated with the lion (Aryeh in Hebrew, Leib in Yiddish) and also had the nickname Yudel. This is the source of such family names as Yudelson, Leibson, Leibowicz, and Lefkowitz ("son of little Leib"). Benjamin was associated with the wolf (Wolf in Yiddish, Volk in Slavic languages, Farkas in Hungarian) from which come the names Wolfson, Volkovich, Wouk, and so on. Naphtali was associated with the gazelle (Zvi in Hebrew, Hirsh or Hersh in Yiddish), creating such patronymics as Hershenson and Herszkowicz ("son of little Hersh"). The Ashkenazic family name Moscowitz has nothing to do with the city of Moscow; rather, it comes from the Polish Moszek/Moszko (little Moses). Other animals frequently referred to in Ashkenazic personal names, and later in family names, are the bear (Ber, used in such family names as Berenson, Berkowitz and, in Russian, Medved and Medvedev), the falcon (Falk, Sokol, Sokolovsky), and the eagle (Adler).

Sometimes nonbiblical Hebrew names would be translated into the vernacular and then develop further. Yechiel and Chayim (both based on the root meaning "life") were called Vives and Vital in medieval France, which developed into the Yiddish names Feivush and Feitel. A Moroccan Jew named Ben-Hayim once told me that he had said to his Ashkenazic neighbor, Mr. Feitelson, "We have the same last name"—both names mean "son of life." Another example of two names based in part on patronymics that mean the same thing, though they don't sound at all alike, are the Ashkenazic Rabinowitz and the Iranian Akhamzadeh, both of which mean "son of a rabbi."

Among Ashkenazic Jews, matronymics derived from a mother's name are more common than they are in most societies, which seems surprising given the usual view of Jewish culture as patriarchal. A number of possible explanations for the development of matronymics exist. In some cases, the father had already died; in others, as was common in Eastern Europe, the mother ran the business. In still others, the mother was simply a more memorable person than the father. Examples of matronymics among Ashkenazic Jews are Sarason (son of Sarah), Rifkin (from Rivka [Rebecca]), Chanin (from Chana), Beilis (from Beila), and Goldenson (son of Golda). Some names could be derived from mothers' names or from a different source. For example. Rosenson could derive from roses or from a mother's whose name was Rose. Perlmutter could come either from someone who worked with mother of pearl or from someone whose mother was named Pearl.

Names based on occupations are quite common among Jews, though generally less so than those based on parents' names. A few of these names are derived from Hebrew, like Chait (tailor), Melamed (teacher), Hazan (cantor), and Katzoff (butcher), but most are derived from the vernacular. For that reason, Jewish names in various parts of the world do not sound related even when they have the same meaning. Among Ashkenazic Jews, the most common trade immortalized in family names is that of the tailor. Besides Chait, mentioned above, there is Schneider (from German or Yiddish, sometimes Americanized to Snyder), Kravitz (from Polish Krawiec), Kravchik (from Ukrainian), and Portnoy (from Russian). There are also many roundabout ways of including the tailoring profession in a family name. Examples of this are Nadelman or Nudelman (needleman), Sherman (from Yiddish Sher, "scissors"), and Fingerhut (thimble). Other trades found in Ashkenazic Jewish names are butcher (Fleisher, Metzger, Katzoff, Reznick), glazier (Glass, Glazer, Sklar), tinsmith (Blecher), blacksmith (Schmidt, Kovalsky), furrier (Futterman, Kirshner, Peltz), and scribe (Sofer, Schreiber).

Similar patterns but very different sounds are found among Jews in other parts of the world. In Arab-speaking countries, there are Abitbol or Boutboul or Teboul (drummer), Abulafia (doctor), Alalouf (seller of fodder), Almozeg (glazier), Asayag (goldsmith), Siton (wholesale grain dealer), and Tabib (doctor). In Iran the name Hakimi (doctor) seems to be typically Jewish.

The third category, nicknames based on personal characteristics, seems somewhat less common among Jews than are the first two categories. Some examples of Ashkenazic names of this type are Schwarz (black), Klein (small), Roth (red), Graubart (graybeard), Geduldig (patient), Dicker (fat), and Schoen (good-looking). It has been humorously suggested that all Hungarian Jews were named Weiss (white), Schwarz (black), Gross (big), and Klein (small) because the government officials picked names at random. Some Arabic examples are Assouline (noble), Elkyess (smart), and Tawil (long or tall). Some Italian Jewish ones are Pacifici (peaceful, a translation of Shalom) and Rossi (redhead). Sephardic family names from nicknames include Azulay (blue), Caro (beloved), Castel (castle), Cordozo (hearty), Esformes (beautiful), Galante (galant), and Pardo (brown).

The final category, found in many different cultures, derives from place names. This type of name is more common among Jews than among most other cultures for a simple reason: Jews were more likely to move from place to place, either because of persecution or because of business opportunities, than were farmers, who were the majority in most societies.

Some Jewish names are easy to trace because they come from well-known cities in the same region where the family lived. Among Ashkenazic Jews , some obvious examples are Berliner, Minsky (from Minsk), Prager (from Prague) and Vilner (from Vilna). Frankfurter, Hamburger, and Wiener (from Vienna) also derive from city names, not names of deli foods. Often the same city can give rise to different family names. So Warsaw gives the names Warschauer (the German form) and Warszawski (the Polish form). For Pinsk, there is Pinsky and Pinsker; for Vilna, Vilner and Wilensky. In other parts of the world, the cities after which Jews are named are naturally different. In Iraq we might find Bagdadi and Basri (from Basra); in Iran, Tehrani, Isfahani, and Shirazi; in Arab countries names like Alfasi (from Fez), Masri (from Egypt), and Adni (from Aden). Sometimes Jews imported their names from the "Old Country." So Jews in Morocco or Syria or Turkey could be named after cities in Spain: Toledano (from Toledo), Cordovero (from Cordova), and Alkalay (from Alcala). Some names are surprising, like the Ashkenazic names London (common in Eastern Europe) and Schottlander (literally Scot, but actually deriving from Altschottland, a suburb of Danzig).

Place names are commonly used as Italian Jewish family names. Many names derive from small Italian cities, such as Bassani (from Bassano), Castelnuovo, Finzi (from Faenza), Modigliani (from Modigliano), Sinigaglia, and Viterbi (from Viterbo). Others were imported by Jews immigrating from other countries. From southern France came Lattes and Foa (Foix in French). Many Ashkenazic Jews settled in Italy in the sixteenth century and later and often Italianized their place names of origin. So, many Italian Jews were named Morpurgo (from Marburg), Ottolenghi (from Ettlingen), Luzzatti or Luzzatto (from the region of Lausitz or Lusatia), Treves (Trier in German), Tedesco (German), or Polacco (Polish).

Among Ashkenazic Jews, some of the most widespread names come from very obscure places. Among the first Ashkenazic Jews to take family names were rabbis proud of their family origins. Many of their names derive from relatively small localities. The ancient Jewish community of Speyer on the Rhine is the origin of Shapiro and Spiro. Others took their names from the small towns named

Günzburg (the origin of Ginzburg) in Bavaria, Eppstein in Hesse, Heilbronn (from which comes Halpern), Hořovice (origin of Horowitz) near Prague, Landau which is south of Speyer, and even Katzenellenbogen, on the Rhine northwest of Frankfurt. The city of Trier, from which Italian Jews acquired the name Treves, also gave Alsatian and southwest German Jews the name Dreyfus. Some Eastern European Jews ended up with Italian-derived names like Padwa and Rappaport (from Porto).

Some names came from countries or regions. Ashkenazic Jews often had names like Deutsch (German), Ungar (Hungarian), Litvak (Lithuanian), Pollack (Pole), Russ (Russian), and even Spanier (Spaniard), Franzos (French), and Italiener (Italian). Regions represented include Franconia (Frankel), Hesse (Hess), Silesia (Schlesinger), and Swabia (Schwab). Some of these names are found mainly outside the country from which they derive. Most Deutsches lived in Hungary, not Germany. There were Sarfatis (French) in Italy and North Africa and Eskenazis (Germans) in Greece.

The four patterns mentioned up to now are shared by Jews and non-Jews. There are, however, several forms that seem specifically Jewish. The first group is made up of tribal and priestly names like Cohen and Levy and their derivatives. In Italy the name Sacerdote (priest) was a typically Jewish name, the equivalent of Cohen in other countries. Among Ashkenazim these names often have alternative forms. For Cohen (spelled many different ways, including Kohn, Kohen, and Cohn), there was the Aramaic equivalent Kahan or Kahana, with various spellings. Another form based on Cohen or Kahan is Kahn (which also means "rowboat" in German). Sometimes the idea of priesthood was "translated" into the vernacular in forms like Kaplan (literally, "chaplain"). In the Russian language, which has no *h*, the *h* was written down as a *g*, creating such forms of Cohen as Cogen, Kagan, and Kagana. For Levy there are such fancied up forms as Levitt, Levine, Levitus, and Löwy.

A widespread equivalent of Cohen—Katz—introduces a new category of names that seem to be found almost only among Jews: names derived from abbreviations. This form is especially easy for Jews to create because the Hebrew language writes only the consonants and uses diacritical marks for the vowels.

Therefore a string of consonants can be pronounced by the addition of vowels that do not have to be written. Katz, which means "cat" in Yiddish but has nothing to do with felines, is an abbreviation of Kohen Tzedek (righteous priest). KTz was pronounced as if it contained the vowel "a." The name Katz could also be expanded to form Katzman, Katzenstein, Katzenberg, and so on.

There are many other names that derive from abbreviations, especially among Ashkenazic Jews. These include Babad (son of the chief rabbi—Ben Av Bet Din), Barash (Ben Reb Shmuel or Ben Reb Shlomo, son of Samuel or son of Solomon), Bril (Ben Reb Yehuda Leib, son of Judah Leib), and my favorite, Shalit (Sheyichye Leorech Yamim Tovim, "may he live many long days").

Invented Names

You may have noticed that the discussion of Jewish names has so far left out some of the most common American Jewish names. These belong to one of the more important categories of family names among Ashkenazic Jews, a group which is of relatively recent vintage. These names, which Jews took on order of the government, signal an extremely important change in the status of Jews in the Western world. Until the eighteenth century, Jews in most of the world were dealt with by governments more as a collectivity than as individuals. They lived under special laws that differed from those of other citizens and were governed by the Jewish community, which assessed taxes, judged internal disputes, and regulated daily life. Governments often assessed global taxes on the entire Jewish community of a town and left it to the Jewish leadership to decide how much each family should pay. Bureaucratic functions for which governments today keep track of individuals and their vital statistics—taxation, education, the military draft, welfare—were either handled by the Jewish community or did not apply to Jews. Therefore the government was not disturbed by the fact that most European Jews did not have family names.

This situation began to change in the eighteenth century. First in Germany and France and then in other European countries, governments began to implement a policy of integrating the Jews instead of segregating them, as they had done previously. Jews were brought under the general law of the state, Jewish communal bodies lost their governmental powers, and Jews were promised that if they proved worthy, they would be granted the full rights of citizenship. In almost every region, one of the first conditions for granting the Jews new rights was that they take permanent family names in order for the government to monitor them, as they were already monitoring their non-Jewish subjects.

In most countries, Jews were given three to six months to choose a permanent family name. In a few places, such as Galicia, they were told that the government would choose names for them. Some governments put restrictions on what names Jews could choose, excluding names of noblemen in some places and in others forbidding Hebrew names or typically Gentile names. Within these restrictions the Jews had a choice. One can imagine the dilemma that many European Jews faced when they learned of the requirement to choose a family name quickly, a name that would now accompany all their descendants. Many Jews simply took the patronymic, nickname, or place name they had been using previously and registered them as their family names. Others, however, either because they did not have or did not like their nickname, made up new names. These newly invented names, known in German as *Modenamen* or "fashionable names," were generally combinations of words that seemed beautiful sounding at the time. It's easy to imagine them putting together names from various words by picking "one from column A and one from column B."

Column A	Column B
Rosen- (roses)	-berg (hill)
Blumen- (flowers)	-thal (valley)
Gold-	- man
Loewen- (lions)	-baum (tree)
Fein- (fine)	-wasser (water)
Silber- (silver)	-blatt (leaf)
Schoen- (beautiful)	-stein (stone)

From Rosen- they could create such names as Rosenberg (rose hill), Rosenthal (rose valley), Rosenman (rose man), Rosenbaum (rose tree), Rosenwasser (rose water), Rosenblatt (rose leaf), and Rosenstein (rose stone). Almost every imaginable tree (and some that are purely fantastic) became the source of a Jewish family name: Appelbaum (apple tree), Birnbaum or Barenboim (pear tree), Kirschenbaum (cherry tree), Kestenbaum (chestnut tree), Eichenbaum (oak tree), Flumenbaum (plum tree), Tannenbaum (fir tree), Lindenbaum (linden tree), Feigenbaum (fig tree), Teitelbaum (date tree), and even Goldbaum (gold tree) and just plain Baum. There was often no requirement that members of the same family choose the same last name. So two brothers might chose completely different names (like Schoen and Lang, for instance), while many people who were unrelated could independently choose to be named Goldberg.

Since the Russian alphabet lacked an *h*, an entire series of doublets was created, which are really the same name: Hendler/Gendler, Horowitz/Gurevitch, Galpern/Halpern, Heller/Geller, and Hirshenson/Gershenson. In some Yiddish dialects the *h* was dropped, as in Cockney English, so Halpert became Alpert and Hungerleider became Ungerleider. Sometimes an *h* was added where it didn't originally exist, resulting in Helfand/Gelfand/Elfant, which all mean "elephant."

Because the permanent family names were imposed as part of centralization and modernization by European states, they never became completely "naturalized" in traditional Ashkenazic society. This differs from the situation in Sephardic Jewry, in which family names have been around for hundreds of years and still have official Jewish status. Many non-Ashkenazic Jewish groups, but no Ashkenazic ones, use the family name for calls to the Torah: "Ya'amod hashem hatov kevod rebi Moshe Toledano" ("the honorable Mr. Moshe Toledano is called to rise to come to the Torah"), whereas Ashkenazim still use the ancient "Moshe ben Shmuel" ("Moses the son of Samuel"). In an East European synagogue "Ya'amod Moshe Shapiro" ("Moshe Shapiro is called to rise to come to the Torah") would have seemed odd indeed. Not only were family names not admitted into the religious service, many people simply didn't use them in daily life. To greet Moshe Shapiro on the street, you would say in Yiddish, "Sholem Aleichem" or "Gut Morgn Reb Moshe" ("Hello, Mr. Moshe"), using the first name only. In fact, many shtetl dwellers were unaware of their neighbors' last names since these names were used only to deal with the government. Moshe Shapiro might very well be known to his neighbors by such nicknames as *Moyshe Shloyme dem Bekers* (Moses the son of Solomon the baker) or *der hoykher Moyshe* (tall Moses) rather than as Shapiro.

The Jewishness of Names

The hereditary family names that did become standard throughout the Jewish world were sometimes distinctively Jewish and sometimes not. Germany is full of non-Jewish people named Gross, Schwarz, Klein, Mayer, and Zimmermann. Similarly, Poland has Kowalskys, Russia has Medvedevs and Sokolovs, and the Ukraine even had a president named Kravchuk. Other names seem Jewish because they are common among Jews but are shared by some non-Jews, such as Jacobson, Löwenstein, and Hamburger in Germany. Even a "typically Jewish" name such as Rosenberg was shared by the notorious Nazi Alfred Rosenberg, who didn't have the slightest hint of a Jewish background. Both a Jew and a non-Jew could, of course, be named after the same place, occupation, or personal quality. Some names, which are typically Jewish in one area, are not considered Jewish at all in others. No one in Norway or Sweden assumes that Mr. Jacobson is a Jew. Krause is a typically non-Jewish name in Germany, but in eastern Europe it is a typically Jewish one.

Often the local population knows what is a typical Jewish name even if to an Ashkenazic Jew it does not sound Jewish. This is the case of many Italian names derived from place names. A former student of mine named Viterbi told me that when a flight attendant on Alitalia heard his name, she immediately replied, "Oh you're Jewish!" To a North African, Ben-Soussan or Kalifa sound like typical Jewish names, but Goldman and Rosenfeld sound German. Sometimes we infer a Jewish connection from a patronymic, so we would guess that Eliashvili was a Georgian Jewish name but that Dzhugashvili (Stalin's real family name) was not Jewish. But this method of determining the Jewishness of a name is never certain.

Even though, in the United States, one way to estimate the Jewish population is to see how many names appear on the "List of Distinctive Jewish Names," this is far from a foolproof method.

Further complicating the idea of Jewish family names is the fact that many Jewish families have changed their original names. In some cases this was done purposely to conceal or at least play down one's Jewishness, as when Kohen became Kovacs in Hungary, Brownstein became Brown, Goldberg became Graham, and Schewelewitz became Smith in the United States. The list of Jews in the theater who took less distinctive stage names is almost endless: in Germany, Max Goldmann became Max Reinhardt; in the United States, Judy Tuwim became Judy Holliday, Isser Danilevich became Kirk Douglas, and Bernie Schwarz became Tony Curtis. Only in contemporary America has the trend been reversed, with a non-Jewish actor helping her career by changing her name from Caryn Johnson to Whoopi Goldberg.

Name changes were not necessarily the result of a desire to assimilate. Often they were simply a by-product of emigrating to a new country. There are many stories and jokes about the names given to Jewish immigrants at Ellis Island, including the old joke about the immigrant who picked a new name and forgot it. When he got to the official who asked his name, he said in Yiddish "Shoyn fargessen" ("I already forgot"), whereupon he emerged as Sean Ferguson. Very often immigration clerks did not have the patience to write down the long and seemingly unspellable names of the immigrants. They simply wrote down Shereshefsky as Sherman, Matyevitz as Matthews, and Galeshevsky as Goldberg. Often they seem to have decided that "I can't spell it but they're Jewish; so I'll call them Cohen or Greenberg or Halpern." Many an American Jewish family no longer knows its original family name.

A similar thing happened in Israel, although there changes were often made for more ideological reasons. Zionist ideology believed in the rejection of the Diaspora and the substitution of Hebrew for the old Jewish vernaculars. Therefore, new immigrants were encouraged to Hebraicize their original names. Many of the leaders of the new Jewish state had new Hebrew names different from their birth names: David Ben Gurion (originally Green), Levi Eshkol (originally Shkolnik), Golda Meir (originally Meyerson), and Zalman Shazar (originally Ruba-schoff). At one point in Israel's history, members of the diplomatic corps were re-quired to Hebraicize their name. Many Israelis translated their original names or picked names that sounded vaguely similar. Lowenstein would be translated as Evenari (lion stone) or Avenary or changed in sound to Lavi. Steinberg would be-come Har Even (stone hill); Goldberg, Har-Paz (gold hill); Gartner, Ginat (gar-den); Benaya, Ben-Naim, and Schoenberg, Shen-Har (the first part sounding like Schoen and the second part translating -*berg* into Hebrew).

Despite the relative recentness of Jewish family names and the fact that many names have been changed in recent times, names continue to be seen as a sign of Jewishness by many people. For some, changing one's name to hide one's Jewishness seems a more serious denial of Jewish attachments than such viola-tions of traditional religious law as eating pork or doing business on Saturday. In a small number of cases, children have gone back to the original family name given up by their parents or grandparents. The authors of *The People's Almanach*, by Irving Wallace and David Wallechinsky, are actually father and son (Wallace is the father and Wallechinsky is the son). Part of this phenomenon is related to the re-vival of ethnicity and the search for roots that is a part of contemporary Ameri-can (and Israeli) culture. In an ironic way, this return to original names, revival of ethnic identity, and search for attachment to the past are the flip side of the process of assimilation and the loss of roots. It is only now, when the organic ties to the past have been weakened by modernity, that the search for roots has be-come a widespread pursuit.

Names continue to be a shorthand way to identify people with an ethnic group, even in our multiethnic, highly mixed contemporary society. They are still used by scholars doing studies of ethnic populations and by members of the group searching for others who share their background. Although family names are certainly no foolproof way of determining who is a Jew and who is not, they are still a convenient marker used by both Jews and non-Jews to tell (or at least guess) if a person is Jewish. They continue to remain the marker of a Jew (in many cases), even when the original source and meaning of the name have long been forgotten, even by the bearers of the names themselves.

Religious Practice

How the Written Tradition Unites and the

Oral Tradition Divides

THE SHARED RELIGIOUS TRADITIONS OF RABBINIC JUDAISM ALLOWED JEWS WHO were spread all over the world to follow similar practices. Many aspects of life were codified in the vast corpus of Jewish law: the outlines of the prayer book, the basic prohibitions of the Sabbath and dietary laws, regulations on married life, the Jewish calendar and its holidays, circumcision, marriage and funeral practices, even which shoe to put on first. Jewish men everywhere wore a prayer shawl (*tallit*) and phylacteries (*tefillin*) every weekday morning and prayed in Hebrew three times a day. Jewish women went to the ritual bath every month after menstruation, lit the Sabbath lights, and (in remembrance of the Temple offerings) burned a portion of the dough they kneaded. All over the world Jews listened to the blowing of the ram's horn on Rosh Hashanah, built huts and ate in them on Sukkot, and sat at the family table on Passover for the annual Seder ritual with matzos, wine, and bitter herbs.

But no tradition, not even the Jewish one, can codify everything. Some aspects of life always escaped the formal legal enactments. Even though rabbinic Jews everywhere shared the same legal written texts, the Bible, Talmud, and Shulchan Aruch, there were still many aspects of these texts that were open to interpretation or that were simply not spelled out. The written tradition might prescribe a festive meal on the Sabbath, but it did not provide a detailed menu. It might require modesty in dress, but it did not give a description of what garments one must wear. It prescribed the texts for prayer but did not determine what melody had to accompany them.

Jews in traditional societies did not see the gaps in the written regulations as an opportunity to escape communal norms; rather than leaving the uncodified areas to individual discretion, they tried to infuse them with religious and cultural meaning. It was characteristic of traditional Jewish societies to fill in the outline of Jewish law with ceremonies, folk beliefs, foods, music, and decoration. Codified Jewish law is like a blueprint that shows the general structure of a house, while the folk tradition is akin to the color scheme, decorations, and personal touches that turn each unit in a row of tract houses into an individualized and personalized home.

As an all-encompassing system, Jewish law itself contains a principle that regulates the relationship between what is codified and what is not. The codified part of Jewish practice, or great tradition, is known as *din* (law); the uncodified practice, or little tradition, is known as *minhag* (custom). The law itself contains the Hebrew maxim "Minhag yisrael kedin hu" ("A Jewish custom has the force of law")—a maxim that the folk tradition magnified in the Yiddish proverb "A minhag brekht a din" ("A custom is stronger than [literally, breaks] a law"). The force of these sayings is to strengthen local custom and make it authoritative. A person brought up with one custom must continue to adhere to that practice; a community must continue its custom rather than adopt the ritual of another place; and within a community there should be a single liturgy and agreed-upon practices.

Because of the authority of local custom, Judaism was marked by dissimilar traditions existing side by side in different places, each equally authoritative, despite the variation in nuance. The law itself requires contrasting local practices: Passover must be seven days in Israel and eight days outside it; Purim falls on the 14th of Adar in most places but on the 15th in walled cities; Eastern European Jews must wait 6 hours after eating meat to eat dairy products, but German Jews need wait only 3 hours and Dutch Jews only 72 minutes; rice is a permitted Passover food for Yemenite or Iraqi Jews but is forbidden for Ashkenazim.

Historically the Jewish legal system has developed in such a way that the unwritten becomes written and custom tends to turn into law. Originally, only biblical law was written; the oral traditions were not allowed to be written down. They could be learned only through direct contact between teacher and disciple. Eventually, after the Roman authorities forbade the Jews to teach the tradition in public, the main oral traditions were written down in the Mishna (c. 200 CE). Later, the oral discussions of the Mishna were written down as the Babylonian Talmud (c. 500), followed by medieval law codes, the most authoritative of which was the Shulchan Aruch (1565). But the process continued even after this final codification, as the replies of each generation of traditional rabbis to new legal questions set new precedents. Often these questions and answers were published, creating a huge responsa literature. Practices that began as customs (sometimes even customs opposed by rabbinic authorities) eventually became codified. Examples of such practices are the bar mitzvah ceremony, the rejoicing of the law of the ninth day of Tabernacles (Simchat Torah), and the *tashlich* ceremony, in which people went to a body of water on the New Year to "throw their sins into the sea."

The Synagogue and Its Service

The dichotomy between uniform laws and diverse customs can be found in virtually all aspects of Jewish religious practice. One area where it is clearly noticeable is in the synagogue service. Throughout the world, traditional Jewish liturgy is characterized by a service virtually completely in Hebrew, and consists of three daily services, an additional Sabbath and holiday service, and a fifth Yom Kippur service. Every service has a set prayer (the Amidah) of nineteen blessings on weekdays, seven on Sabbath and holidays, and nine on the New Year. The Shema Yisrael (Hear O Israel), containing the basic credo of divine unity, is recited twice daily. The Torah scroll is read twice on the Sabbath and once on Monday and Thursday. These are only the most obvious aspects of uniformity.

Despite this unity of basic structure, custom created myriad local rites with many differences of detail and nuance. Though to an outsider the variations might have seemed minor, to traditional Jews they were matters of significance. Disagreement about the order of certain prayers led to a difference in the service. There were also variations in the wording of certain prayers. The liturgy was expanded by the addition of many new prayers and liturgical poems (*piutim*) written mainly in the Middle Ages. These new prayers are rarely universal and usually differ from region to region. The new prayers are not necessarily of minor importance. On the High Holidays they include such significant liturgical compositions as Kol Nidre, *Unetane Tokef* (describing the heavenly court of judgment), and the *Avoda* (a poetic description of the ancient Temple service on Yom Kippur).

Because of these differences, Jewish prayer books appear in different regional versions (*nusachot*). The liturgies are generally grouped into two main traditions, which are then subdivided into further local varieties. The variations among the different liturgies are smallest in the Sabbath and weekday prayers, greater for the festivals, and greatest for the High Holidays and penitential services (Selichot). The two main prayer book traditions are generally traced back to the differences between the traditions of the Land of Israel (Palestinian tradition), from which the Ashkenazic rite descended, and those of Babylonia, from which the Sephardic rite evolved. The Sephardic rite has replaced the former liturgy of a number of areas in the Muslim East far beyond the area where Judeo-Spanish was spoken.

Among Ashkenazic Jews the divisions of the ritual are quite complicated. Originally all Ashkenazic Jews used the Ashkenazic rite, which was divided into two main subgroups—the Western, now known as Nusach Ashkenaz (the German rite), and the Eastern, generally known as Nusach Polin (the Polish rite). When the Hasidic movement developed in the eighteenth century, it made a radical change in liturgy by adopting a version of the Sephardic rite. The Hasidic rite known as Nusach Sfard or Nusach Ha'ari (after the famous mystic Isaac Luria [1534–1572], who was nicknamed Ari [the Lion]), is not to be confused with the real Nusach Sepharad of the Jews of the Mediterranean area. Although its text is close to, but not the same as, the rite of the Sephardim, the Hasidic prayer book is read according to Ashkenazic pronunciation rules and with Ashkenazic musical traditions.

Visitors to traditional synagogue services in various parts of the world would notice a number of regional differences. Probably most noticeable is the difference in musical tradition. The music of the synagogue in Western Europe, and to a considerable extent in Eastern Europe as well, was greatly influenced by Western musical styles. Although there are elements of earlier systems, the melodies of Ashkenazic, Italian, and Dutch Sephardic liturgies tend to be in either major or minor keys. The music of the Jews of the Arab world, of Iran, and of the Sephardim of Southeastern Europe sounds much more Middle Eastern in its chanting style, in its use of "microtones" (sounds in between Western notes), and in its rhythms, which will be discussed further in Chapter 8. These musical differences are very noticeable in Torah reading as well. All rabbinic Jews share the same system of written cantilation symbols, but the method of performing this system of "notation" is completely different. There is an Ashkenazic tradition, which is pentatonic, and a separate Sephardic-Oriental tradition, which has few resemblances to the Ashkenazic system.

The way the prayer leader and congregation interacted also varied regionally. Sephardic, Oriental, and Yemenite services were generally chanted out loud by the cantor or by selected members of the congregation, often with rhythmic choruses of congregational chanting. In Ashkenazic synagogue services the cantor usually sang only the beginnings and ends of prayers, and the congregation murmured the rest of the prayers at a rapid pace. In general, there was less attention to decorum in the traditional Ashkenazic synagogue than in the traditional Oriental one. Certain regions, notably North Africa and Eastern Europe, developed

5.1 Bipolar arrangement of Italian synagogues exemplified by the layout of reader's desk, benches, and ark of the Conegliano Veneto synagogue, 1701, at its present location in Jerusalem.

styles of elaborate cantorial singing in which the prayer leader sang long selections. The Moroccan style, with its many ornaments, resembled Arabic and flamenco singing, while the East European style was more emotional and intended to arouse tears in the congregants.

Although all synagogues had an ark in the front to hold the Torahs, the layout of synagogues differed regionally as well. Synagogues generally faced Jerusalem, which in Europe meant that the "Eastern wall" was the front of the synagogue, but in Iraq or Iran meant that congregants faced in a westerly direction. Traditional Ashkenazic synagogues generally had a cantor's stand (*omud*) in the front and a platform (*bima* or *almemor*) in the center on which the desk for reading the Torah was located. Often the men had individual stands for their books in front of their chairs. Congregants usually faced forward in Ashkenazic synagogues, though in informal Eastern European synagogues the men often sat around tables. In many Sephardic and Oriental synagogues, congregants were grouped in rows on both sides of the hall facing the center. Italian synagogues were arranged in a "bipolar" manner with the Ark in the front and the cantor's desk on an elevated platform in the rear (Illustration 5.1). In the synagogues of southern India there were two cantors' platforms, one on the main floor and the other in front of the women's balcony.

In some countries of the Muslim world, the Jews shared with their neighbors the custom of removing the shoes before entering the sanctuary. In these countries the congregants often sat on the carpeted floor rather than on chairs or benches. Among European Jews, both the removal of shoes and sitting on the floor are associated exclusively with mourning customs and would otherwise be unthinkable in the synagogue.

In the traditional synagogue, women were separated from men by a partition. In Europe, women in many congregations sat in a gallery or balcony behind a latticework and looked down on the proceedings in the "main synagogue." In the synagogues of Carpentras and Cavaillon of southern France, the balcony was set aside for communal dignitaries and ritual objects, and the women originally sat in a room *below* the main sanctuary. In the Muslim countries, some synagogues dispensed with a women's section altogether because women did not generally attend the synagogue. On the rare occasions when they did attend, they simply stood in the back of the synagogue.

Other differences in the public service involved the form of the Torah scroll. Jewish law prescribed that the Five Books of Moses be handwritten in black ink on a single parchment roll, but it did not prescribe what kind of covering this scroll had to have. In the European tradition, practiced by Ashkenazic Jews, as well as by Jews who lived in Italy, southern France, parts of Morocco and Algeria, and among Sephardim in the Ottoman Empire, the scroll was attached to two wooden rollers (Atzei Chaim), and then covered with a decorated mantle of cloth (nowadays generally velvet) (Illustration 5.2). The mantle was usually topped with a silver breastplate and the rollers with a silver crown (Illustration

5.2 (left) Torah with a velvet mantle from Morocco, 18th or 19th century.

5.3 (center) Torah Crown, Vienna, 19th century (silver, repoussé, chased, parcel gilt).

5.4 (right) Torah finials (rimmonim) Turkey, late 18th–early 19th century (silver, repoussé, cast).

5.3) or two finials (*rimmonim*) (Illustration 5.4). In most of Asia and North Africa (including the Samaritan communities), the Torah scroll was enclosed in a wooden or metal case (*tik*), rather than a mantle and had neither crowns nor breastplates. Usually the case was circular, though sometimes it was octagonal or hexagonal. The two halves of the case were connected with hinges to enable the tik to be opened for reading (Illustrations 5.5, 5.6). In some areas the case was covered with a cloth, but in others it remained uncovered. When the Torah was read, European Jews removed the coverings and laid the bare Torah scroll down

5.5 (left) Exterior of a Torah case from India, late 19th–early 20th century (silver, chased, die-stamped, and wood, painted).

5.6 (right) Torah in a case, open for reading, Iraq, 1869.

מפה לכבור התורה
איסתר אישת כמר
שמואל סונינו ::

5.7   *Torah Binder, Italy, 17th century*
      (undyed linen, embroidered in silk thread)

5.8 *Torah Binder (wimpel), Germany, 1733*
      (linen, embroidered with silk thread)

on the reader's desk. Most Jews in the Muslim countries read the Torah with the case in a vertical position, though in Yemen the case was placed in a lying position. The Torah case had several decorated finials, the number varying regionally.

In countries where the Torah was covered with cloth alone, the scroll had to be bound so that it did not unravel. The binders took different forms in various parts of Europe. In Eastern Europe, the Torah was generally bound with a plain, narrow white piece of cloth called a *gartel* (literally, "belt") whose ends were tied in a bow. (In recent years, some forward-looking congregations have replaced this with a new-fangled velcro-attached binder.) In Italy a wider Torah binder was devised, usually decorated with lettering containing the name of its (usually female) donor (Illustration 5.7). The characteristic German Jewish Torah binder, known as the *Wimpel*, was similar to the Italian binder but more elaborate, an example of Ashkenazic German Jews and non-Ashkenazic Italians sharing similar traits. Wimpels were made in honor of the birth of a baby boy and sometimes were fashioned from the diaper used at the circumcision, which was cut into strips that were then sewn end to end. Fashioned in the form of long linen rolls (usually about 6 inches wide and 10 feet long), they contained an embroidered or painted inscription with the newborn's name, birth date and the wish that "God make him grow to (the study of the) Torah, the marriage canopy, and good deeds." Wimpels were often elaborately illuminated with folk designs and illustrations (Illustration 5.8).

Some other local variations in the synagogue involved the prayer shawls and phylacteries that men wore. Among most Oriental Jews, but also among Ashkenazic Jews in Germany, boys began to wear the talit at the age of bar mitzvah (thirteen) or even earlier. In Eastern Europe, on the other hand, the custom grew that only married men wore the talit. In many Mediterranean countries the prayer shawl was made of silk or cotton, while among Ashkenazic Jews wool was the traditional material used. In virtually all countries the talit was white and decorated with a pattern of colored or black stripes, a practice that is not codified but seems to have a common origin, perhaps the decorations on Roman outer garments. Yemen was the one country in which the talit did not have this pattern. But even in Yemen, the Western-style white talit with stripes came into vogue in the twentieth century.

As prescribed by Jewish law, tefillin, black leather boxes containing four specified biblical texts, were bound on the left arm and around the forehead at the hairline. What varied is the way the tefilin were bound. In all areas, Jews bound the arm tefillin seven times around the lower arm and then around the hand and middle fingers. Ashkenazic Jews bound them in a counterclockwise fashion and formed the letter shin, with its apex facing the thumb, on the back of the hand. On the palm of the hand, the letters daled and yud were formed, spelling out a divine name (Illustration 5.9a). Jews in the Muslim world bound their tefillin in a different pattern with crosswise patterns on the back of the hand (Illustration 5.9b). Perhaps Jews in Christian lands avoided such a pattern because of its seem-

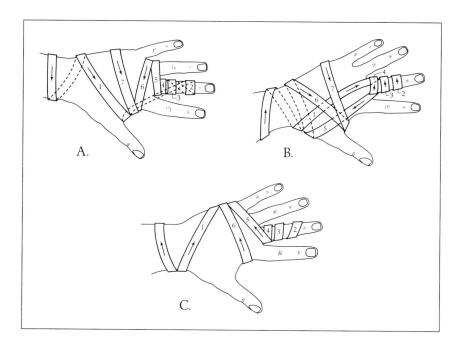

5.9 Different traditions of winding Tefillin on the hand: a) Ashkenazic b) Sephardic-Oriental c) Hasidic

ing resemblance to a cross. Hasidim, Ashkenazic Jews who had adopted certain Sephardic practices, formed the letters shin, dalet, and yud on the hand, but they formed them with the apex away from the thumb and wound their tefilin in a clockwise direction (Illustration 5.9c). These differences may seem minor, but they are examples of systematic geographic and cultural variations.

The Festivals

Geographical diversity in customs was also strongly evident in home celebrations of holidays. Though there are many possible examples of variations, the symbolic foods of Rosh Hashanah and the Passover Seder are sufficient to illustrate the richness of local differences. At the beginning of the New Year, it was customary for

*A*lthough all rabbinic Jews used bitter herbs and haroset at the Seder, the ingredients actually used differed. Many Ashkenazic Jews used sharp-tasting horseradish (sometimes in the form of unground, raw horseradish root) for their bitter herbs, while most non-Ashkenazic Jews used various mildly bitter forms of lettuce. Recipes for haroset, intended to commemorate the mortar used by the Hebrew slaves in their building labors, varied at least as widely. Among Ashkenazic Jews the usual main ingredients of haroset were apples, nuts, cinnamon, and wine, all of which were available (or at least obtainable) in a cold climate. In many parts of the Middle East, Italy, and the Balkans, dates were used instead of apples and other subtropical ingredients were sometimes added, such as orange or orange peel, figs, pine nuts, and pomegranate.

In most parts of the world, haroset was sweet. In Yemen participants at the Seder had a choice of two types of haroset, called dukke—one sweet and one sour. Both types were made with dates, raisins, figs, sesame, pomegranate, almonds and other nuts, pepper, cumin, and ginger. The sweet type was mixed with grape juice and the sour type with wine vinegar.

all persons at the family table to eat foods that were symbolic of blessing for the upcoming year. Among Ashkenazic Jews this custom was often limited to the eating of an apple dipped in honey as a symbol of a sweet year. Less common customs of some Ashkenazic Jews were the eating of the head of a sheep or fish, "so that we shall be the head and not the tail," and also the eating of carrots. The latter food was eaten because its Yiddish name, *mern*, also meant "to increase," and a prayer was said that God should "increase our merits."

All these symbolic Ashkenazic foods are rudimentary compared to the Rosh Hashana ceremony among Sephardic and Oriental Jews. Among them, the eating of symbolic foods was a *Seder* (set ritual) with a host of special dishes. Sephardic Jews in Greece and Turkey ate apples, leeks, beets, dates, squash, fish, and the head of a fish. Each food was accompanied by a short prayer (*yehi ratson*) recited in both Hebrew and Ladino. Some of the prayers were based on puns involving the name of the food and the wish uttered for the New Year. In Arabic-speaking countries, the foods eaten were somewhat different because the plays on words between the foods name and its symbolic meaning were different in Judeo-Arabic than in Ladino.

Even more elaborate local customs were associated with the Seder ceremony at the beginning of Passover. There were, of course, many aspects of the Seder service prescribed by religious law that did not vary from place to place. These included the three matzos, the four cups of wine, the use of bitter herbs and their garnish (*haroset*), the symbols of an egg and a bone, the structure of the main part of the Hagada (Seder prayer book) before the meal, and the practice of reclining on cushions during the ceremony. Still, the regional variations were striking. The use of the vernacular was much greater at the Seder than at most Jewish ceremonies; in some places, the entire ritual and accompanying songs were recited in the vernacular, sometimes instead of, but usually in addition to, Hebrew.

The placement of the ritual foods for the Seder also differed culturally. Ashkenazic Jews grouped them on a special plate, while Jews in Tunisia and Libya placed them in a wicker basket. In Bukhara the foods were displayed on a silk, embroidered cloth. In Yemen, the table itself became the "Seder plate." A small, round wooden or metal table was covered with a layer of large-leaved radishes, over which were placed layers of parsley and lettuce. Plates of haroset and of meat and egg were placed in the middle of the table in a space left free of leaves (Illustration 5.10). During the parts of the ceremony when Jews in other countries lifted the Seder plate, Yemenites lifted the entire table.

5.10 Yemenite seder table with layers of greens around the edge and other ritual foods in the center.

5.11 Passing the Seder plate over the heads of the participants—
Benaroch family of Meknes, Morocco.

The text of the Hagada varied as well, especially in the part after the festive meal. A series of songs that became favorites in the Ashkenazic rite (*Adir Hu, Ehad Mi Yodea, Had Gadya*) were absent from the ritual of many Jews in Asia, though in some parts of Asia and North Africa they were recited in the Judeo-Arabic or Judeo-Spanish vernacular. The Ashkenazic custom of pouring a fifth cup of wine and opening the door for the prophet Elijah was unknown in Yemen, India, and Kurdistan but was practiced in Bukhara. The recitation of the four questions by a child, a centerpiece of the Ashkenazic Seder, was not customary in Tunisia, Cochin, or Aden, where everyone recites the questions in unison, but it was customary in Yemen, where children did the recitation in both Hebrew and Arabic (*ma kebar*).

Various customs were introduced to make the ceremony more interesting to children, but most of them were not universal. The custom of having a child "steal" and hold the *afikoman* (piece of matzo needed to complete the ceremony) for ransom was common in Europe and in Kurdistan but not in Tunisia, India, or Iran. In parts of North Africa (Morocco, Tunisia) it was customary to pass the

Seder plate three times over the heads of the guests as a sign of blessing at the beginning of the Seder (Illustration 5.11). In some places this was done by the head
of the household; in others, by the oldest unmarried daughter or by a son. One
European Jewish traveler to North Africa tells of his discomfiture during the
Seder when he stood up at the wrong time and knocked over the plate being
passed over his head.

In Kurdistan, the Caucasus, and Yemen, and in parts of North Africa, too, the
Seder leader placed the matzo over his shoulders and walked around the table
(or went outside), saying "So did our forefathers leave Egypt." In the Kurdistani
and Caucasian version this ceremony was greatly elaborated. In some towns there
was a dialogue: "Where are you from? Egypt. What are you bringing? The dough
of our fathers from Egypt. They had no time to bake it. Come, I will tell you the
story that God performed for our fathers." In some places a boy acted out the
scene, coming to the door wearing a beard and limping into the house. (Pesach,
usually translated as "Passover," can also mean "limping.")

The Seder song "Dayenu" ("It Would Have Been Enough") was enacted in different ways in different areas. In Yemen, the table was picked up off the floor at
each refrain of "Dayenu." In Iran and in some neighboring parts of Iraqi Kurdistan, the celebrants beat each other with leeks or scallions during the recital of
"Dayenu." This was intended to memorialize the beating of the Hebrew slaves
but often resulted in raucous hilarity. I remember attending a student model
Seder in Los Angeles at which the rabbis were Ashkenazi but many of the students were Iranian. When the children started to hit each other with scallions, the
rabbis tried in vain to quell the "disturbance."

Local Festivals

Besides the holidays celebrated by Jews around the world, there are some holidays known only to particular subgroups of Jews. All rabbinic Jews celebrated the
festival of Purim on the 14th of Adar to commemorate the deliverance of the

Jews from massacre in the Persian Empire, as related in the biblical book of Esther. But in many parts of the world, an additional local Purim was celebrated as well. In the Middle Ages and even in modern times, it became customary for specific communities, or even families, that had been saved from imminent danger to institute such a local Purim celebrated only in that locality or family. In some of these local Purims there were even special synagogue services with the reading of a scroll commemorating the deliverance. One such local Purim, called Purim Vinz, took place in Frankfurt, Germany, to commemorate the return of the Jews to the city in 1616 after their expulsion by rebels led by Vincenz (Vinz) Fettmilch. Fettmilch's execution was compared to the hanging of Haman, the villain of the biblical Purim story. A special scroll, Megilas Vinz, recounting the event, was written in Hebrew and Yiddish. Another special Purim was celebrated in a number of Italian cities to commemorate their rescue from French bombardments during the wars of the 1790s. In Prague the "Curtain Purim" celebrated the rescue of a communal official in 1622 from hanging after being accused of hiding stolen curtains. The Brandeis family of Mlada Boleslav, Bohemia, celebrated the 10th of Adar as Powidl Purim ("plum jam Purim") because the family was cleared of the charge of poisoning Gentiles with plum jam in 1731.

A different kind of localized festival that has gained popularity in Israel in recent years is the Mimouna. Originally celebrated in North Africa on the night

5.12 The Seged ceremony as held in Ethiopia in 1984. Women climbing the mountain with stones on their heads as a symbol of penitence.

(and day) following the end of Passover, today it is the great "ethnic festival" of Moroccans in Israel, which no politician would miss in an election year. The origins of the festival and the meaning of the word "Mimouna" are obscure. The first written references to the festival date only to the eighteenth century. Practices connected with the Mimouna vary from place to place but include at least some of the following: eating the first leavened food immediately after Passover (generally pancakes [*mufleta*] or couscous); putting fish (sometimes live fish in a bowl) on the table; placing a cup filled with oil on a plate of flour; placing greens in the home; beating household members with green twigs; gathering at a spring or a river on the morning of the Mimouna; and eating dairy foods.

Ethiopian Jews, who were not followers of the rabbinic tradition, observed a number of holidays unknown to rabbinic Jews. The most famous of these was the Seged, which has become the ethnic festival of Ethiopians in Israel. On the 29th day of the eighth month, Ethiopian Jews went to the top of a hill to hear the priests (*kessim*) read excerpts from the Bible and expound them (Illustrations 5.12, 5.13). They bowed to the earth many times. The priests were generally separated from the people by a cloth or a circle of stones. The first half of the Seged day was a fast, and the second half was a time for dancing and feasting on meat and other good foods.

Another type of Jewish festival common in many parts of the world was held

5.13 The Seged ceremony as held in Ethiopia in 1984. Men returning down the hill after the ceremony.

in honor of deceased holy individuals. Although official Jewish philosophy has no place for saints or intercessors between humans and God, a number of Jewish folk cultures placed a high value on the holy man. The Hasidim of Eastern Europe and the Jews of North Africa, although widely separated geographically, both celebrated the anniversaries of the death of holy men and venerated their graves. In both traditions the death of the pious was not considered a sad occasion, since the holy person, now in the spiritual realm, could intervene on behalf of those left behind. Many Hasidic groups celebrated the *yahrzeit* (anniversary of death) of departed *rebbes* (Hasidic leaders) with gatherings where they ate, drank, sang, and told stories about the departed. Pilgrimages to the rebbe's grave became a common event among Hasidim. In post-Communist Eastern Europe, pilgrimages of Hasidim to holy sites have been revived (increasing tourist income, to the delight of the Polish and Ukrainian governments). Among Habad (Lubavitch) Hasidim there were also special festivals, including the 19th of Kislev, which commemorated the freeing of the first Lubavitcher rebbe, Shneur Zalman of Liady, from imprisonment in 1799.

The veneration of holy rabbis in North Africa was similar in form to the Hasidic yahrzeit of the rebbe, but had a somewhat different background, since it was similar to the practice of North African Muslims of venerating a holy man (*marabout*). North African Jews, too, made the anniversary of death (called *hilula* [literally, "wedding"]) an occasion for gathering, feasting, and celebration. Many areas had local holy graves, which became sites for pilgrimages. Besides honoring local great rabbis—for example, the rabbis of the Abu Hatzeira family—a hilula could also celebrate great rabbis of the ancient past. The greatest hilula of all, celebrated not only in North Africa but throughout most of the non-Ashkenazic Jewish world (and to some extent among Ashkenazim as well), is the hilula of the second century rabbi Shimon bar Yohai, who is traditionally identified as the author of the central book of Jewish mysticism, the Zohar. This celebration, held on the 18th of Iyar, coincided with the traditional minor Jewish festival of Lag Ba'omer. In Israel today, the hilula at the traditional gravesite of Rabbi Shimon in Meron is a huge event, with bonfires, roasting of meat, prayers, and singing. Both Ashkenazim and non-Ashkenazim attend; Hasidim mark the occasion with the first haircut of young boys (at age three). In honor of Rabbi Shimon, Jews in the Muslim countries sing a special song, "Bar Yohai" not only at the hilula, but also on virtually any happy occasion.

Folk Beliefs and "Superstitions"

The practice of showing a degree of veneration for special individuals is a good example of a widespread folk practice that seems to be at odds with the Jewish philosophical tradition. Similarly the rabbinic tradition had at least some qualms about belief in miraculous or magical cures and powers. All the great monotheistic religions try to draw a line between the accepted doctrine of the religion and the "superstitious" practices of the masses, but the line is not always clear. Many a rabbi, in talmudic times and later, was said to have special powers to intervene with the divine, effect cures, bring rain, or avert disasters. In medieval and later Ashkenazic Jewry, a rabbi who was said to have such powers was known as a *ba'al shem* (literally, a "master of the Name"). The most famous of these miracle workers was the founder of the Hasidic movement, Rabbi Israel (c. 1700–c. 1760), who was given the title Baal Shem Tov (the "good miracle worker") as a sign of his preeminence over other such "masters of the Name." In Germany, where the Hasidic movement made virtually no inroads, the most famous recent Baal Shem was Seckel Loeb Wormser (d. 1846), known as the Baal Shem of Michelstadt (a town just south of Frankfurt). Stories about this Baal Shem were told by village Jews throughout southern Germany even into the twentieth century.

Besides faith in the power of holy men, Jewish folk beliefs included the use of amulets, special prayers, and recitations to ward off illness, bad luck, or the "evil eye." Belief in the evil eye was widespread in the Middle East and the Mediterranean world among Christians, Jews, and Muslims. Generally it was considered to be a result of jealousy, which could be aroused by mentioning good luck, beauty, or other good qualities. A common verbal protection against bad luck was to state "no evil eye" after mentioning some good thing. So in Yiddish one would say, "*a sheyn kind, kenehore*" (a "beautiful child, no evil eye"). In German culture and among many Ashkenazic Jews, bad luck came through hearing rather than seeing; therefore one said "unberufen" or "unbeschrien" ("not bewitched" [literally, "not called out"]). These verbal protections were sometimes accompanied by ritualized spitting noises.

Other common methods used in Eastern Europe for protecting against bad luck were tying a red ribbon on a child's crib or carriage, or tying garlic or camphor around the neck to protect from disease. For certain kinds of disease, one might recite a special formula to get rid of the evil eye ("opshprekhn an ayin hore"). Sometimes various types of "sympathetic magic" were used to bring about some event. During difficult childbirths, Ashkenazic Jews would sometimes tie the belt of the Torah around the woman's waist or untie all the knots in the house. Pregnant women would bite off the tip (*pitom*) of the etrog fruit used on Sukkot as a charm for an easy birth. To avert plagues, such methods as measuring the cemetery with a string and then donating the string for wicks for the synagogue candles, or burying a lock and key to "lock up the plague," were sometimes attempted.

An amulet was a more formal way of averting bad fortune and usually enlisted Kabbalistic beliefs. Though an amulet could be either with or without inscriptions, many Jewish amulets were sheets of paper with letters or words written on them, sometimes in a specific geometric configuration, such as a seven-branched candelabrum (Illustration 5.14). Sometimes the letters did not have any obvious meaning, but at other times they spelled out phrases such as "Adam and Eve inside, Lilith outside"—a common formula against Lilith, an evil spirit who harmed newborns. In the Muslim countries, both Jews and Muslims often used necklaces in the shape of a hand called a *hamsa* (from the Arabic word for "five") to ward off bad luck.

Responses by the rabbinic leaders of official Judaism to these various types of folk belief were ambivalent. On the one hand, Judaism could not tolerate calling on any power other than God. On the other hand, the Talmud and much of rabbinic literature do recognize the existence of harmful spirits (shedim and *mazikim*), and Kabbalistic literature emphasizes the titanic struggle between good and evil forces in this world. Pre-modern rabbis often fought against witchcraft and against magical practices that were reminiscent of idolatrous practices. They attacked those whose amulets seemed to display reliance on heretical ideas, but they did not generally reject the idea that amulets served a purpose and that the supernatural forces could be called upon to fight the evil eye or evil spirits. Rabbis were ambiguous in their acceptance or rejection of astrology and of predictions of the future. Though

5.14 Amulet in the shape of a star by Rabbi Abdallah Joseph Somekh, North Africa (Morocco) (parchment).

the Talmud contains the expression "En Mazal Le'Yisrael" (literally, "Israel has no constellation"),* to imply that astrology did not have any power over the Jewish people, rabbis generally tolerated most of the folk beliefs designed to protect against the evil forces. They were on their guard, however, lest these beliefs cross the line into heresy, magic, or idolatry. Similar attitudes can be found among Christian and Muslim leaders in the Middle Ages as well.

Life Cycle Events

In connection with the life cycle, folk Judaism added numerous practices to the ceremonies required by religious law. The main ceremonies required by official Jewish law at the birth of a boy are circumcision on the eighth day after birth and the redemption of firstborn boys on the thirtieth day (unless they are the children of a Cohen or Levite). For the birth of a girl, no ceremony was required. In

---

*Because mazal is the Yiddish word for "luck," the saying was sometimes translated humorously as "Jews have no luck."

most parts of the world, however, Jewish people wanted a more elaborate cele-bration of a birth. In many places a ceremony was introduced for celebrating the birth of a girl, though it was usually a very pale substitute for the elaborate feast-ing and celebration at a boy's circumcision. Celebration of a girl's birth was gen-erally restricted to calling the father to the Torah (often on a weekday) and formally giving a name to the newborn girl. Among some Sephardic Jews this ceremony was elaborated somewhat and given the title Zeved Habat.

In medieval Germany an additional naming ceremony called Holekrash de-veloped, whose origins are disputed. Some scholars connect it to a pagan German ceremony to ward off the evil goddess Holle, while others connect it with the Hebrew word *chol* ("nonsacred," since the secular name is given at the cere-mony). In the nineteenth and twentieth centuries the Holekrash ceremony was celebrated only in southern Germany, Alsace, and Switzerland and generally took place six weeks after birth of a child. In some places it was for both boys and girls, in others only for girls, and in still others only for boys. All children under the age of twelve were invited; they lifted the baby's cradle, recited "Holekrash, how shall the child be called?" and gave the child its nonsacred (non-Hebrew) name. The ceremony sometimes included biblical verses and generally concluded with giv-ing the children large conical bags of candy (Illustration 5.15).

Many additional folk traditions were created among Ashkenazic Jews either to celebrate the birth of a boy or to protect him against evil forces. More celebra-tory than protective was the *zocher* or *sholem zocher* ("peace to the male"), held on the Friday night before the circumcision and accompanied by modest refresh-ments. More protective was the *wachnacht*, or vigil on the night before a circum-cision. Groups of men or children remained awake all night and studied Torah to ward off the danger. In a modified version, children came on the eve of the cir-cumcision to recite the Shema prayer together (*krishme leyenen*).

Various practices were also developed to "fool" the evil forces. Sometimes a child would be named Alter or Alte ("old one") with the hope that the Angel of Death, searching for a baby to kill, would think the baby was an old man or woman. Another method, used especially in Hasidic circles, was to allow a boy's hair to remain unshorn until age three. As the hair grew long, they believed the

5.15 Holekrash: Central European Jewish baby naming ceremony in an oil painting by Alis Guggenheim, Lengnau, Switzerland.

Angel of Death would be fooled into thinking that the little boy was a girl and would leave him alone.

In many parts of the world a ceremony developed to celebrate a boy's first day of school. In Ashkenazic Jewry, the alphabet, which the boy began to learn, was coated with honey, which he then was allowed to lick off the paper.

Another life cycle event, the bar mitzvah, now a universal part of official Judaism, began as a folk ceremony. Although the Talmud states that a boy attains legal adulthood at the age of thirteen, it does not prescribe any ritual for the occasion. Among Ashkenazic Jews, the custom grew that a boy demonstrated his entrance into full participation in the religious service by reading a portion of the Torah or the prophetic reading (*haftara*) at a Sabbath service. In many parts of the Muslim world, however, the essential demonstration of manly obligations was the putting on of tefilin, a practice done only on weekdays. Therefore, among Jews in the Muslim countries, the bar mitzvah was usually held on a Monday or Thursday (weekdays on which the Torah was read) rather than on the Sabbath. Additional practices associated with the bar mitzvah found in various parts of the world include the bar mitzvah discourse and the dinner in celebration of the event. In Cochin, India, the first haftara recited by a young boy (around the age of six) was a bigger celebration than the coming-of-age ceremony at age thirteen, which they called the *bar minyan* (since the boy could now be counted as part of the prayer quorum, or *minyan*).

In most traditional societies the bar mitzvah celebration was essentially a family or communal affair. Only in recent years, especially in the United States, has it become an extravaganza with increasingly elaborate feasting, decorations, and music. Someone once described these modern bar mitzvahs as "more bar than mitzvah." Within the last sixty years, the *bat mitzvah* for girls and the adult bar and bat mitzvah have been introduced, ceremonies that have gained great currency in American Jewry but were unknown before the twentieth century.

The next great life cycle event in Jewish life after the bar mitzvah is marriage. In most traditional societies (Jewish and non-Jewish), marriages were arranged between families, with only the most perfunctory consultation with the couple-to-be, and often involved complex financial arrangements such as dowries and trousseaus. In the Middle Ages the age at marriage seems to have been around puberty throughout the Jewish world, but this began to change in the seventeenth century in Western Europe. In the decades before World War I, the average age of marriage for Jewish brides in Eastern Europe rose from about seventeen to twenty-three. In many parts of the Muslim world, on the other hand, very early marriage, especially for brides, remained common among Jews well into the twentieth century.

Originally Jewish law permitted men to have multiple wives, though women were not allowed to practice polygamy. The Bible narratives are full of the complex problems that arose from relationships in the polygamous households of the Patriarchs. In medieval Christian Europe, the Jews' continued acceptance of polygamy clashed with the mores of their neighbors, and in tenth century Germany, Rabbenu Gershom prohibited polygamy. This prohibition, however, was held to be binding only by Ashkenazic Jewry. Jewish religious practice in other parts of the world still permitted men to have more than one wife, although economic and social conditions made polygamy rare. In some Muslim countries, Jewish women had a clause put into their marriage contracts forbidding their husbands to take another wife without their permission. By modern times, polygamy was rarely practiced by Jews, but it still existed in some parts of the Middle East. The Israeli government handled the touchy problem of what to do about this practice by validating the multiple marriages of immigrant men already married to more than one wife but forbidding them to take an additional wife after arriving in Israel.

Marriage ceremonies in different parts of the traditional Jewish world looked and sounded very different, despite the many common legal enactments. Originally the Jewish marriage consisted of two separate ceremonies—*kiddushin* (betrothal) and *nisuin* (marriage), which were often many months apart. In most of the Jewish world, these two ceremonies are now performed on the same day, one after the other. The basic element of the kiddushin ceremony is the transfer of an item of value from the groom to the bride. In modern times it has become customary for the groom to give the bride a ring, though Syrian Jews still use a coin that is later made into a ring. After the kiddushin ceremony, the marriage contract (*ketuba*) is read (in the Ashkenazic and some other traditions), after which the seven blessings of the nisuin ceremony are recited.

Since talmudic times, the nisuin ceremony has taken place in conjunction with a *chuppa*. Originally this seems to have been a decorated marriage chamber, but in most of the Jewish world today, it has taken the symbolic form of a marriage canopy. Among Yemenites the original marriage chamber is still used, and a canopy is not customary. In Cochin, India, and in parts of Iraq, the bride was seated on a chair near the Ark containing the Torah scrolls and a white silk or linen veil was suspended above the chair to cover the bride's face, but there was no canopy. In many parts of the Middle East, but also in Germany and Holland, a prayer shawl was spread over the bride and groom in addition to (or instead of) a marriage canopy. In the Ashkenazic tradition the bride and groom stood under the chuppa, and in many non-Ashkenazic traditions they were seated under the chuppa.

The practice of the bride wearing a white wedding dress is now common in many cultures around the world, including the Jewish community. But this practice is of relatively recent vintage. Although premodern pictures of traditional Ashkenazic weddings often depict the bride wearing a thick veil, they do not show a white dress with a train. In North Africa, the wedding dress (*keswa al kabira*) was an embroidered black and colored dress in the style of a Spanish costume. In Yemen, the bride wore an extremely elaborate costume whose exact form differed from town to town. In the capital, San'a, the bride's costume consisted of embroidered leggings, a red underdress, and a white one, and a gold brocade coat, along with many rows of necklaces made of silver, gilded silver, coins, coral beads, and pearls, as well as many bracelets and rings. On her head the bride wore a high triangular tiara of pearls adorned with flowers (Illustration 5.16). The entire outfit was so heavy that the bride could barely move.

5.16 *Traditional Yemenite bridal outfit, San'a, Yemen, 1930s.*

The wedding ceremony itself was often only one part of a series of celebrations lasting for many days. In Eastern Europe, the wedding was preceded by the *badekn* ceremony, at which the groom placed the veil on his bride's face; it was followed by seven days of banqueting to which at least one new person had to be invited. In Germany until the nineteenth century, the ceremony of *Mahnführen* was performed before the wedding. Wheat was thrown at the bride as a symbol of fertility.

5.17, 5.18 Chuppastein: Marriage stone built into the wall of synagogues in South Germany against which the groom smashed a glass at the wedding. Inscriptions include abbreviated form of the verse "the voice of gladness, the voice of joy, the voice of the bridegroom, the voice of the bride." Left: From the synagogue in Bingen. Right: From the synagogue in Edelfingen.

The tradition of the groom breaking a glass during the wedding ceremony was performed differently in various parts of the world. Its origins are said to be in mourning for the destroyed Temple at Jerusalem, but since it is often accompanied by cries of "Mazel tov" ("congratulations"), anthropologists have suggested other explanations for the custom. In a number of villages in southern Germany, where weddings were customarily performed in front of the synagogue, a *chuppastein* was incorporated in the outside wall of the synagogue. This was a stone with an inscription referring to the joy of the wedding (Illustrations 5.17, 5.18). The groom took the wineglass used for the benedictions of the wedding and threw it against the stone, smashing it. This contrasts with the more usual practice of breaking the glass by stepping on it.

In many parts of the Middle East, one of the practices associated with weddings is the henna ceremony, which is practiced by Jews and Muslims alike. Brown henna dye is applied to the fingers, the toes, and sometimes the face of the bride, and sometimes to those of the guests and the groom as well. Generally thought to symbolize fertility, the painting of henna generally took place before the wedding and was often accompanied by feasting, singing, and dancing. In the Middle East as well, Jewish women, like their Muslim counterparts, showed their joy at weddings and other festive occasions by uttering high-pitched cries of "you-you-you" that sound vaguely like the way Indian attacks were depicted in old-fashioned Western movies.

In Yemen, the traditional wedding often lasted for two weeks. The actual marriage ceremony, usually held on a Thursday, took place after a week of preliminary celebrations and was followed by a week of feasting. On the Thursday before the wedding, the groom was taken to be bathed, and the room in his house where the wedding was to take place was decorated. On Saturday night, the rabbis came to dress him in his wedding costume. Monday and Tuesday were devoted to the application of henna dyes, first to women in the bride's house, then to women in the groom's house, and finally to the groom himself. Wednesday began with the celebration of the groom's gifts to the bride and ended with the betrothal ceremony (*erusin*) in the bride's house in the evening. The actual wedding took place in the groom's house on Thursday. After the seven days of postmarriage feasting were completed, smaller celebrations were held on the Sabbath for five weeks after the wedding.

In most Jewish folk cultures, weddings were accompanied by singing and dancing. In accordance with tradition, men and women usually danced separately. In Yemen, where the separation of the sexes was particularly strictly enforced, men's and women's dances and songs differed almost completely, since festivities for men and women took place in separate houses or rooms. The music, language of singing (Hebrew vs. Arabic), dance steps, rhythms, and styles of men and women bore little resemblance to each other.

In the Ashkenazic tradition, the separation of the sexes was less rigidly enforced, though men and women in Eastern Europe still danced separately. At weddings, however, the groom and the male guests were permitted to dance with the bride. In this special dance (*mitzva tanz*), the groom or guest did not actually touch the bride. Rather, they held opposite ends of a handkerchief during the dance. Other dances at Eastern European Jewish weddings sometimes included a dance holding a twisted festive loaf of bread (*koyletch*), as well as a *broygez tanz* (an "angry dance"), a dance of the two mothers-in-law, and a *mezinke tanz*, which was performed when the last daughter in the family was married off.

The last life cycle events, of course, are those related to death. The basic outlines of Jewish mourning practices after a relative's death—tearing one's clothes,
sitting on the floor, and remaining at home for a week—were the same throughout traditional Judaism, but many details varied from place to place. It was traditional, for example, after the funeral to eat a food that was round in shape.
Among Ashkenazic Jews this usually was an egg or a bagel; among Yemenite Jews
the mourning food was grapes. The Jewish code of law both requires certain
mourning practices (like rending one's clothes) and forbids others (like cutting or
scratching one's skin). In some Jewish cultures in the Middle East, however, cutting one's skin, though forbidden by halacha, was a widespread practice. In general, Jews in contact with modern European cultures tend to express their grief in
a less public and more restrained manner than those in contact with Middle Eastern cultures. German Jews sometimes expressed disdain for the loud wailing and
crying they claimed were the rule in Eastern European funerals; Jews of Eastern
European origin living in Israel often had the same reaction to the unrestrained
mourning of Jews from Muslim lands.

In order not to emphasize social differences at the time of death, the Talmud
placed restrictions on ostentatious funerals. The deceased was to be buried in a
simple white shroud as quickly after death as possible and with no elaborate cas-
ket. The bier on which the body was placed was to be carried to the grave (wherever possible) by pious members of the community. The communal members
and male relatives were to fill in the grave after the funeral. Unlike the Romans,
the Jews did not cremate their deceased. Though the basic simplicity of the practice was the rule in Jewish traditional funerals, its method varied from place to
place.

The traditional practice of Jews throughout the world was to bury the deceased in the ground as quickly as possible and in a manner that would not retard
decomposition of the body. In most of the Old World this meant that the body
was wrapped in a shroud and placed on a bier but not in an enclosed coffin. In
Western countries in modern times, such practices were generally frowned upon
or declared illegal by governments worried about health problems. Therefore in
American Orthodox funerals, the deceased is placed in a plain coffin of unplaned

5.19 Sargenes (men's shroud worn on the High Holidays) from Alsace with the characteristic West European separate wide collar, from an engraving by Alfonse Levy.

5.20 Women's shroud from Alsace with striped blouse.

pine. In Israel, on the other hand, where all Jewish funerals are under the control of religious rather than secular authorities, coffins are used only for military funerals. A story related to this cultural difference is as follows: An American businessman wished to invest in Israel. After doing a market study, he found out that there was no coffin factory in Israel. Luckily, someone tipped him off before he invested his money in a nonexistent market niche.

Traditional Jewish shrouds are white, but their form varies from culture to culture. Often the deceased is dressed in a costume that is now archaic but was once common. The chief item of Ashkenazic shrouds was the *kittel* (called *sargenes* in Germany), a white linen robe with a cloth belt but no pockets. (The Yiddish equivalent of the English proverb "You can't take it with you" is "Shrouds have no pockets.") The Eastern European kittel opened in front and was fastened with buttons or snaps, while the German sargenes had an opening only at the neck and was put on over the head. Unlike the Eastern European version, it also had a detachable broad white collar that was tied around the neck over the robe, much like the separate collar or ruff worn by eighteenth century German Jewish men over their long black robes. As late as the twentieth century, the deceased were buried in this archaic costume in Germany (Illustration 5.19). Women's shrouds were often equally archaic. An Alsatian Jewish set of female shrouds in the Israel Museum contains the Gan Eden Reckle ("little Garden of Eden dress"), with a striped blouse and apron over the white robe bearing a striking resemblance to the old-fashioned Central European peasant dress (Illustration 5.20).

Traditionally, Ashkenazic Jews, like their Christian neighbors, placed upright gravestones with inscriptions over the graves of the deceased. Among Sephardic

5.21 (left) Jewish tombstone (in Georgian) from Georgia containing photos of the deceased, Kareli, 1967.

5.22 (right) Jewish tombstone (in Hebrew) from Georgia containing portrait of the deceased.

and Oriental Jews, the tombstones were generally horizontal, parallel to the ground. For distinguished individuals, Ashkenazic Jews built elaborate box-shaped monuments called an *ohel* (tent), which often had inscriptions on all sides. In traditional Ashkenazic cemeteries flowers were not permitted on the grave, nor were they allowed at funerals. Instead, those who came to the cemetery put small stones on the graves of their loved ones to symbolize their visit. In some Central Asian communities, Jews, in recent times have shared the custom of their non-Jewish neighbors of putting a photograph of the deceased on the tombstone, a practice that would shock traditional Ashkenazic Jews (Illustrations 5.21, 5.22).

✦ ✦ ✦

Funeral and mourning customs are the final acts in the rites of the life cycle. But Jewish tradition does not permit a chapter to end on a sad note. Therefore it is fitting to conclude with some general remarks about popular Jewish religious practices. In contrast to most modern Jews, who see the code of Jewish law as too restrictive and all-encompassing, traditional Jews saw it as too limited and unspecific. The popular imagination was constantly adding to Jewish rituals, celebrations, and observances. There are many motivations for popular additions to the requirements of Jewish law, including the desire to fill in the blanks left by the law; the need to cope with fears about the dangers of death, disease, and bad luck; and the influence of the practices of non-Jewish neighbors. Sometimes popular practices came into conflict with the law, while at other times they ignored the law or reinforced it. Jewish legal sages saw popular practices both as a sign of piety and as a potential danger to the restraints of the law against superstition. They sanctioned most practices but were on the lookout for those that smacked of magic, were too similar to non-Jewish practices, or violated technical requirements of the law. Sometimes their prohibitions were heeded by the bulk of their followers, but sometimes they were ignored. Such practices as *kaparot* (a pre-Yom Kippur ritual involving the slaughter of a chicken), which were originally opposed by the rabbis, eventually received their encouragement and acceptance.

Jewish customary practices varied not only from place to place but also from period to period. In every era, new practices were invented and old customs allowed to fall into disuse. Many a practice mentioned in the Talmud is no longer performed anywhere in the Jewish world today. For instance, women no longer dance in the fields on the 15th of Av for men to choose their brides, nor is covering one's head still used as a mourning custom. Such medieval customs as the hanging of the afikomen matzoh in the synagogue, the avoidance of building a house on a site where an oven once stood, and the use of a wedding ring decorated with a three-dimensional tower have also long since disappeared. This constant coming and going of Jewish customary practices enabled Jewish religious life to continue without becoming bloated with too many ceremonies or impoverished with too few.

In modern times, this process has changed. It is not that new Jewish customs and practices are not being created today. Quite the contrary! We need only think of the bat mitzvah, the feminist Seder, observances of Yom Hashoah (Holocaust Remembrance Day), or new celebrations for the birth of a girl to see that the impetus to create new rituals is very much alive. However, the context in which the new customs arise is different. The new ceremonies seem to be created in a much more conscious, less spontaneous way than were the traditional customs. (Perhaps this is only an illusion of perspective, since we were not present when the older customs came into being.) Second, the ceremonies are no longer seen as a customary supplement to a shared legal framework that Jews everywhere consider binding. They seem to be individual or collective responses to issues that seem relevant today,which are then given the form of ritual. They are often conscious reforms of the ritual rather than unconscious expansions of it.

Cuisine

Gefilte Fish and Cholent Meet

Malawach and Couscous

TRADITIONAL JEWISH CUISINE, LIKE OTHER ASPECTS OF JEWISH POPULAR CULTURE, has some basic structures that are similar among all Jews, but also a variety of local eating traditions that make them unrecognizable to each other. The basic structures shared by all Jews were the limitations imposed by the kosher laws, the restrictions on cooking on the Sabbath, and the need to celebrate the holidays with the choicest foods. The specific recipes for a holiday dish in a particular area depended on climate, the availability of staples, and local non-Jewish traditions, as well as local Jewish religious customs. Each group of Jews, being cut off from direct contact with others, naturally assumed that all Jews ate the same "Jewish food" as they did. But this was not at all the case; with very few exceptions, such as wine and challah for kiddush and matzo for Passover, the foods of one region were completely foreign in other areas. The gefilte fish, cholent, and kugel of Eastern European Jewry bear little resemblance to the couscous, the meatballs and peas, and the tajine popular among Jews in North Africa. The tastes and smells of one type of Jewish cuisine often seem strange, and sometimes unappetizing, to Jews from a different part of the world.

These tremendous regional differences might lead us to believe that Eastern European Jewish cooking is just the regular cuisine of Poland or Russia or that Moroccan Jewish food is no different from Moroccan Muslim food. But this is not the case. Jewish patterns of food preparation were often distinct from those of their non-Jewish neighbors. These differences resulted not only from the restrictions of the Jewish dietary laws, but were also caused by the different migration patterns and cultural contacts of Jewish and non-Jewish populations. Even when the Jews adopted recipes from their neighbors, they modified them to conform to the laws of Kashruth or associated them with a Jewish holiday or ritual. In so doing, they "Judaized" the borrowed dish and made it an integral part of Jewish culture. Once the function of the particular food was a Jewish one, the fact that it was similar to a dish eaten by non-Jewish neighbors was considered relatively unimportant.

The Restrictions of Jewish Law

The laws of Kashruth outlined in the Bible, and greatly elaborated in the rabbinic tradition, put many restrictions on Jewish culinary preparations. First, certain foods were forbidden under all circumstances. Pigs were proscribed, as were all mammals that did not both chew their cud and have split hooves (such as horses, camels, and rabbits, as well as dogs and cats). Also forbidden were all shellfish and any other fish lacking both fins and scales (such as shark and catfish). Only the most common fowl, like chicken, duck, goose, squab, and turkey, were permitted.

Cattle, sheep, lamb, calves, and goats had to be slaughtered according to ritual law, the animal's veins and blood had to be removed, and the sciatic nerve had to be extracted from the hindquarters. In countries where the last procedure was considered too cumbersome, Jews were only permitted to eat meat from the forequarters of the animal. A similar procedure applied to birds, except for the rule about the sciatic nerve.

More restrictive than any of the aforementioned prohibitions was the required separation of meat and dairy products. The biblical passage "Thou shalt not seethe a goat in its mother's milk" was interpreted to forbid the eating of any milk product (including butter, cheese, and whey) with any meat product (even extended from mammals to poultry) at the same meal. Separate utensils were required for meat and milk products. These rules made it necessary for Jews to substitute for either the milk product or the meat in dishes where local non-Jewish recipes mixed them. This excludes the possibility of a kosher cheeseburger.

In addition to these restrictions, which applied at all times, there were dietary limitations that applied to certain times, but not to others. On the Sabbath it was forbidden to cook or bake, but rabbinic tradition encouraged the consumption of warm food. Only food whose cooking had begun before sundown on Friday could be eaten on the Sabbath. Considerable culinary ingenuity was needed to invent dishes that could cook slowly overnight or could be kept warm without spoiling.

Excluding days of fasting, the most stringent of all dietary restrictions applied to Passover. During the eight days of the holiday (seven in Israel), no food that had undergone leavening could be eaten, nor could any food that contained even a tiny amount of leavened dough be used or even kept in one's possession. The legal definition of leavened food accepted by all rabbinic Jews is more or less the following: any food in which wheat, oats, barley, rye, or spelt (a variety of wheat) comes into contact with water and ferments or rises. This excludes all bread, beer, pasta, and whiskey, and most kinds of cake and crackers from the Passover table. The staple of the holiday—matzo—is made by rapidly mixing water and flour and baking it quickly before it has time to rise. All of these restrictions lead to a Passover cuisine that is very characteristically Jewish. Some regional Jewish traditions added to these universal official restrictions and also forbade additional foods, such as rice and beans, on Passover.

The Changing Availability of Foods

The changing availability of certain foods was responsible for many of the variations in Jewish eating habits. With rapid and refrigerated international shipping today, it is easy to forget how restricted the availability of many fruits, vegetables, and other staples was in earlier times. Only foods grown in the immediate region were readily available, and only the very rich could afford to import a product from far away.

Many products that later became integral to Jewish cuisine were simply unknown in the Old World before Columbus and his successors brought them from the Americas. Before the sixteenth century the potato was unknown in Europe, and in most places it was not introduced until the eighteenth or even the nineteenth century. As a result, many of the most "traditional" Ashkenazic Jewish foods could not have existed until about 250 years ago. Potato pancakes (*latkes*), traditionally eaten on Chanukah, could not date back to the Maccabees who originated the Chanukah holiday, but had to have been introduced as a holiday food relatively recently. Similarly, potato *kugel*, potato *knishes*, *cholent* with potatoes, and any of the other "typically Jewish" Eastern European foods made with potatoes are fairly recent recipes. Other products unknown in Europe and Asia before the voyage of Columbus were corn, tomatoes, sweet potatoes, and chocolate. Coffee, rice, and other "necessities" were introduced from the East in post-biblical times, and noodles and other pasta products were unknown in Europe before the Middle Ages.

Climate and growing conditions were important limitations on culinary possibilities. Figs, dates, olives, lemons, and oranges could be included in the Mediterranean Jewish cuisine, but such products were not available in Northern Europe. In Eastern Europe, eggplants were available in the relatively warm Romania and Ukraine, but not in the much colder Lithuania. Some parts of the world grew mainly rice, while others specialized in rye or barley. Eastern Europeans ate many dishes made of buckwheat (*kasha*), a grain not cultivated in most other areas where Jews lived. Romania was one of the few countries of Europe where corn was grown for human consumption—as the base for the area's most characteristic food, *mamaliga* (corn meal porridge). Wine was an important part of the diet in Italy and other Mediterranean countries, but in Eastern Europe it was hard to acquire. Therefore Ashkenazic Jews commonly used whiskey instead of wine even for the obligatory kiddush on the Sabbath or boiled up an ersatz wine made out of raisins. The most typically Jewish food in Italy, *carcciofi a la giudea* (deep-fried artichokes, Jewish style) could never have originated in Central and Eastern European countries, where artichokes were not grown.

Foods Borrowed But Changed

Jews borrowed both the recipes and the names of foods commonly used by their non-Jewish neighbors. So North African Jews ate *couscous* like their Muslim neighbors, and German Jews and German Christians both ate *Sauerbraten*. At a Polish or Ukrainian restaurant you can find the equivalent of Jewish *blintzes*, *pirogen*, *varenikes*, *knishes*, and stuffed cabbage, often with names not very different from those used in Yiddish. Jews ate their version of the Romanian *pastrama*, Polish *kielbasa* (sausage), and Algerian *merguez* (sausage), suitably modified to fit into the dietary laws. In Italy they ate pasta, in Iran they ate yogurt, and in much of the Arab world they ate meats roasted on a spit, as was typical in the region.

Despite the similarities in recipes and names, Jewish and non-Jewish foods were by no means identical. In North Africa and Iraq, for instance, it seems that Jews preferred beef in dishes in which Muslims ate lamb, even though both are kosher. Jews in the Muslim countries also drank wine and such distinctive liquors as anisette or arak (*raki*), whereas Muslims who drank these would violate Muslim religious law. Eastern European Jewish cuisine included not only foods borrowed from Slavic cookery, like blintzes or knishes, but also foods they had imported from Germany or Austria, like *strudel*, *kreplach*, and *farfel*.

Even when the same food was eaten by Jews and Gentiles, it was accompa-

nied by different associations. A complex set of changes in both recipe and meaning can be illustrated by the Ashkenazic food kreplach. The word *kreplach* itself
comes from the German *krapfen* or its dialect equivalent, *krepl*. Some claim that
the word is cognate with the elegant French *crepe* (rolled pancake). It has a number of differing meanings in German but is generally a type of donut or yeast pastry, associated in many parts of the country with the pre-Lenten Carnival.
Carnival, or Shrove Tuesday, generally takes place in late February or early March
at around the time of the Jewish feast of Purim. Although the original meanings
of Carnival and Purim are unrelated, they have taken on certain similar festivities—masquerades, merrymaking, and drinking. It would seem that the carnival
krapfen (*Fastnachtskrapfen*) became a Purim food. When Jews migrated to Eastern Europe, the food changed form for unknown reasons and became a type of
ravioli filled with either chopped meat or cheese. The food went from being
eaten on Purim alone to being enjoyed at, and then associated with, Purim,
Hoshana Rabba, and the eve of Yom Kippur. Folk tradition even explained that
you eat kreplach when you beat something: "Haman on Purim, the willow leaves
on Hoshana Rabba, and yourself in penitence for Yom Kippur."

In the case of cholent, there are areas that share a similar name but a different
recipe for the food, and others where the recipe is rather similar but the names
are totally different. Derived from an Old French word that means "warming up,"
the term *cholent* was applied by Ashkenazic Jews to the food that cooked from
Friday night until it was eaten at lunch on Saturday. What ingredients were in the
original recipe for cholent no one knows, but by modern times the forms of the
food differed widely. They shared a name and could be characterized as a kind of
stew or casserole, but their recipes had little in common from region to region.

The term *cholent* (and its variants) was found among all Ashkenazic Jews.
Foods that resembled cholent but had unrelated names were also found in most
non-Ashkenazic Jewish communities. In many parts of the Jewish world the hot
Sabbath food was given a name based on the talmudic Aramaic word *hamin* (literally, "warmed"). In some places the original term *hamin* was kept, but in others
it was translated into the vernacular (*cholent* in Yiddish, *s'khina* in Moroccan Arabic). In a few areas another Talmudic term, *tamun* ("sealed up"), was used and

translated into the vernacular (*tfina* in North Africa). In many Jewish cultures in the Muslim world a key ingredient in the hamin was hard-boiled eggs that cooked together with the meat and grains or beans all night and acquired the taste of the meat. In the Balkans these eggs were called *huevos haminados*.

Gefilte fish, a typically Ashkenazic food, may owe its origin to a fine point of Sabbath law. Religious tradition forbids winnowing (separating the wheat from the chaff) on the Sabbath. This prohibition was expanded to include separating the inedible from the edible part of any food, which was interpreted as forbidding removal of the bones from fish on the Sabbath—a rather dangerous proposition. To avoid this danger, the fish was taken out of its skin before the Sabbath, the bones were removed, and the fish was ground with matzo meal and replaced in the skin. This "pious" explanation of gefilte fish has a rival, more secular, explanation. This version explains that since fish was scarce, housewives "stretched" it by mixing it with cheaper meal so that there was enough to feed all persons at the table. This explanation is supported by the existence of recipes for fish stuffed in a similar manner in a number of non-Jewish cultures as well.

Gefilte fish became a staple of Eastern European Jewish cuisine but was unknown elsewhere (at least until the invention of "gefilte fish in a jar" in America). In Poland it was called "Jewish fish." But not all gefilte fish was alike. In fact there was an important regional difference that has never been fully explained. East of the sixteenth century border between Poland and Lithuania, gefilte fish was seasoned with salt and pepper, but to the west it was made sweet, with sugar rather than pepper. On either side of the "frontier," Jews thought that the rival recipe for gefilte fish was barbaric.

Differences in Passover Foods

The greatest variety of all in Jewish cuisine is found in Passover foods, despite the fact that the presence of matzo and the absence of bread and year-round cake were features everywhere. On Passover the traditional Jewish laity was even stricter than the law required in avoiding even the slightest hint of leavening. Eventually these customary restrictions acquired the force of religious law. The most famous of these additional restrictions is the Ashkenazic ban on *kitniyot* (legumes). Although the Talmud concludes that legumes are permitted on Passover, Ashkenazic tradition banned rice, corn, peas, beans of all kinds, and even peanuts. Also banned, although less consistently, were oils made from most of these products. In the folkways of Ashkenazic Judaism, rice or beans were considered just as *hametz* (prohibited for Passover) as bread or beer. Yet Jews in other countries, such as Yemen and Iraq, permitted kitniyot and even served rice at the Seder. In some countries like Morocco, rice was banned as too similar to other grains, but beans were permitted.

In their extreme restrictions, Ashkenazic Jews were aided by the introduction of the potato in early modern times. In the Ashkenazic home, potatoes and eggs became staples of the holiday season, especially for families that followed Hasidic traditions that began in the eighteenth century. Fearing that matzos were not totally baked through, Hasidim worried that in case a tiny bit of flour remained uncooked, it might combine with liquid and rise. Therefore the Hasidim forbade the use on Passover of all foods made out of matzo combined with any liquid. This meant that matzo meal (ground matzo used to make baked goods) could not be used for most cooking and baking. Some traditional holiday foods like matzo balls (*knaidlach*) were simply banned, while others underwent a change in recipe. Cakes and baked goods made of matzo meal were reformulated to use potato starch instead. This modification can be seen in regional differences in the recipes for the Passover pancakes called *chremzlach*. In Lithuania (a non-Hasidic area) they were made with matzo meal and in Germany they were made with soaked matzos, but in Hasidic Galicia and Hungary they were transformed into potato puffs. So one way you can tell if a family comes from the Hasidic tradition is by the contents of their chremzlach recipe.

There is an additional twist to the story of the Hasidic stringency about matzo meal. For the Hasidim the potato became the "staff of life" for Passover. In the Balkans, however, the Sephardic Jews felt differently about the potato when it was introduced. To them it seemed too much like dough-producing grains, and therefore the rule was "Sweet potatoes are permitted but not white potatoes." The food of the Hasidim would not have been accepted on Passover tables in Salonika or Istanbul.

Different Cooking Styles

Since Jewish cooks tried to develop as much variety as possible in their cuisine within the restrictions of religion, availability, and custom, it is difficult to give an overall characterization of each particular regional Jewish cuisine. Nevertheless, some general characteristics are noticeable. Most Jewish cooking in North Africa and Asia uses a variety of strong spices, such as pepper, cumin, and cilantro, and some main dishes are accompanied by very hot, peppery sauces. This doesn't mean that all "Oriental" Jewish dishes are spicy. The couscous made by North African Jews is based on the mild tastes of its main ingredients: semolina grain, meat, and assorted vegetables. Ashkenazic food, at least in Eastern Europe, also used strong flavorings, but they were based on onions, garlic, or horseradish. The free use of garlic in Jewish cuisine in Central and Eastern Europe was the target of much anti-Semitic ridicule. Garlic was more commonly used in the Mediterranean area than in Northern Europe, where it was generally absent from non-Jewish cuisine. Not only non-Jewish Germans and Poles, but sometimes even Sephardic Jews and Karaites, made fun of the "smelly" Ashkenazic foods. In the twentieth century some German Jews were so intimidated by the ridicule of anti-Semites that they dropped the item from their pantries; some could barely stand to hear the word "garlic."

Another distinction between traditional food habits involves the source of fat for frying and baking. In the Mediterranean regions, where a number of foods were deep fried, olive oil was a much-used staple, sometimes supplemented or replaced by other vegetable oils like sesame oil. In Northern Europe, where olive oil was unavailable and vegetable oils were introduced relatively recently, animal shortenings tended to be used for baking and frying. While Christians in Northern Europe made much use of lard or butter, Jews could not use the former at all, and their use of butter was restricted to dishes not eaten with meat or poultry. As a result, Ashkenazic Jews made heavy use of chicken and goose fat. A by-product of the rendering of the chicken or goose fat was *gribenes* (fried skin), a favorite delicacy of European Jews in the days when no one worried about cholesterol.

Sometimes changes in the availability of foods—for instance, the introduction of coffee—made possible new forms of religious practice. Certain Jewish religious practices, such as the midnight mourning ritual for the destroyed Temple (Tikkun Hatzot) and the nighttime study vigils on Shavuot and Hoshana Rabba (the seventh day of Sukkot), were introduced by Kabbalists at the time of the Renaissance. It is no coincidence that such late-night rituals replaced older early morning rituals among Italian Jews at precisely the same time that coffee gained widespread popularity.

Bread and Matzo

Two foods that unite Jews all over the world are the Sabbath loaf and the unleavened Passover matzo. But even these foods have plenty of regional differences. In Judaism bread is not only the "staff of life" but also *kove'a s'uda* (makes food into a meal). Before bread is eaten, tradition requires ritual washing of the hands and a special blessing. But the word "bread" means different things in different parts of the world. In much of the Middle East, bread comes mainly in a round, flat form today called "pita." This looks and tastes very different from the oblong high loaves common in many parts of Europe. In Northern and Eastern Europe, everyday bread for the masses was made of dark, hearty grains like rye, and white bread, made from wheat, was only for the wealthy.

No matter where rabbinic Jews lived or what kind of bread they usually ate, they made a blessing over two loaves of bread on the Sabbath. Among Ashkenazic Jews, the custom developed that the Sabbath bread should be braided and made from white wheat flour. Among Ashkenazic Jews in Eastern Europe and

Holland, these loaves were known as *challah*. In much of Central Europe, however, they were called *berches* or *barches* (in the area around Frankfurt am Main, *datcher*) and were generally made with a great deal of yeast, with a thick hard crust, and without eggs. This contrasted with the softer egg challe of much of Eastern Europe. In parts of Germany, the berches had only a braided strip on top rather than being totally braided. Many Jews in the Mediterranean lands, on the other hand, made Sabbath loaves that were not twisted at all. In some countries these loaves had added herbs or spices to make them special.

The matzos, too, took different forms in different lands. In most countries traditional matzos were round, the natural shape formed by flattening dough with a rolling pin. Today's machine-made matzos are generally square because the machine cuts separate pieces from long ribbons of dough on conveyor belts. This shape also makes matzos easier to fit into a standing box. Today matzos are relatively thin, but in some countries it was once customary to make them very thick. The Talmud and medieval rabbinic literature describe matzos as being as much as 1 inch thick or even more. In North Africa and Italy, where the holes in the matzos were made by hand, the finished matzos have cutouts that made them look like doilies. By contrast, Ashkenazic matzos were made with a special roller that left tiny holes in a straight-line pattern.

In almost all parts of the world, matzos were baked before the beginning of Passover for the entire festival and stored. In Yemen, where it was customary all year round to bake bread fresh every day, it was the custom to do the same with matzos on Passover. Yemenite Jews kneaded flour and water and baked matzos each day throughout the festival, something unknown to all other Jewish groups.

Some Favorite Jewish Dishes in Different Parts of the World

Until modern times, Jews tended to eat the foods common to their own region and not mix Jewish cuisines from other parts of the world. Jews who ate gefilte fish and kreplach did not eat couscous or falafel or malawach. This situation has

When I decided to create a selection of Jewish recipes from various parts of the world to illustrate the many differences in style, I wasn't aware of how complicated a task this would be. This is not because there aren't enough Jewish cookbooks or recipes in print; in fact, there are so many that it's impossible to read them all. The problem arose when I tried to locate the most authentic recipes clearly identified with a particular place, because cookbooks have a different purpose than this book. Purchasers of cookbooks are usually looking for suggestions to vary their cooking repertoire, and they are less interested in the history or geography of a particular dish than in a convenient and efficient way to prepare a complicated dish without sacrificing taste or attractiveness. Rather than describe how the dishes were traditionally cooked over an open fire, in a clay oven, or with a wicker basket, the cookbooks generally adapt recipes so that they can be made on a modern electric or gas stove, in a crock pot or an electric heating tray, or even in a microwave oven. Recipes that take many hours, or even days, with the traditional cooking method are rewritten so that they can be prepared in a few hours or even a few minutes. Cookbooks are also more likely to describe fancy and exotic foods than to concentrate on the simple, basic foods that were everyday staples. That's why printed recipes for cholent, the staple Sabbath food of Eastern Europe, are much less common than recipes for cakes, pastries, and fancier dishes. All these circumstances make cookbooks less than ideal sources for traditional Jewish cooking. In the following selection of recipes, I have tried to use sources that are as authentic as possible, but I do not claim that these recipes are "the way grandma used to make them" in Yemen, Poland, or Morocco. Nevertheless, I hope that trying them will at least give you an idea of how different the cooking styles of various Jewish communities were.

One last caution: Every cook had his or her own way of making a particular dish. An ambitious cook might make several versions of the same food so as not to bore the family. So, the recipe for a particular food given here may not be the same as the one you have inherited from your family. The examples that follow are only the tip of the iceberg. But if you try even some of the recipes, you'll be able to "eat and be satisfied."

changed tremendously. Not only have migrations brought people with different eating traditions together in the same place, but printed cookbooks, radio, and television have promoted the spread of various culinary traditions far beyond their former territorial limits. Today, almost no one in the Jewish world eats foods prepared only the way that they were in the Old Country. Now, it is more common to "mix and match" recipes from various parts of the world for family menus.

Since the most distinctively Jewish recipes are associated with the Sabbath and with Passover, that is where we will start. The Sabbath and holidays were times for eating much better food than usual. Fish and meat were especially honored as Sabbath foods, and in many families the Sabbath was the only time meat or chicken appeared on the table. Often many courses were served at the two main Sabbath meals on Friday night and Saturday at noon, including appetizers, soups, main dishes, and desserts. The third obligatory Sabbath meal on Saturday afternoon was generally a much simpler snack of cold foods.

Saturday lunch foods were especially distinctive because of the religious requirement that warm food (hamin) be served, despite the fact that cooking on the Sabbath was forbidden. Generations of Jewish housewives in various countries came up with a host of ingenious solutions to the problem. In Eastern Europe, the two foods that were staples of the Saturday lunch table were cholent and kugel. A basic recipe for cholent includes:

6 small potatoes	*½ cup navy beans*
1 lb. meat cut into cubes	*water*
1 onion	*salt*
½ cup kidney beans	*pepper*
½ cup lima beans	*garlic powder*

Peel the potatoes, leaving small ones whole and cutting larger ones in half. Rinse the meat and beans, peel the onion, and place them in a large pot. Add plenty of water until the pot is about three-quarters full. Add salt, pepper, and garlic powder. Bring to a boil; then reduce the heat and let it simmer, the longer the better. Keep the pot uncovered and keep adding water if necessary. Once the beans have expanded, they won't absorb the water so rapidly. Before the Sabbath, make sure that you have enough water in the pot, about 1 inch above the ingredients. Cover the pot tightly and place it on the blech (an aluminum sheet that covers the burners of the stove so that the pot does not come into direct contact with the flame). Cook overnight.

There are a number of variations on the cholent recipe. Some, especially those of Hungarian Jews, omit the potatoes; others include barley or vary the kinds of beans used. All traditional recipes include the requirement to cook the dish overnight over a low flame. In Bohemia-Moravia, *sholet* was a dish of goose, rice, and peas. In southern Germany and neighboring parts of Western Europe, the recipe for *schalet* was quite different from that of the meat stew described above. Despite the fact that the term *schalet* resembles *cholent* and comes from the same root, schalet took the form of a casserole resembling a pie or pudding and was quite unlike a meat stew.

Schalet could be made from various ingredients including potatoes or noodles, but there were many other varieties as well, such as *weckschalet*, a kind of bread pudding made from stale bread or rolls, *matzo schalet*, and *apple schalet*, for which the recipe follows.

DOUGH	FILLING
10 heaping teaspoons flour	*apples, finely cut*
3 teaspoons stirred goose fat, beef fat, or margarine	*sugar*
2–3 teaspoons sugar	*cinnamon*
1–2 eggs	*raisins*
1 shot glass of cherry or plum brandy	*lemon peel, orange peel, and*
pinch of cinnamon	*sliced almonds (optional)*

Combine dough ingredients with water to form a smooth dough. Roll it out several times and, after it has rested for a while, cut it in half. Cut one of the halves in half again. Grease a deep, round iron pot with goose fat and place the larger piece of dough, rolled out into a circle, in it so that the floor and walls of the pot are covered and the dough hangs out over the top about the thickness of a thumb. Cover the dough with finely cut, strongly sugared apples mixed with cinnamon and raisins (optional addition: lemon peel, orange peel, and coarsely cut almonds) to a thickness of two thumb breadths. Roll out the smaller piece of dough into two round layers as wide as the pot. Cover the apples with one of the dough layers, then a layer of apples as above, then the second layer of dough, and then the remaining apples. The third piece of dough is rolled out to form a round pot cover, placed over the apples, pressed down, and then attached securely with the end of the first piece of dough, which was hanging down but is now turned inward. Optionally, the top can be smeared with goose fat. The schalet is placed in the oven for 1¼ to 1½ hours.

More similar to Eastern European cholent in function than schalet was the German Jewish *gesetzte Supp'*. This thick soup, which cooked overnight, could take many different forms, including white bean soup, pea soup, barley soup, and rice soup. The most distinctively German Jewish form was *Gruenkernsuppe*, made from a special kind of green-kerneled wheat called *Gruenkern* or *Dinkel*. The kernels of grain could either be ground or served whole. A recipe for Gruenkernsuppe follows.

1½ lbs. bones and marrow bones
1½ lbs. meat: tongue (Schlund) *or brisket* (Brustkern)
1 teaspoon flour
large quantity of Gruenkern (1 heaping spoonful per person)
salt
1 celery root
water to cover

Place all ingredients in a deep iron pot. Bring them to a boil. Place the dish in the oven or special Sabbath oven and let it cook slowly for six to eight hours, after which it will be thick and have a hearty taste.

Ashkenazic Jews who prepared cholent or its German equivalent, gesetzte Supp', often did not have a proper oven for cooking their Sabbath food. It was therefore customary to place the pots of cholent or soup in a communal oven in the bakery and to seal up the oven on the eve of the Sabbath so that no one would be tempted to adjust the flame or otherwise engage in cooking on the Sabbath. Each pot was marked for identification and then picked up by a member of the family or a servant on Saturday at noon (Illustration 6.1).

6.1 Housewives in Bialystok carry cholent, a dish of meat, potatoes, and beans, to the baker's oven on Friday afternoon.

The same principle that governed cholent also applied to its equivalents made by non-Ashkenazic Jews in various parts of Southeastern Europe, Asia, and North Africa. What follows are a few regional versions of the Sabbath noonday main dish. In North Africa there were two main forms: s'khina in Morocco and tefina in Morocco, Algeria, Tunisia, and Libya.

One recipe for s'khina [spelled Scheena by the author of the cookbook] is as follows:

3 lbs. small potatoes
1 cup dried chick peas, soaked in water overnight, drained
1 lb. beef chuck, cut into 1-inch cubes
2 lbs. beef shin bones, cut into 2- or 3-inch pieces
1 lb. ground beef mixed with 1/4 teaspoon pepper and shaped into a loaf
8 raw eggs in the shell
1 teaspoon salt

Put the potatoes and chick peas in a clay or metal pot large enough to contain all the ingredients. Add the the beef cubes and bones on top. Place the ground beef loaf on one side, the eggs all around the pot and sprinkle salt on all.

Cover the mixture completely with water. Bring to a boil on top of the stove and cook over low heat for 15 minutes.. Put the pan in the oven and bake at the lowest heat, about 200 F, for 8 to 10 hours or overnight.

Serve warm on the Sabbath about noon, after returning from synagogue. Serves 8.

Two Tunisian versions of T'fina, called T'fina Camounia, are as follows: the first, vegetarian, version is not for the sabbath, but the second meat version is.

1 lb. dried white beans
4 cups water
5 garlic cloves, put through the press
3 teaspoons ground cumin seed
1 1/4 teaspoons salt
2 teaspoons paprika
1 ripe tomato, chopped fine (1/2 cup)
3 tablespoons corn oil
1 pound potatoes (about three), cooked in their skins until soft, peeled
3 large eggs, beaten
1/8 teaspoon ground turmeric

Soak the beans in water, covered, overnight, then drain. Put the 4 cups of water and beans in a large pan, and cook them over a low heat until they are soft but not disintegrating, for about 45 minutes.

Mix together the garlic, cumin seed, 1 teaspoon salt, paprika, tomato paste, and chopped tomato. Heat the oil in a skillet, add the mixture, and stir-fry over moderate heat for 5 minutes. Add to the simmering bean pan and continue to cool slowly for 10 minutes.

Mash the potatoes, but not too smoothly. Add the beaten eggs, 1/4 teaspoon salt, and the turmeric and mix. This is the dumpling mixture. For each dumpling, take 1 heaping tablespoon of the mix and drop it into the simmering bean pan. Do this with all the potato puree. Cover the pan and cook at a low heat for 15 minutes.

The Sabbath version includes the vegetarian bean ingredients, but adds

> *2 lbs. beef chuck, cut into 8 pieces*
> *8 eggs in the shell*
> *4 small potatoes (1 pound), peeled*

In this version the beans are not soaked overnight. Put the white beans, the 4 cups water, garlic, cumin seed, salt, paprika, tomato paste, and ripe tomato into the pot. Place the pieces of beef over this. Arrange the eggs and potatoes around the top of the meat. Cover the pan and bring to a boil over moderate heat. Reduce heat to very low and cook, if using the traditional method, all of Friday evening, to be served warm about midday Saturday. Serves 8.

In Iraq and surrounding areas, the main form of the hamin served on Saturday was completely different. It was called *t'beet* [spelled tabit by the author of the cookbook]:

> *2 tablespoons corn oil*
> *1 medium onion, chopped (1/2 cup)*
> *1 chicken, 3 pounds, cut into 6 pieces, loose skin and fat discarded*
> *3 1/2 cups water*
> *1 teaspoon salt, or to taste*
> *1/8 teaspoon pepper*
> *2 tablespoons tomato paste*
> *2 cups raw rice, well rinsed*

Heat the oil in a pan, add the onion and chicken, and saute over moderate heat for 10 minutes or until brown. Add the water, salt, pepper, and tomato paste and bring to a boil.

Add the rice, turn heat to low, and cook for about 1 hour without stirring. Test the rice for doneness, and if too firm add 2 or 3 tablespoons of water. Turn heat off and let stand for 10 minutes before serving. [If prepared for the Sabbath, the chicken and rice are put ino an oven turned to the lowest heat and baked overnight from Friday afternoon until Saturday.]

In almost all the non-Ashkenazic recipes, hard-boiled eggs cooked all night are an integral part of the Saturday lunch meal. These are either cooked together with the main warm Sabbath dish, as shown above, or they are boiled separately. A recipe for *huevos haminados* (eggs in the hamin) from Rhodes includes the following ingredients:

1 dozen eggs	*¼ cup olive oil*
water to cover	*1 teaspoon salt*
outer skins of 6–10 brown onions	*1 teaspoon pepper*

Place water, onion skins, oil, salt, and pepper in a 4–6 quart pan. Add eggs carefully so as not to crack the shells. Bring to a boil, cover and cook over low heat for approximately 1 hour. Place pan in a 225° oven for 3 or more hours or overnight.

Another Sephardic recipe suggests the addition of coffee grounds to help make the eggs brown.

Among Ashkenazic Jews the cholent or other hot meat dish was generally accompanied by kugel. Recipes for kugel vary widely. All kugels are baked dishes, but with differing main ingredients. The most common types of kugel are made from noodles or potatoes (and from matzos on Passover). In some regions the kugel, especially noodle kugel, is sweet, and in others it is not. The following kugel recipe has come to be known as *Jerusalem kugel*.

12 ounces thin vermicelli	*salt*
oil	*pepper*
3 tablespoons sugar	*4 tablespoons oil*
3–4 eggs	*¼ cup water*

Boil noodles, drain, and set aside. Put the sugar in a small saucepan and brown it in oil over a low flame for 2–3 minutes, watching it carefully so that it does not burn. As soon as the sugar turns a caramel color, add the water. It will get hard immediately. Boil on a low flame for a couple of minutes until it becomes syrupy. Add the syrup to the cooked noodles. Mix well until all noodles are coated. In a separate saucepan heat 4 tablespoons oil. While it is hot or still warm, add the noodles. Mix in. Then add eggs and seasoning. Kugel may be prepared either by greasing a deep pot and baking it in the oven at 375° for 1 hour or by frying it well on both sides.

Kugels are usually eaten as a side dish on Friday night or Saturday lunch and are served either cold or warm. They were eaten by both Eastern European and German Jews. As you may have noticed, however, the German recipe for schalet resembled kugel much more than it did the cholent recipe. In southern Germany the chief difference between kugel and schalet was that kugel was "sharp" and made with beef fat, while schalet was usually sweet. Otherwise they were virtually the same.

No part of the year's Jewish cuisine is as distinctive as the holiday food for Passover. Jewish cooks have had to find ways to make their menus interesting without such staples as bread, flour, pasta, and, in much of the world, without rice or beans. In some places, unleavened matzo substituted for bread or dough in various pies and soups. In other areas, matzo was pounded into meal, which was then used much like flour to produce various types of baked goods. The results varied widely in different parts of the world. The following three examples are only a tiny selection of the thousands of Passover recipes in existence.

MINA DE CORDERO (MATZO PIE WITH LAMB FILLING) FROM GREECE AND TURKEY

2 lbs. shoulder of lamb	*8 matzos*
3–4 green onions, finely chopped	*oil for sprinkling*
2 eggs	*salt and pepper to taste*

Place the lamb in the pot and simmer it very slowly until tender. (It will create its own gravy.) Cool it, trim off all fat, and cut it into tiny pieces. Add green onions, salt, and pepper. Beat 1 egg and fold it into the meat mixture. Wet the matzos to soften them; then blot them between paper towels to absorb the moisture. Preheat the oven to 400°F and place a generously greased baking pan, large enough to be lined with 4 matzos, in the oven until the oil is very hot. This will prevent the matzos from sticking. Line the bottom of the pan with matzos; spread the meat mixture and top with the remaining matzos. Sprinkle the top with oil and beat another egg; pour over all. Bake until browned on top, approximately one-half hour. Serves eight to ten persons.

A staple Jewish dish comes from Germany.

MATZEKLÖSS' (MATZO DUMPLINGS).

6–7 matzos	*muscat*
parsley	*salt*
onions	*pepper*
4–6 eggs	*enough matzo meal so that dumplings don't stick to hands*
ginger	

Soak matzos and press them to remove the liquid. Cook with parsley and chopped onions in fat or oil. Cool down. Add spices, eggs, and matzo meal. Form large balls (about 2–3 inches in diameter). Cook in salt water. Leftovers can be fried the following day in oil with onions.

Matzeklöss are different from the matzo balls made by all Ashkenazic Jews, which are cooked in chicken soup. Matzo balls, called *knaydlakh* in Eastern Europe, and *klössle* in southern Germany, are made of matzo meal, fat, eggs, and water.

A traditional dish from Uzbekistan is *Passover soup.*

1 tablespoon oil	*½ cup chopped coriander*
2 medium onions, chopped	*1 teaspoon salt*
1 lb. boneless beef chuck, cut into 1 inch cubes	*¼ teaspoon pepper*
½ lb. beef bones	*1 medium potato, cut into 1/2 inch cubes*
1 small carrot	*4 eggs, beaten*
8 cups water	*matzo*
1 ripe tomato, cut into cubes	

Heat the oil in a large pan and stir-fry the onions, beef, bones, and carrot over moderate heat for 3 minutes. Add the water, tomato, coriander, salt, and pepper and bring to a boil. Cook, covered, over moderately low heat for 1 hour.

Add the potato. Cook for 15 minutes. Just prior to serving, add the eggs in a steady stream to the simmering soup, stirring them in. Serve hot, breaking as much matzo as wanted into each soup plate.

For the "minor holidays" of Purim and Chanukah, various baked goods were traditional. These varied from place to place, though in America the Eastern European versions—*homentashen* for Purim and *latkes* for Chanukah—have become the norm.

Homentashen were triangular pastries filled with poppy seeds, plum jam, or other fruit fillings. They could be made from yeast dough or cookie dough. Though the name of the food seems to mean "Haman's pockets," there are a number of reasons to believe that this was not the original name. In Hebrew they are called *ozney haman*, which means "Haman's ears." One theory is that the pastry was originally called *Mohntaschen* (German for poppy-seed pockets) but was later associated with Haman, the villain of the Purim story, whereupon they became a Purim food. In southern Germany the traditional Purim pastry was called a *Haman* and was made from yeast dough. After the dough rose twice, it was rolled out on a flour-covered board to the thickness of one-half of a finger. Human figures were cut out of the dough, and their eyes, mouth, and nose were marked with raisins, almonds, and lemon peel. They were then placed on a tin oiled cookie sheet, allowed to rise again, painted with egg, and baked. Sometimes an extra piece of dough was placed across the neck of the dough figures in remembrance of the gallows on which Haman was hanged.

The feast of Chanukah was also associated with special foods, which varied regionally. In the former Czarist Russia, the predominant Chanukah delicacy was latkes or potato pancakes. Because of the mass Jewish immigration of Russian Jews to America, this became the almost exclusive Chanukah food for Jews in the United States. A basic recipe for latkes is:

5 large Idaho potatoes	*salt and pepper*
1 large onion	*oil for frying*
4 eggs	*pinch baking powder (optional)*
¼ cup matzo meal or flour	

Grate the potatoes and strain them through a colander. Grate the onion. Add the grated onion and eggs to the potatoes. Mix well. Add the matzo meal and seasoning. Mix well. Heat oil in a frying pan and add the mixture, one tablespoon at a time, to the oil. When the latkes are golden brown, turn them over and brown the other side.

In other parts of Eastern Europe, notably Romania, deep-fried jelly doughnuts were the typical Chanukah food. Called *sufganiyot* in Hebrew, these have become the predominant Chanukah food in Israel. Among Sephardic Jews in the Balkans and Turkey, a third type of Chanukah baked good, called *bimuelos,* was common for the holiday. The following recipe comes from the island of Rhodes:

1⅓ cup warm water	cinnamon to sprinkle
2 cakes yeast (room temperature)	oil for deep frying
1 egg	
½ teaspoon salt	SYRUP
1 tablespoon oil	24 oz. honey
3 cups flour, unsifted	¼ cup water

Combine the honey and water for syrup. Bring to a boil. Dissolve yeast in ½ cup of the warm water. Add beaten egg, salt, and oil to the mixture. Add to flour all at once and stir, adding the remaining water gradually. Allow the mixture to rise for at least 1 hour. Heat shortening to 375° and drop the dough from a tablespoon that has first been dipped in oil into the hot fat. Bimuelos puff up and should be turned over until evenly golden. Drain them on paper towels. Dip them in warm syrup and sprinkle them generously with cinnamon. They are best served warm and preferably immediately, but they can be fried ahead of time and dipped in the hot syrup just before serving. This recipe makes about forty-five. Serve a minimum of two or three per person.

Though latkes, sufganiyot, and bimuelos are quite different, they are all made with oil. Some explain that this is done to symbolize the Chanukah miracle of the olive oil that was only enough for one day and burned for eight days. More down-to-earth explanations trace it to the extension, by Ashkenazic Jews to Chanukah, of the Central European custom of eating a holiday goose for Christmas. The latkes or jelly doughnuts were then made with the leftover Chanukah goose fat.

Eastern European cooking features many different types of baked goods for various occasions, many of them filled with vegetables, fruit, meat, or cheese. Blintzes and knishes, two popular foods now considered characteristically Jewish, are examples of Jewish modifications of foods eaten by their Christian neighbors.

Probably the most common form of blintzes are *cheese blintzes,* made as follows:

BATTER	FILLING
4 eggs	*1½ pounds dry cottage cheese*
1 cup flour	*2 egg yolks*
1 teaspoon salt	*sugar and cinnamon to taste*
1 cup milk or water	
oil for frying	

Beat the eggs and salt. Add flour alternately with milk. Heat oil in a frying pan. Pour only enough batter into the pan to make a very thin pancake, tipping the pan in all directions so that the batter covers the pan. Fry the pancake on one side until it blisters. Shake it onto waxed paper.

Combine the filling ingredients and place one tablespoon of the mixture on the browned side of each pancake. Fold in the sides to form a square. Brown it in a frying pan or broiler. Serve it hot with sour cream or apple sauce.

There are many different kinds of knishes as well as different kinds of blintzes. The following, *kasha knishes*, is a variety made with kasha, or buckwheat groats.

DOUGH	FILLING
2 cups flour, sifted	*2 cups cooked kasha (1 cup raw)*
½ teaspoon salt	*1 egg*
1 teaspoon baking powder	*1 onion, diced and sautéed*
1 tablespoon oil	
2 tablespoons water	
2 eggs, well beaten	

Mix the dry ingredients for the dough. Form a well and add all liquid ingredients. Mix to form a smooth dough. Roll out to a ½ inch thickness. Then prepare and mix together the kasha filling. (Raw kasha is first mixed with boiling water and cooked for 20 minutes over medium heat). Fill the dough with the mixture. Roll it up as you would a jelly roll. Moisten the edges and fold them over. Place the knishes in a pan greased with oil. Bake at 350° until brown and crisp. Slice.

Borekas, a favorite food of the Sephardic Jews of Greece and Turkey, has now become a very popular food in Israel. Related to the Turkish food borek, it consists of a triangular or semicircular crispy pastry with a variety of fillings, such as cheese, spinach, or potatoes. The following is a recipe for *cheese borekas.*

PASTRY

¼ cup corn oil
¼ cup cold water
2 cups flour
¼ teaspoon salt

FILLING

¼ pound farmer cheese, mashed
¼ pound feta cheese, mashed
¼ teaspoon pepper
1 egg, beaten

TURNOVER

1 egg beaten
2 tablespoons grated kashkaval cheese
oil for baking sheet

Mix the pastry ingredients together with enough water to make a soft, pliable dough. Knead the dough for several minutes to produce this consistency, dusting it with flour when necessary. Cover and set it aside.

Mix the filling ingredients together until smooth. Set aside.

Divide the pastry into walnut-size pieces, each rolled into a ball. Roll out each ball into a disc about 4 inches in diameter. Put 1 tablespoon of the cheese filling onto the end closest to you, fold it over, moistening the rim with water, and press down the edges all around. Using an empty can 3 to 4 inches in diameter, press down the folded turnover to cut off the excess dough and seal the edges.

Brush the top of each boreka with the beaten egg. Dip the moist brush in the grated kashkaval cheese and rub it over the top. Bake the borekas on an oiled baking sheet in a 350° oven for 35 to 40 minutes or until their tops and bottoms are light brown. Remove and cool them. Serve at room temperature. Makes twenty-two.

One of the characteristic baked delicacies of the Yemenite Jews is *malawach* (fried bread pancake). A dough ball (*ajin*) is prepared as follows:

4 cups flour
2 tablespoons oil or butter

2 tablespoons vinegar
1 teaspoon salt
1 teaspoon sugar
2 cups water
¼ pound margarine, room temperature

Mix all ingredients except the margarine and knead the dough a bit. Then let the dough rest, covered, for 3 hours. Divide the dough into eight pieces. Flatten out one piece to about 6 inches in diameter. Incorporate about 2 teaspoons of margarine into the dough circle, pushing and kneading it in but maintaining the circle.

Cut a line open from the center of the circle to the outside edge. Take one end and roll it around counterclockwise into a ball.

To make the ajin into malawach, flatten it into a pancake about 10 inches in diameter and not more than ¼ inch thick. Melt 2 teaspoons of margarine or butter in a heated skillet over moderate heat. Fry the pancake until brown and crisp, about 5 minutes on each side.

A typical Iraqi baked dish is the sambusak. There are versions made with meat, others made with cheese, and still others, like the following, are filled with chick peas:

DOUGH:

3 cups flour
¼ teaspoon salt
1 cup water
Stuffing:
2 tablespoons corn oil
2 medium onions, sliced very thin (1 cup)
2 cups cooked chick peas (canned are satisfactory), pureed
¼ teaspoon salt
2 teaspoons ground cumin seed
oil for deep frying, about 1 cup

Mix flour, salt, and water together into a soft dough, adjusting flour and water to achieve a manageable consistency. Set aside, covered, for 1/2 hour.

To make the stuffing: Heat the oil in a skilled, add the onions, and stir fry over moderate heat until just turning light brown. Add the chick pea puree, salt, and cumin seed, and continue to stir-fry over low heat until the mixture is quite dry. [Turn out into a dish and cook well.]

Prepare a round disc from the dough according to the size you like. In family-style restaurants, the disc is about 8 inches in diameter and 1/4 inh thick. Fill this size with 1/2 cup stuffing, fold over into a half-moon shape, and seal the dough with a wet finger. Heat the oil until moderately hot and fry the turnover on both sides until golden brown. Drain on papertowels. Makes 6 large turnovers.

To my mind, one of the most unusual items of Jewish cuisine comes from Italy. Carcioffi alla giudea (deep-fried artichokes), an invention of Roman Jewish cooking, is one of the few Jewish foods that is considered a gourmet delight. The quite complex recipe that follows is presented by one of the leading experts on Italian fine cuisine, Marcella Hazan. The most complicated part of the recipe is the trimming of the artichoke.

6 medium artichokes,	*black pepper, freshly ground from the mill*
* as young and fresh as possible*	*½ lemon*
vegetable oil	*salt*

In preparing any artichoke, it is essential to discard all the tough, inedible leaves and portions of leaves. Begin by bending back the outer leaves, pulling them down toward the base of the artichoke, and snapping them off just above the base. Do not take the paler bottom end of the leaf off because at that point it is tender and quite edible. As you take more leaves off and get deeper into the artichoke, the tender part at which the leaves will snap will be farther and farther from the base. Keep pulling off single leaves until you expose a central cone of leaves that are green only at the tip and whose paler, whitish base is at least 1½ inches high.

Slice at least 1 inch off the top of that central cone to eliminate all of the tough green part. Take the half lemon and rub the cut portions of the artichoke, squeezing juice over them to keep them from discoloring. Look into the exposed center of the artichoke. At the bottom, you will see very small leaves with prickly tips curving inward. Cut off all those leaves and scrape away the fuzzy "choke" beneath them, being careful not to cut away any of the tender bottom. If you have a small knife with a rounded point, use it to do this part of the trimming. Return to the outside of the artichoke and, where you have snapped off the outer leaves, pare away any of the tough green part that remains. Cut off all of the stem except for a short stump. As you snap off the hard outer leaves, keep them progressively longer at the base, giving the artichoke the look of a thick, fleshy rosebud. Rub all the exposed cut surfaces with lemon juice.

Turn the artichoke bottom up, gently spread the leaves outward, and press them against a board or other work surface, flattening them as much as possible without going so far as to crack them. Turn the artichoke right side up and sprinkle it with salt and a few grindings of pepper.

Choose a deep skillet or sauté pan and pour oil into it 1½ inches deep. Turn the heat to medium, and, when the oil is hot, slip in the artichokes, bottoms up. Cook them for 5 minutes or so, then turn them over. Turn them again, from time to time, as they cook. They are done when the thick part of the bottom feels tender at the pricking of a fork. This may take 15 minutes or longer, depending on how young and fresh the artichokes are. Regulate the heat to make sure that the oil is not overheating and frying the artichokes too quickly.

When the artichokes are done, transfer them to a board or other work surface, bottoms up, and press them with a wooden spoon or spatula to flatten them some more.

Turn on the heat to high under the pan. Place a bowl with cold water near the stove. As soon as the oil is very hot, slip in the artichokes, bottoms up. After frying them for just a few minutes, turn them over, dip your hand in the bowl of water, and sprinkle the artichokes. Stay at arm's length from the pan because the oil will sizzle and splatter.

As soon as the oil stops sputtering, transfer the artichokes, face down, to paper towels or to a cooling rack to drain them. Serve them with the leaves facing up. Do not refrigerate or reheat.

Summing up the Jewish culinary tradition is a virtually impossible task. The number and variety of dishes prepared by traditional Jewish cooks in various parts of the worlds are much too great. No particular style, spice, or taste is common to all Jewish foods. Jewish food can be spicy or bland, heavy or light, full of meat or largely vegetarian, depending on the season, region, or individual cook. A typical Jewish food in one part of the world is totally unknown to Jews in another area. Ashkenazic Jews who are offered unfamiliar Jewish foods from the Middle East might think them exotic, horrible, or delicious but might not recognize them as Jewish. Typically Jewish foods in America like bagels and lox or pastrami sandwiches are rare in Israel and in kosher restaurants in France or Italy.

What united Jewish cuisine all over the world was not a particular dish or style, but a shared function and a shared religious tradition. Traditional Jewish cooking followed the laws of Kashruth. In general, what was kosher in one part of the world was kosher everywhere else. There were a few exceptions, however. Some Middle Eastern Jews ate locust, a food no European Jew would consider acceptable. Ashkenazic Jews would not permit beans or rice on Passover even though Middle Eastern Jews would. Besides the common dietary rules that forbade the mixing of meat and milk and the use of pork or seafood, there were shared Jewish holidays that required festive foods but sometimes limited the methods by which they could be prepared. These gave Jews everywhere in the world the same structural needs when it came to preparing foods: They needed to have warm food on the Sabbath, unleavened food for Passover, and something symbolic of the blessings of the New Year on Rosh Hashana. But since they were not in direct contact, did not have the same ingredients available, and lived among peoples with their own varied culinary traditions, Jewish cooks in various parts of the world came up with dishes that did not resemble the dishes made elsewhere. Like all other elements of traditional Jewish culture, Jewish cuisine shared a common core of meaning and structure but differed so much regionally as to be unrecognizable from one area to another.

Costume

Not Just a Long Black Coat

MOST JEWISH CULTURAL TRADITIONS WERE PRIVATE, INTENDED FOR THE INTERNAL circle of family, friends, and synagogue, and did not have much impact on the outside world. Costume and hairstyles, however, marked Jews visually. Not only did they affect how Jews saw themselves, but they also played an important role in determining how the non-Jewish world viewed the Jews, and how Jews and their non-Jewish neighbors related to one another.

As in other aspects of Jewish cultural life, the great tradition played a role in determining how Jews dressed, but this role was much smaller than the role played by climate, fashions of the surrounding culture, available materials, and the relationship between Jews and Gentiles. Aside from Jewish religious requirements regarding dress, such as rules of modesty and head coverings, there were two possible attitudes Jewish and non-Jewish populations could have about how Jews should dress. One option was to minimize the differences between their dress and that of their neighbors so that they could blend into the general population. After all, differences in religion don't have to be visible, and the relationship between individual Jews and God is a private matter.

The second option was to make the differences between Jews and non-Jews as visible as possible. Historically there were a number of different sources and motivations for emphasizing religious differences in costume. One source was Jewish pride. To make one's Jewishness visible to all was considered a mark of honor. A second motive was the desire to prevent unauthorized mixing of Jews and non-Jews. If Jews were recognizable at first glance, the chance for them to become romantically involved with non-Jews would be lessened. This led both rabbinical and non-Jewish authorities to encourage Jews to dress in a distinctive way. Finally, visual differentiation—making the Jews wear a special hat, hairstyle, or badge—could be enforced by the non-Jewish authorities as a way of humiliating Jews and demonstrating their lowly position in society.

There were also more neutral reasons for Jews and non-Jews to dress differently. People of different nationalities, ethnic groups, and social classes all bring different traditions and practical needs to bear in choosing how to dress. They may not consciously desire to look different from or the same as members of other groups and yet still be recognizable because of their different mode of life or patterns of migration.

In the various societies in which Jews of the Diaspora have lived, these considerations have all helped form the ways Jews presented themselves in public. Sometimes there were clear notes of ambivalence in Jewish attitudes, a mixture of pride in their distinctiveness and fear or shame of being visibly Jewish in a hostile society. No single Jewish attitude has existed over time with regard to dress. It is not necessarily true that they would have dressed like everyone else, had they not been forced to wear a special garb, or that they necessarily wanted to look different at all times. The range of attitudes differed widely from one society to another.

This chapter looks at many examples of Jewish costume. It is important to keep in mind that national costumes often differ from everyday dress. As we all know, the same individual can dress very differently for different occasions. Usually the most picturesque costumes, the ones that artists depict and that appear in books on costume, are worn only on special occasions—for church or synagogue, at weddings, festivals, or in processions. Ordinary clothes tend to be less picturesque and often less distinctive than national costumes. In many parts of Europe today, local costumes are preserved by special societies and worn only at festivals, to church, and to impress visiting tourists. Similarly the traditional costumes in which Jews were depicted were often worn only on the Sabbath, for weddings, or on other special occasions. The preserved examples are usually the most different, the most beautiful, or the most exotic. The clothes worn by Jews on weekdays may have been somewhat distinctive, but they were not necessarily considered worthy of depicting in art and probably were not as different from non-Jewish costume as special-occasion clothing was.

Jewish Religious Law and Jewish Dress

Biblical and rabbinic law dictates a number of aspects of Jewish dress. In some cases the rules are clear, uniform, and unchanging, but more frequently, they are open to interpretation and are implemented in very different ways in various societies. Certain rules regulated matters that were invisible to outsiders or restricted to worship. For instance, it was not readily visible that Jews did not wear sha'atnez, a mixture of linen and wool forbidden by the Bible. In the days when most clothing was made at home, the law against sha'atnez was easy to obey, since people knew what their clothing was made of. In the modern world of ready-made clothing and wool blends, it is not always obvious if a garment contains the forbidden mixture. Orthodox Jews of today solved this "problem" by creating "sha'atnez laboratories" where garments can be examined chemically or microscopically to determine if they contain sha'atnez.

Less esoteric than the prohibition on sha'atnez is the biblical requirement that Israelites place fringes on the four corners of their garments. According to rabbinic interpretation, this regulation applies only to males and only to a garment that actually is rectangular and therefore has four corners. Although the letter of the law does not absolutely require it, pious Jewish men always wore a special four-cornered garment (*arba kanfot*) with *tzitzit* (fringes), four doubled strings that are wound and tied in a prescribed manner, at each corner. Though the Bible prescribes that the fringes include a blue thread (*techelet*), almost all Jews since the destruction of the Second Temple, over 1900 years ago, have worn fringes that are exclusively white. This is because the rabbis preferred to forego the required blue dye made from a rare snail altogether rather than allow an imitation vegetable coloring to be used. Some groups in recent times have attempted to restore the blue thread, but most pious Jews have not followed them.

In general, the arba kanfot is worn underneath one's outer clothing. Those Jews who have interpreted the verse "And you shall see them and remember my commandments" to mean that the fringes have to be visible either wear the arba kanfot as an outer garment or ensure that the fringes themselves stick out visibly from their outer clothing (Illustration 7.1). In addition to the arba kanfot (sometimes also called *talit katan* "small talit"), men also wore a large four-cornered, fringed garment, referred to as a *talit*, as a prayer shawl during the daily morning service.

Because they deal with clearly visible aspects of dress, the rules concerning men's beards and hairstyles, women's modesty, and head coverings for both men and women have a much greater impact on the daily life of the individual Jew and have been subject to great variations in interpretation. Several passages in the Bible prescribe in rather unspecific terms how Jewish men should wear their hair and beards. Included are prohibitions against "rounding the corner of your head" (*pe'at roshekha*) and against "destroying the corner of your beard" (*pe'at zekanekha*) (Leviticus 19:27). Rabbinic tradition defines "destroying the corner of your beard" using another biblical passage, which forbids priests from "shaving the corners of their beard" (Leviticus 21:5). This is ultimately interpreted to mean that using a razor to shave the beard is what the Bible forbids.

7.1 Talit katan (arba kanfot)—four-cornered garment with fringes usually worn by religiously observant males under their shirts, worn in a visible manner by Hasidic Jews.

Depending on the time and place, these prohibitions have been carried out in very different ways. Some Jewish societies interpreted the first prohibition merely as forbidding the total removal (rounding) of the sideburns, while others have forbidden even the trimming of the sidelocks (*pe'ot*). The Hasidim of Eastern Europe and the Yemenite Jews were two widely separated groups who grew long sidelocks. Some Hasidim combed their sidelocks behind their ears, but other Hasidic groups allowed their sidelocks to hang down in long ringlets. In such cases, the pe'ot were not merely part of the beard but were clearly visible as separate sidecurls (Illustration 7.2). Some Jewish societies merely required that the beard not be removed totally, while others, like the Hasidim, frowned upon even trimming the beard. In much of the Muslim world and parts of Eastern Europe,

7.2   *Pe'ot (sidelocks) worn by Hasidic man and boy at traditional first haircut at age 3. The man is wearing the traditional streimel (fur hat).*

Jews' beards were not particularly distinctive since most Gentile men also retained their beards, but for many centuries Jewish men in Western and Central Europe were the only ones to wear beards. In the folklore of many European societies the Jews' beards were considered sinister, a sign of resemblance to the Devil or to goats and other animals. In the seventeenth and eighteenth centuries, many European Jews began to trim their beards into goatees or narrow strips at the jaw line. Since only shaving with a razor was prohibited, some religious Jews used clippers or depilatory powders to remove their beards. Finally, with the invention of the electric shaver, whose double blades work like clippers, unlike a straight razor, many modern Orthodox Jews began to appear clean-shaven in public without formally violating the biblical prohibition.

The rules concerning women's dress were also interpreted differently from one Jewish society to another. The basic regulations, which are found in rabbinic law, though not explicit in the Bible, were that women should dress modestly and that married women should cover their hair. The requirement to dress modestly, that is, in a way not interpreted as sexually arousing, applied in theory to men as well as women, but almost all regulations were applied only to women's clothing. To some extent modesty is in the eye of the beholder, and the definitions of what was "covering that part of the body that should be covered" varied. The required length of the sleeves, hemline, or neckline was different in various parts of the Jewish community.

With regard to covering the hair, custom also varied. In some places it was interpreted as requiring some sort of headdress, while in others it meant that no hair should be visible. Some societies interpreted the requirement as forbidding the showing of any kind of hair, while others permitted the use of artificial hair. Among Ashkenazic Jews in modern times, this has taken the form of the *sheitel* (wig) made either of artificial hair or even from the natural hair of the wearer. A woman's natural hair was cut short under the wig or, in some very pious Eastern European communities, shaved off entirely. When the sheitel first developed, it was denounced by rabbis as a violation of the essence of the law, but eventually it was accepted in most Ashkenazic communities. By the late nineteenth and early twentieth centuries the sheitel was the mark of the pious Ashkenazic Jewish matron. By contrast, Jewish women in parts of North Africa wore elaborate headdresses, usually in the form of artificial braids. In Yemen, women wore the *gargush*, a cloth headdress covering their hair entirely. The front of the gargush was made of fringed material, sometimes covered with metal, that came down over the upper forehead (Illustration 7.3).

The practice of Jewish men covering their heads at all times is of later origin than the requirements concerning married women. Whatever its origin, the practice was interpreted as a mark of respect for God, a symbol that there is "something above me." This etiquette is exactly the opposite of Christian practice, where the removal of the hat is considered a sign of respect. The requirement for a head covering was most strictly enforced during religious services, but in most places it was customary for Jewish men to keep their heads covered at all times.

7.3 Jewish couple in San'a, Yemen, 1937–38. The man wears long sidelocks and the woman's hair is covered by the gargush.

Though Jewish law did not prescribe the shape, size, or color of the head covering, these matters took on considerable importance in the various local Jewish cultures.

A final biblical law concerning clothing forbade cross-dressing between men and women. This regulation was generally interpreted as requiring a clear difference in the clothing of the two sexes. In Western society, from the Middle Ages to the twentieth century at least, this meant that men "wore the pants" and women wore skirts. But this was not the universal practice. In some societies, everyone wore robes or skirts, while in others, such as parts of the Arab world, women wore leggings (the source of "harem pants"), while the men often did not. The ancient Greeks thought that the wearing of trousers was typical of "barbarians." Only today does Orthodox practice oppose women's wearing of pants, though many modern Orthodox women ignore the regulation. Even today, rabbis from the Middle East are less insistent about this than Ashkenazic rabbis, perhaps because they remember the old Middle Eastern practices.

Women's Seclusion Among Jews, Christians, and Muslims

By the standards of today's Western society, traditional Judaism was quite restrictive concerning the position of women. Not only were married women required to keep their hair covered and dress modestly, but a man and a woman could not be alone together unless they were husband and wife. Men and women were forbidden to dance together, and women were not even permitted to sing in the presence of men. In the synagogue, women sat in a separate section and did not take an active part in the service. All of these measures were meant to prevent sexual temptation for the men.

When we compare the position of women in Jewish society with that of contemporary women in Christian and Muslim society, the picture becomes more complicated. In general, Jewish women were less restricted than Muslim women but more restricted than Christian women, who generally did not have to cover their hair or face or avoid appearing in public. In most Western countries, women's clothes were far less revealing than many twentieth century fashions, but there were times when plunging necklines (though rarely short hemlines) did bare quite a bit of the female anatomy. In traditional Jewish society, women were not necessarily confined to the home. Among Ashkenazic Jews especially, it was quite common for Jewish women, even more than Christian women, to have their own businesses. If the cut of their clothing differed at all from that of Christian women, it was in the direction of less revealing styles. Christian women generally wore hats, but these hats did not cover all their natural hair, as did those of Jewish women.

In the Muslim world, the tradition of female modesty was even stricter than that of the Jews. Covering the head and the entire body was common for all

7.4 The various degrees of modesty required by Christians, Jews, and Muslims from the Ottoman Empire, 1873. From left to right: a Jewish woman from Salonica, a Bulgarian (Christian) woman from Perlepe, a Muslim woman from Salonica in her outdoor clothing. Muslim women were not veiled in such a manner within the house.

women, married and unmarried. In many Muslim countries, women were not permitted to appear in public unless their faces were veiled (Illustration 7.4). In the strictest Muslim societies, a woman on the street uncovered only one eye and kept the rest of her face veiled. Jewish women in Muslim countries were generally not subject to such strict regulations and generally covered their hair but not their faces. However, they often found it advisable to veil their faces when walking through Muslim quarters.

Jewish women in Muslim countries were not entirely free from Muslim regulation of their apparel. In Yemen, for instance, the government required Jewish women to cover all of their hair while allowing Muslim women to leave a small portion of their hair uncovered. In some small Yemenite towns, Jewish women resented these attempts by Muslim authorities to prevent them from showing their hair and did what they could to evade the regulations. In Iran, the opposite situation occurred. Jewish women were forbidden to veil their faces, thus making them instant targets for the unwanted attention of Muslim men on the street. This prohibition on veiling was naturally humiliating to Jewish women.

Anti-Jewish Legislation

Non-Jewish regulations of Jewish dress did not only apply to women; frequently they also affected men. Sometimes government regulations required Jews to obey Jewish religious traditions that made them look different. For instance, eighteenth century laws in various German-speaking countries required married Jewish men to wear beards. In Yemen, men were required to wear long, visible sidelocks. In both cases, Jews were made to look different at first glance. Many Jews found such regulations deeply humiliating, since they could easily become targets of anti-Jewish aggression. On the other hand, government regulations sometimes forbade certain dress codified by Jewish law or custom. Nineteenth century Czarist Russian regulations forbidding Jewish men to wear sidelocks, beards, or long coats and proposed Yemen laws to force Jews to appear bareheaded fall into this category.

The earliest laws forcing Jews (and other "infidels") to dress differently than the "faithful" were proclaimed by the Muslims. Jews were required to wear black or yellow turbans, (never green ones, since that color symbolized the prophet Muhammed) and to tie their clothes with a rope (*zunnar*) rather than a belt. In some Muslim countries, such as precolonial Morocco, Jews were forbidden to wear regular shoes and instead had to wear slippers in the Muslim quarters.

7.5 *A drawing of the special Jewish badge, "Judenzeichen," Jews in Germany had to wear.*

WORMS

J U D E N.

ZWEITE HÄLFTE DES 16. JAHRHUNDERTS.

7.6 *The special Jewish badge in Germany worn by a Jewish couple in Worms, Germany, in the second half of the 16th century.*

Similar discriminatory laws on Jewish clothing soon appeared in Christian countries, especially after the enactments of the Catholic Church's Lateran Council in 1215. In medieval France, England, Germany, and Italy, Jews were forced to wear special badges or hats. The badge consisted of the tablets of the law or of a yellow ring sewn to the front of one's outer garment (Illustrations 7.5, 7.6). In parts of Germany the ring-shaped badge remained in effect until the eighteenth century. And in the twentieth century the Nazis revived the medieval Jewish badge in the form of the infamous yellow Star of David, which they forced Jews to wear. The special Jewish hat took various forms. In Italy, Jews were often required to tie a red cloth to their hats. In Germany, where the Jewish hat was required for a particularly long time, its form varied from a high conical hat

7.7 *Jewish rider wearing the Jewish pointed hat.*

(similar to a dunce cap), to a brimmed hat that came to a point at the top, to a hat whose pointed top was "crowned" with a small ball-shaped form (Illustration 7.7). In some countries the Jewish hat had to be yellow.

How Jews Dressed in Various Societies

Although the requirements of Jewish religious law and the restricted position of the Jews in most premodern countries created certain common parameters for Jewish clothing, Jewish costume differed widely from one area to another. In most places it would be fairer to call the costume of the Jews a variation on the local non-Jewish costume than to present it as a variant of a worldwide Jewish way of dressing. Visual documentation shows that the way Jews dressed in a particular country changed conspicuously over the ages. If there was a common thread beyond the restrictions mentioned above, it was that Jews in many countries tended to wear more subdued colors than their neighbors, who often wore brightly colored costumes. There also seems to have been a tendency, especially in the European countries, for Jewish costume to lag behind current fashions. Items of clothing that were once popular among the general population were retained, in modified form, by Jews long after the bulk of the population abandoned them. A well-known example of this is the *caftan* (long coat) of Eastern European Jews; less well-known is the practice of seventeenth and eighteenth century German Jewish men and women of wearing a white ruff or wide starched collar, which was common among Christians at least a century earlier. Even today, Orthodox Jews in the West seem distinctive because they continue to wear items of clothing once widely used but now generally obsolete, such as the dark suit jackets and black hats worn by many yeshiva students today.

Among the regions that had their own distinctive type of Jewish costume in premodern times were Yemen, Turkey, Tunisia, Morocco, Germany, and Eastern Europe. Though in each particular region these costumes were considered the mark of a Jew, they differed almost totally from Jewish costumes in the other regions. In Yemen, Jewish women were distinguished by their distinctive head coverings, a particular kind of embroidery on their daily costumes, the wearing of black dresses, and special colors and decorations on their festive leggings. Men were distinguished by their long sidelocks and their low, dark caps with a checkered cloth wound around them, rather than the fez or turban, which they were forbidden to wear. At weddings, Yemenite grooms and especially Yemenite brides wore elaborate costumes. The adornment of the bride both differed from that of Muslim brides and varied from town to town (Illustration 7.8).

In Turkey, Judezmo-speaking Jews wore costumes that differed from place to place but that showed some distinctive features. Common among Jewish men was the *kaveze*, a combination fez and turban, which consisted of a cylindrical

7.8 *Yemenite bride's dress from outside San'a. The photo was taken in Israel, at a wedding that took place six weeks after the arrival of the couple from Heidan, the north of Yemen. Compare to Illustration 5.16.*

7.9 *Jews in Bursa, Turkey, 1873. The man is wearing a kaveze on his head and the woman on the left wears a fotoz. The woman on the right is dressed as she would be for going out of the house.*

cardboard crown of black with a piece of light-colored material rolled around it. Jewish men in Turkey also sometimes wore the fez or the turban, generally in subdued colors. Women's headdresses varied; in some places they wore the *fotoz*, a large, dome-shaped cushion of cloth covered with jewels (Illustration 7.9). In the street they covered the fotoz with a white veil or cloth, which was then folded in front of the neck. Other Turkish Jewish women wore a *yemeni*, a square colored kerchief with a lace fringe that completely covered their hair.

Pictures of Tunisian Jews from the nineteenth and early twentieth centuries show very distinctive Jewish dress. Jewish men wore black or dark blue turbans; over their leggings and short jackets, they wore a cloak of a light color. Tunisian Jewish women often wore light-colored pants, a small gold-embroidered jacket

7.10 Jews in traditional costume at a wedding in Tunis. Postcard, late 19th century.

with a hip-length cloak over it, and a huge pointed velvet hat (*kufia* or *sarma*) (Illustration 7.10). In Algeria, Jewish women also wore very high hats, often covered by white veils on festive occasions, and unlike Tunisian Jewish women, they wore long, floor-length robes. In nearby Morocco, Jewish costumes were quite different. Men wore black skull caps, belted tunics, and long robes. Muslim law required them to wear backless slippers rather than regular shoes. Jewish women's daily costumes were not very different from the clothes of Muslim women, though they were less strictly veiled than Muslims, but their ceremonial dress was unique. Known as the *keswa el kbira* ("great outfit"), it was derived from Spanish costume and was presumably brought to Morocco by the expelled Spanish Jews. The keswa el kbira was often elaborately decorated, made of velvet, green in some towns and red in others, and sometimes embroidered with gold. It consisted of a tight bodice, a sash, and a fuller skirt, and was often worn with separate wide sleeves or a large veil (Illustration 7.11). The design of the ceremonial dress varied from town to town, as did the way Jewish women wore their hair.

7.11 Keswa el kbira—Jewish woman in traditional festive costume, Tetuan, Morocco, late 19th century.

Married women wore various types of hats, large head scarves, and braids made of imitation hair.

Although both German and Eastern European Jews were Ashkenazim, their traditional costumes were noticeably different. Until the eighteenth century, both German Jewish men and women wore large white ruffs of a type no longer worn by Gentiles. Both men's and women's costumes were mainly black and white, and both sexes wore a long sleeveless cloak (*schulmantel* or *sarbal*) to the synagogue. Men wore large flat hats (*barretts*) (Illustration 7.12). Married men were also conspicuous because, unlike virtually all Christian men, they wore beards. The traditional German Jewish costume began to disappear in the eighteenth century as Jews began to wear the costume of non-Jews. Still, there are depictions of elements of this traditional costume being worn by men in the synagogue in southern Germany around 1800 and even a few decades later (Illustration 7.13).

Even in the twentieth century, vestiges of the obsolete German Jewish costume survived in one special context—shrouds for the dead, worn by traditional Jewish men to the synagogue on the High Holidays. The men's costume consisted of a white robe (*sargenes*) open only at the top and put on over the head; a separate wide, white collar that reached the ends of the shoulders; and a soft white cap like a nightcap. Except for the color of the robe, this bears a striking resemblance to eighteenth century Jewish costumes. Women's shrouds did not in-

7.12 *Jewish wedding in 18th century Germany. Note the white ruffs worn by both men and women.*

7.13 *Scenes from German Jewish life c.1820. The Sabbath pictures (upper row left, middle row left, and right) depict elements of traditional Jewish dress, as do the hats in the picture in the lower row left depicting the fast of Tish'a B'av. The other scenes mainly depict weekday scenes in which Jewish costume is not distinctive.*

clude the old white collar but instead had an unusual black and white striped breastcloth worn over the white robe (see Illustrations 5.19 and 5.20).

Aside from shrouds, no remnant of a special German-Jewish costume survived after the first decades of the nineteenth century. Some early nineteenth century pictures do show Jews wearing elements of general eighteenth century garb, especially three-cornered hats, which non-Jews had abandoned earlier, but such distinctiveness disappeared soon thereafter.

The traditional Eastern European Jewish costume for men is so familiar today that many assume that it was the traditional costume of Jews everywhere. In Poland and Lithuania, traditional Jewish men wore long black coats tied with a cloth belt at the waist. They generally wore their beards long and untrimmed, with long sidelocks (Illustrations 7.14, 7.15). There were various types of male headdress, some of which varied regionally. Among these were the high fur hat

7.14 *Traditional Jewish costume in Eastern Europe, early 19th century. From left to right: a married woman with covered hair, an unmarried woman, a married man.*

7.15 *Jewish costume from Warsaw, 1846.*

7.16, 7.17 Two types of Hasidic fur hats. Left, the spodik; above, the shtreimel.

7.18 Yeshiva students in Warsaw wearing the typical Jewish cap (yidish hitl) of Central Poland.

(*spodik*) (Illustration 7.16) and the saucer-shaped hat with a fur brim (*shtreimel*) (Illustration 7.17) worn mainly on the Sabbath and for special occasions. In the house or underneath their regular hats, men wore a skullcap (*yarmulka* or *kapl*). Originally, the wearing of a skullcap was not a specifically Jewish practice. The word *yarmulka* itself is of Ukrainian origin, and non-Jews in Germany, France, and East-Central Europe in the nineteenth century (as well as the Roman Catholic clergy for a much longer period) sometimes wore flat or pillbox-shaped skullcaps indoors. Because of its connection with Jewish religious custom, however, the yarmulka became a Jewish symbol in modern times. This is especially true because, unlike Christians, Jews wore head coverings both in the synagogue and during meals. Indoors, it was simply more convenient to wear a skullcap rather than a larger hat. On weekdays, Eastern European Jewish men generally wore less elaborate forms of outdoor head coverings than on the Sabbath. This was sometimes known in Yiddish as a *yidish hitl* (Jewish cap), and it varied from region to region. In the Warsaw area, the Jewish cap looked like a pillbox skullcap with a tiny brim in front (Illustration 7.18). In Lithuania and the Ukraine, on the other hand, the Jewish cap had a larger brim and a different shape and was not very different from the caps worn by non-Jewish workers.

Jewish women's dress in Eastern Europe was less distinctive than men's. Unlike men, they did not restrict themselves to black. Their dress styles were much like those of Christian women. What was distinctive about Jewish women's dress was the *brusttuch*, an embroidered piece of cloth worn in front of the blouse, and the headdress (Illustration 7.19). In many parts of Eastern Europe in the nineteenth century, Jewish women completely covered their hair with a lace cap or a *shterntikhl*, a forehead band, which was often richly embroidered or covered with pearls. On less formal occasions, they undoubtedly used kerchiefs that resembled those of their non-Jewish neighbors (Illustration 7.20).

What was once the general costume of Eastern European Jewish men is now generally thought of as Hasidic garb, an association brought about by decrees of the Czarist Russian government in 1850 forbidding Jewish men to wear sidelocks and long black coats and, a year later, forbidding Jewish women to shave off their hair at marriage. In much of the Czar's realm Jews obeyed the new laws, though

7.19 Painting of a Jewish woman wearing the distinctive Jewish Brusttuch [breast cloth], Poland.

7.20 A Jewish couple (Peysekh and Leye Zilberman) in Bar, Ukraine. The wife is wearing a kerchief that completely covers her hair.

reluctantly, believing that the prohibited items of dress were not requirements of Jewish law. The Hasidic sect, on the other hand, took a very different view. They refused to accept the decree and fought it with every means at their disposal. Consequently, the Hasidim were the only ones who retained the traditional Eastern European Jewish costume. However, even the pious students of the Lithuanian yeshivas, who were not Hasidim, generally dressed in a version of Western costume.

It is frequently said that Eastern European Jewish dress is nothing but the costume of the medieval Polish upper class. Like many popular beliefs about Jewish culture, this one contains some elements of truth, but it not completely correct. What is true is that the traditional costume of Eastern European Christians, especially those of the upper classes, was based on the *kaftan* (long robe), rather than on the Western short coat and trousers or hose. The belted coat and the fur hat also seem to have been elements of traditional costume in much of Slavic Eastern Europe (Illustration 7.21). Some of the names used for items of Polish or Ukrainian traditional dress, like *kapota* or *yarmulka*, were the same as those used in Yiddish. But several factors distinguish the Jewish costume from medieval Christian ones. The most obvious difference seems to be color. Jewish men wore black coats and black belts. When the early Hasidim wore white instead of black, it was considered highly anomalous by non-Hasidic Jews. The costumes of Christians, on the other hand, were often decorated with embroidery and were brightly colored. Male Christian peasants often wore white

7.21 Jewish male costume from eighteenth-century Poland

shirts and pants, quite different from the Jewish costume in Eastern Europe. Everyday costumes of Jewish and non-Jewish town folk in the nineteenth century seem much more similar than the traditional costumes. Photos of Ukrainians in their everyday dress, wearing coats hanging below the knees and caps with brims, look much more like pictures of Jews in their daily dress, though there are still noticeable differences (Illustration 7.22).

In recent times, two developments have taken place in Jewish dress. Most widespread is the transition of Jews in most parts of the world from a distinctively Jewish costume to one that is indistinguishable from that of their non-Jewish neighbors. In many parts of the world, this transformation has been completed, though in some places, remnants of Jewish dress have been kept or new habits have been created. In Tunisia and among the very pious in the United States, Jews wear their hats or caps further back on their head than do non-Jews.

7.22 West Ukrainian town dwellers. The men are wearing long, dark coats with outside belts.

7.23 Ashkenazic yeshiva student in Jerusalem wearing tefillin and a hat pushed back on his head.

One practical explanation for this is that the tefilin worn in prayer are worn at the top of the forehead, and a worshipper wearing a hat would have to push it back in order to accommodate them. This habit may have been carried over into daily life as well (Illustration 7.23).

The other modern phenomenon with regard to Jewish dress is the development of a kind of worldwide costume by Orthodox Jews. To a considerable extent, this has been influenced by Eastern European traditions. Very Orthodox rabbis, even those coming from Middle Eastern countries, frequently dress in long black coats and broad-brimmed black hats to symbolize their office. The skullcap (*yarmulka* or *kipa*) has become part of the costume of modern Orthodox men both for street wear and at home. Degrees of Orthodoxy can easily be determined from the type of headgear worn, especially in Israel. The black hat ranks as most extreme or pious, a black velvet or silk skullcap is somewhat more moderate, and a knitted skullcap (*kipa seruga*) marks the modern wing of Orthodoxy. Among Orthodox women there is no specific item of Jewish dress, but there has been a noticeable revival in recent years of conspicuously modest dress and hair coverings.

Music

The Religious and the Secular

UNTIL VERY RECENT TIMES, MOST JEWISH MUSICAL TRADITIONS WERE transmitted by purely oral means. Very rarely was any kind of musical notation used; most singers of Jewish religious and secular music could not even read musical notes. One learned the traditions by hearing them and repeating them, but because the music was not written down, it did not remain rigidly fixed. A singer could give his or her own variation of a familiar melody. New melodies were invented or borrowed from non-Jewish cultures all the time. The repertoire of Jewish music changed over the centuries, with old and new musical styles being blended to-

gether. A religious service might include melodies composed in the present century along with melodies hundreds of years old.

What Is Jewish Music?

The definition of Jewish music is itself a much debated question. Is any music
written by a Jew Jewish music? Is only synagogue music Jewish? What makes
Jewish music distinctive? If Hasidim borrowed a Ukrainian shepherd's tune and
set religious words to it, does that make the melody Jewish? Does the fact that

8.1 Ma'oz Zur

> W riting about music has an inherent difficulty: reading a description of music is not the same as listening to it. In order to really understand the similarities and differences among local Jewish traditions, it is necessary to refer to actual musical examples. For those of you who can read musical notation, this chapter will include some examples written as sheet music. Unfortunately, this is not the same as hearing the music itself.

the opening bars of the Ashkenazic melody for the Chanukah hymn "Ma'oz Zur" ("Rock of Ages") are identical to the opening bars of Martin Luther's "Nun freut euch lieben Christeng'mein" ("Rejoice O dear Christian Community") invalidate "Ma'oz Zur" as a Jewish melody (Illustration 8.1)?

We know that much Jewish folk music, whether secular or religious, is borrowed from, or at least influenced by, the musical traditions of the people among whom the Jews lived. Does that mean that Hasidic music is purely Slavic and Yemenite music is purely Arabic? Or is there some common element found in all Jewish music, some common ancestor from which the various regional traditions descend? These questions are ideologically laden ones fraught with emotional implications. If Jewish music is merely borrowed from non-Jewish cultures, does that mean that this aspect of Jewish culture is merely derivative and not creative? Or is it a tribute to the ability of Jews to adapt to various cultures and make them their own? Does Jewish music have to go back to an ancient tradition in the Holy Land in order to be authentic, or is it just as authentic if it was invented in the various medieval diasporas?

One of the pioneers of the comparative study of Jewish music, A. Z. Idelsohn, a strong Zionist, was firmly convinced that the Jewish traditions in such widely separated places as Yemen, Germany, Morocco, and Poland had common roots. For him, authentic Jewish music was "Semitic-Oriental" song, and the later additions, such as German influences on the Ashkenazic tradition, were dilutions of the authentic tradition. Later scholars tended to be more skeptical about the common roots of all Jewish music, although they too sometimes found points of similarity.

The definition of Jewish music I will use includes both liturgical and secular music. The discussion of Jewish secular music will be limited to music that is either in a Jewish vernacular language, used for a specifically Jewish occasion (for instance, wedding music), or has a specifically Jewish theme. Only music of the Jewish folk tradition will be included, excluding music by well-known Jewish composers of the modern period.

Anyone who listens to a cross-section of Jewish music from around the world is first struck by the *dissimilarity* of the various traditions. Any characteristic one might use to describe the music of one particular geographic branch of Jewish music—for instance, the plaintive minor tone of East European Jewish music—does not exist in Jewish music in other parts of the world. The dissimilarity is greatest in the nonliturgical music. Jewish folk songs in the vernacular and Jewish wedding dance tunes rarely share the same words, melodies, rhythms, or any other characteristics. The music of the religious service is the most likely to contain common elements, if indeed there are any such elements to be found.

Jewish Religious Music

To trace any Jewish music back to a common ancestor, it is necessary to look at what religious music existed before the destruction of the Temple. A number of biblical texts provide evidence that the Temple service was accompanied by musical instruments, including the lyre, the drum, cymbals, and wind instruments, as well as singing by the Levites. There is, of course, no notation to tell us what the music of the ancient Temple sounded like. It is certain, however, that after the destruction of the Second Temple by the Romans in 70 CE, the use of instrumental accompaniment in Jewish religious services came to an end. With few exceptions, the Jewish service, until modern times, was chanted or sung by the unaccompanied solo or congregational voice, usually consisting of male voices only.

The singing of psalms remained a part of Jewish ritual even after the destruction of the Temple, as well as playing a prominent part in Christian liturgy. The psalms can be given all sorts of possible music settings, and in fact, most forms of psalm singing (psalmody) are completely unrelated to each other. Scholars of Jewish music have discovered, however, that in widely separated parts of the Jewish world the psalms are chanted in a simple manner that has certain characteristics in common. There is a remarkable similarity between psalm recitation in Germany and that of various "Oriental" communities, including those of Persia and Morocco, countries not usually noted for their close ties to Germany. It could be that these communities retain a remnant of an ancient tradition, but it is also possible that they borrowed from a much more recent source.

Another type of musical tradition shared throughout the Jewish world is cantillation of the Bible. Jewish tradition prescribes a particular way of chanting biblical texts in the religious service, midway between reading and singing. This cantillation seems to be quite different from the way other religious traditions, such as the Muslim or Christian ones, read or chant their scriptures. Unlike all other Jewish traditional music, the cantillation system has a written tradition well over 1000 years old. The cantillation signs are not notes, but rather motifs (usually one per word) that have both grammatical and musical functions. Each motif contains a number of notes. In some ways, the cantillation signs act like the commas, colons, and periods of our writing system. Scholars believe that the written signs derived from hand signals that were given to the reader to direct him to the correct phraseology. Cantillation signs are either conjunctive or disjunctive; the disjunctive signs tend to be more elaborate, while the conjunctive signs help join the parts of the sentence and are usually simpler (Illustration 8.2). Somewhat similar signs were used in medieval notation both in Western and Central Europe and in the Byzantine Christian churches, where they were known as *neumes*.

The fact that Jews all over the world have Bibles with identical printed cantillation signs (they are not written in the Torah scrolls themselves) does not mean that they sing the biblical text to the same melody. In fact, even in a single local tradition, the same signs are sung differently, depending on the book or the occasion. Ashkenazic Jews, for instance, have separate *trops* or cantillation melodies for reading the Torah, the Haftara (prophetic reading), the Book of Esther, the Book of Lamentations, and the Torah reading on the High Holidays. Some Ashke-

Lords or Disjunctives

	Trope	Hebrew Name	Transliteration	Literal Meaning
1	⊺	סוֹף ־פָּסוּק	sof pawsuk = end of sentence	
2	ᚷ	אֶתְנַחְתָּא	esnachtaw = to rest	
3	∴	סֶגּוֹל	segol = cluster of three dots: also a vowel sign	
4	⊥	שַׁלְשֶׁלֶת	shalsheles = chain	
5	⊥:	זָקֵף גָּדוֹל	zawkef-gawdol = full, upright (chironomic sign)	
6	⊥̇	קָטוֹן or זָקֵף קָטוֹן	zawkef-koton or koton ‑ ‑lesser upright (chironomic sign)	
7	⌐	טִפְחָא	tipchaw = hand-breath (chironomic sign)	
8	∴	רְבִיעַ	revia = four-square	
9	≅	זַרְקָא	zarkaw = scattered	
10	⌐	פַּשְׁטָא	pashtaw = extending (chironomic sign)	
11	≼	יְתִיב	yesiv = staying	

8.2 Cantillation signs

	Trope		Hebrew Name	Transliteration	Literal Meaning
12	⌐		גֶּרֶשׁ	– geresh = to chase (when milel)	
13	⌐		אַזְלָא	– azlaw = going on (when milra)	
14	⌐⌐		גֵּרְשַׁיִם	– gershayim = double geresh	
15	⌐		תְּבִיר	– tevir = broken	
16	⊻		פָּזֵר	– pawzer = to scatter	
17	⊻⊻		קַרְנֵי־פָרָה	– karne fawraw = horns of a heifer	
18	⊻		תְּלִישָׁא גְדוֹלָה	– t'lishaw g'dolaw = big t'lishaw	
19	⌐		מוּנַח לְגַרְמֵיה	– munach legarme = independent munach	

Servants and Conjunctives

20	⌐		מוּנַח	– munach = sustained	
21	⋝		מַהְפַּך	– mahpach = reversed	
22	⎺		דַּרְגָּא	– dargaw = stepwise	
23	⌐		מֵירְכָא	– merchaw = to lengthen	

8.3 Eastern Ashkenazic cantillation of the Torah

nazic groups have an additional trop for the Song of Songs, Ecclesiastes, and the Book of Ruth.

For the reading of the Torah, there are a number of regional traditions. One tradition is used by all Ashkenazic Jews, though there are noticeable variations between the Western (German, French, British) and the Eastern subtradition (Illustration 8.3). A second tradition, also with local subvariants, is found in such widely separated areas as Morocco, Italy, Persia, Iraq, Syria, and the Sephardic community of Amsterdam (Illustration 8.4). Still different is the cantillation of Yemen. In a few areas, like Bukhara, the art of cantillation was lost and was replaced with a simple chant. Some Hungarian Jews read the Haftara (but not the

8.4 Sephardic cantillation of the Torah

Pentateuch) in a chant with little cantillation. Each of these main traditions seems musically unrelated to each of the others, though generally the relative length of motifs is consistent across all traditions. One puzzling discovery is that in Lithuania, where the Ashkenazic Torah trop was in use, Ecclesiastes, the Book of Ruth, and the Song of Songs were chanted to a special melody similar to that used by most Jews in the Middle East and the Mediterranean for the Torah (Illustration 8.5). It is similar, but not the same, since a change of one note puts the melody in the Western major scale rather than in a Middle Eastern mode. Is this a borrowing and adaptation of a Sephardic tradition or is it a remnant of the original Torah trop that Ashkenazic Jews later abandoned?

8.5 Lithuanian cantillation of Song of Songs

The modern Ashkenazic Torah trop differs greatly from all the others. Like certain other types of folk music, such as Celtic music, it uses a mainly pentatonic scale. (The best way to explain this is that there are only five notes to each octave—rather like playing a melody exclusively on the black keys of the piano.) It sounds more "major" and more European than do the trops used in the Middle East. Even though it differs from other Jewish musical traditions, the Ashkenazic Torah cantillation has a long documented history. It was first written down in Western musical notation in the late fifteenth and early sixteenth centuries by Christian scholars interested in the proper reading of the Bible. Analysis shows that, despite changes in the melody over the past 400 years, it is still clearly recognizable as the same basic system. The German subvariants of the Ashkenazic tradition are especially close to the forms noted down during the Renaissance, perhaps because the scholars who recorded them lived in Germany.

A final characteristic seemingly shared by all traditions of Jewish liturgical music is the use of modes. Today, most music in Europe and America is either in a major or a minor scale. In much of the Middle East, the eastern Mediterranean, Iran, and India, on the other hand, music does not generally fall into major or minor scales but rather follows a mode (a series of musical motifs in a particular scale). Because Jewish traditional music, even in Europe, is often modal rather than major or minor, some have used this as an argument that even Ashkenazic or Italian Jewish music is basically Middle Eastern (and therefore "authentic"). A weakness in this argument is the fact that European music, until about the seventeenth century was also mainly modal. Not only the ancient Greek modes, but also the modes of the medieval Catholic Church, were important in the development of Western musical traditions.

The use of modes is extremely widespread in the Jewish music of the Middle East, but it is also found in Ashkenazic religious music. This is especially true of the parts of the Sabbath and weekday services chanted by the cantor. Some of these modes (also called by the Yiddish name *Steiger*) were named for particular prayers—for instance, the Mogen Ovos mode or the Ahavo Rabbo mode. The Ahavo Rabbo mode is the plaintive style made familiar in much of Eastern European cantorial music. Some have claimed that this type of mode is the most authentically Jewish of all. However, scholars have pointed out that this mode was rarely used by Jews in Germany, Yemen, Morocco, or Italy. Perhaps this supposedly most Jewish prayer mode was, in fact, an innovation borrowed by Eastern European Jews from their non-Jewish neighbors.

Whether or not their music actually had ancient roots, Jews tended to believe that their synagogue melodies were of great antiquity. They pointed to a particular melody of the priestly blessing as "going back to the Second Temple," even though it has a clearly Eastern European sound. Nowhere is this tradition of antiquity as strong as in the Ashkenazic tradition of "Misinai melodies" (melodies from Sinai). These melodies, mainly used on the High Holidays of Rosh Hashana and Yom Kippur, are solemn chants shared by all Ashkenazic Jews. Among these Misinai melodies are the High Holiday chants for the evening "Barechu" (the call to prayer), for "Alenu" as recited in the Musaf service (in the morning), the introductory Kaddish, and, most famous of all, "Kol Nidre." Musical scholars examining the "melodies from Sinai" of the Ashkenazic Jews quickly came to the conclusion that they are not only much later than "Sinai," but in fact are later than the simpler and less impressive modes of psalmody and Sabbath prayer. Bearing the closest similarity to the music of medieval Christian Europe, several of the melodies are recognizably akin to chants used in the Catholic Church.

The relationship between traditional Jewish and traditional Catholic music is complex. It is not just a matter of borrowing in one direction. The Catholic Church itself grew out of Judaism and considered itself the true heir of ancient Israel. Many of its prayer texts came from the Hebrew Bible. It would not be surprising if certain musical traditions had a common ancestry. But there is also plenty of evidence of direct borrowing. The Ashkenazic introductory "Barechu"

8.6 Comparison of Ashkenazic Barechu with Gregorian chant Iste Confessor

of the High Holidays is very similar to a Gregorian melody to the Latin words *Iste confessor domine colentes*. Could Ashkenazic Jews have borrowed it from their neighbors (Illustration 8.6). If they did, then borrowing certainly went in the opposite direction as well. The melody of "Alenu" for the High Holidays is also to be found in sections of the Ninth Mass of the Virgin. The borrowing is attributed in a medieval Jewish chronicle to the tragic martyrdom of the Jews of Blois, France, in the year 1171. As the Jews were being burned at the stake they sang "Alenu" as their final song, which Christians later adopted for their own religious worship.

In other cases, the relationship may have been even more complicated. In the Ashkenazic tradition, the song "Eli Zion" concludes the dirges sung on Tisha B'av, the memorial fast for the destruction of the two Jerusalem Temples. The melody for this hymn is shared by all Ashkenazic Jews, a sign of antiquity. This melody is similar to those of two Christian hymns, one a Latin Christmas carol, "Puer natus in Bethlehem" ("A Child Is Born in Bethlehem"), and the other a melody sung by pilgrims to the shrine of St. James of Compostella in Spain. Perhaps the oppressed medieval Jews heard the joyful songs of Christian pilgrims and, viewing them as extremely sad signs of their own low status, then used them for the liturgy of the saddest day in the Jewish calendar.

Worshippers' desire to view the melodies they used as being of great antiquity was not confined to the Middle Ages. A melody that has became very popular among Jews in modern times is "Sholom Aleichem," the hymn welcoming the guardian Sabbath angels sung on Friday night at home. The slow, plaintive melody seems to many to be deeply traditional. Not only Ashkenazic Jews, but even Jews from as far away as India, have claimed that this song was sung traditionally by their ancestors. The history of the melody proves otherwise. It was composed in May 1918, on the steps of Low Library at Columbia University in New York City, by Israel Goldfarb, a cantorial student at the Jewish Theological Seminary. The borrowing of non-Jewish melodies was not merely the result of assimilatory tendencies. The Hasidim were a traditionalist group that borrowed melodies from other cultures, often deliberately. Among Chabad Hasidim, for instance, the solemn Yom Kippur services are concluded with the joyous singing and dancing of what the Hasidim themselves call "Napoleon's March." The melody is based on the French army anthem "Chant du Depart," sung by Napoleon's soldiers during their Russian campaign of 1812 and heard by the Hasidim. They continue to use the melody, which they have transformed into a song of victory over Satan and the evil inclination, to this day. The same Hasidic group also sings various Belarussian drinking songs that they have reinterpreted as having religious meaning. A similar case is the Hungarian Hasidic use of the Hungarian folk song "Szol a kokos mar" ("The Rooster Is Crowing"). This mournful tune is interpreted by the Hasidim as referring to the longing of the Jew for the Divine Presence. Sometimes several languages are used in the same Hasidic song as in (Ukrainian:) "A mi piom tai hulia-em" ("And We Drink and Rejoice") and (Hebrew) "Vatoh tishma min hashomayim" ("And You Will Hear from the Heavens"). A very different use of a known non-Jewish melody for Jewish religious purposes is found among German Jews. The aria "Se vuol ballare" from Mozart's *Marriage of Figaro* is used as the tune for the liturgical "Lecha Dodi" during the period of semi-mourning between Passover and Shavuot.

Jewish Secular Music

Although Jewish music is easiest to trace in liturgical music, there were many other uses for music in Jewish culture. In many countries this music was also distinctively Jewish in one way or another. We can distinguish several different types of secular Jewish folk music based on function. There were love songs, lullabies, songs for family celebration and mourning, and dance music for weddings and other joyous occasions.

The use of the various types of folk music differed greatly among Jews in different parts of the world. We can see this by examining some of the characteristics of three groups—Sephardim, Yemenites, and Ashkenazim. The Sephardic repertoire of secular music is very well developed and has many characteristics that are different from those of other Jewish traditions. Among the Jews of Spanish origin, many songs continue to circulate that were originally part of the medieval Spanish *Romancero* cycles. Some of these Sephardic songs preserve texts long lost among contemporary Spanish speakers, while others preserve different variants of songs known from other sources. The *Romansas*, often sung by women, preserve tales of Spanish folk heros, knights in shining armor, and star-crossed lovers. Often the only thing Jewish about them is that they are preserved only by Jews and are sung in Djudezmo. These songs are sometimes used in surprising ways in Jewish ritual, as in the use of mournful songs about Don Juan or the "Seven Princes of Lara" ("Siete Infantes de Lara") on Tish'a Be'av when the destruction of the Jerusalem Temple is mourned.

Besides the Romansas, with their clear Spanish origin and parallels, Djudezmo-

TAMBIEN DE LA MADRUGADA

Yo me le - van - tí un lu - nes,
Un lu - nes por la ma - ña - na, To - mí ar - co
en mi ma - no Y me hué por
la se - ga - da, Tam - bién de la ma - dru - ga - da.

2
Así biva el Nikotchirí,
Que vayga por la plasa,
Que me merque harina blanca,
Por hazer el pan de caza,
    También de la madrugada.

3
El marido por la puerta,
El enamorado por la ventana,
– Avridme, mi blanca niña,
Avridme, mi blanca dama,
    También de la madrugada.

4
Los piés tengo en la nieve,
La cavesa en la helada,
– Ah! Mujer, la mi mujer,
A quien daš tanta palavra?
    También de la madrugada.

5
– Al moso del panadero,
Que los malos años haga,
Harina no tengo en caza,
Levadura me demanda,
    También de la madrugada.

6
"Donde te escondo mi alma?
Donde te escondo mi vista?"
Lo escondió en una caša,
Y la caša era de pimienta,
    También de la madrugada.

7
El marido que viniera,
El enamorado que sarnudara:
  Ah! Mujer, la mi mujer,
Quien sarnuda en esta caša?
    También de la madrugada.

8
– El gato de la vezina,
Que a los ratones alcansa.'
Tomó la balta en su mano,
Y rompió la linda caša.
    También de la madrugada.

9
"Vezinas, las mis vezinas,
Venid, vereš gato con barva,
Mustachico ruvio tiene,
Y sapatetica entravada,
    También de la madrugada."

10
Tomó la balta en su mano
La cavesa le cortava ...
Quien tiene mujer hermoza,
Que la tenga bien guadrada,
Porque se la yevan de la cama
Y se queda el sin nada.
    También de la madrugada.

8.7

speaking Jews had a wide repertoire of popular songs. Some of these were turned into art songs for concert performance in the twentieth century. Included among Jewish folk songs are many quite explicit love songs with lines like "Nude and without Shoes You Went into the Garden" or "The Husband Went Out the Door and the Lover Came in the Window" (Illustration 8.7). These songs are often sung by pious elderly women without the slightest hint of impropriety.

Vernacular songs have found a greater place in the liturgy of the Sephardim than among the Ashkenazim. When the Torah is removed from the Ark, the con-

CUANDO EL REY NIMROD

8.8

gregation sings "Bendicho su nombre de el senyor de el mundo" ("Blessed Be the Name of the Lord of the World") in Ladino. The concluding "En Kelohenu" is often sung alternately in Hebrew and Ladino ("Non Como muestro Dio"). At bar mitzvahs and other life cycle events, the song "Cuando el rey Nimrod" is sung. This song about the birth of Abraham has many similarities to the wording of Christmas carols. Like King Herod searching the sky for the star announcing

Jesus' birth, King Nimrod looks at the sky for a star that announces the birth of Father Abraham (Illustration 8.8).

There is often a noticeable difference between the music of the Sephardic liturgy in Hebrew and that of of Judeo-Spanish folk songs. The liturgical music often sounds quite Middle Eastern, with microtones, many melismas (several notes per syllable), and a throaty singing voice. The folk songs, on the other hand, are sung in various styles, some of them distinctly Spanish and others quite similar to the folk music of the Balkans (Greece, Yugoslavia, Bulgaria, and Turkey). The music is generally more rhythmic and lyrical than the liturgical music.

The Yemenite musical tradition has many points of difference from the music of Jews in other Arabic countries. There is a rich tradition of nonliturgical and semiliturgical music in Arabic and Hebrew among Yemenite Jews. One of the most striking characteristics of Yemenite music is the sharp dichotomy between the repertoires of men and women. Since the sexes were rigidly separated at all public events, including wedding celebrations, they developed singing traditions that were quite distinct. While men sang in both Hebrew and Judeo-Arabic, sometimes mixing both languages in the same song, women sang exclusively in Judeo-Arabic. Though they used only one language, women's songs often stitched together different tunes and rhythms, while men's songs did not. Men tended to sing songs from a written text, while women improvised their songs in oral form only. Many of the women's songs were accompanied by the drum and the *saham* (a flat metal platter tapped with a key or another metal object) held by the two lead singers. Both men's and women's songs were often accompanied by dancing.

Ashkenazic folk music, too, underwent a great deal of development, especially in the nineteenth and early twentieth centuries. Hasidic music has already been mentioned. Outside of formal worship, Hasidic music was most commonly sung at the third meal of the Sabbath and at gatherings with the rebbe. Hasidic music comes in several different styles. Some is without rhythm and some is strongly rhythmic, some is mournful and some is ecstatic. Some Hasidic tunes are in a minor key but others sound quite Westernized. Certain Hasidic dynasties, like

8.9 *Jewish musicians at a Polish wedding in Lachwa (The Jewish Forward Art Section, January 9, 1927).*

the Modzitzer rebbes, had a particular penchant for Western march and waltz music, and many of their tunes are heavily influenced by those styles.

The Yiddish folk repertoire of non-Hasidic Jews developed in many different directions. Lullabies and love songs in Yiddish were often sung by women. Unlike the Judezmo love songs, Yiddish songs were romantic, though rarely explicit. Explicitly sexual songs were usually reserved for crude parodies. With the development of Yiddish theater in the late nineteenth century, a repertoire of Yiddish operetta developed. Many of its songs, especially those by Abraham Goldfaden, became virtual folk songs and enjoyed great popularity. Musically, most Yiddish folk songs were in a minor key. Much of this music used the interval of the augmented second. The note was one and one-half notes away from the previous note (for instance, a G sharp was followed by a B or a C by an E flat). This produced a sound that sounded plaintive and "Eastern" to a Western ear.

Besides the vocal music of Eastern European Jewry, a style of instrumental playing called *klezmer* music was popular in the nineteenth and twentieth centuries. *Klezmer* comes from the Hebrew word for instruments (*klei zemer*). The typical Jewish folk orchestra consisted of a few strings (usually violins), a clarinet, perhaps a flute, a horn, and a dulcimer. Such Jewish family names as Fiedler, Zimbalist (cymbal player), and Pauker (drummer) probably come from the instruments the family members played. Because much of their music was for dancing, klezmorim (the plural of *klezmer*) played mainly at weddings and were often employed by Christians as well as Jews in Eastern Europe (Illustration 8.9). The "wailing clarinet" was considered a special hallmark of the klezmer style. Klezmer music enjoyed a worldwide revival in the last two decades of the twentieth century.

On the first hearing, Jewish music seems to owe more to the local cultural context than to any common musical tradition. In many cases, the direct borrowing of specific non-Jewish tunes is well known and easily documented. A question therefore arises: Does Jewish music (especially in secular contexts) have any particular characteristics? This is often a difficult question to answer because most discussions of Jewish music occur without a systematic comparison to the local non-Jewish traditions.

Where attempts to compare Jewish with non-Jewish music in the same locality have been made, a few differences have been noted. In Eastern Europe, for instance, it was found that Jewish singing tended to be solo or in unison, with little trace of the elaborate choral harmony traditions of the Ukraine and Russia. Although to many Western ears Russian music sounds "Jewish," Russian Christian composers often detected a specifically Jewish nuance that differed from ordinary Russian music. One well-known example is Sergei Prokofief's *Overture on Hebrew Themes*, which uses the klezmer style. Students of Sephardic music have shown the importance of Balkan influence and the relatively limited influence of Spanish melodies on much of the Ladino song tradition, but they do not seem to have analyzed how Sephardic musical traditions differ from those of the Balkans. We know that Jewish music in Yemen was distinctive in using only drums, metal plates, and cans because the government limited all other musical instruments to the royal entourage. It is likely, but impossible to prove at present, that other differences existed between Jewish and Muslim musical styles in Yemen.

Modern Developments In Jewish Music

In the twentieth century, a new Jewish musical tradition grew up in Israel. To some extent, the Israeli musical culture developed out of the cultures of the Jewish immigrants to Israel. "Hevenu Shalom Aleichem," an early Israeli folk song, was based on a Hasidic melody. Romanian folk music influenced the Israeli national anthem, "Hatikvah," and contributed the hora, which became the national dance of Israel. Other influences on Israeli music were the native Arabic music of Palestine, as well as the Middle Eastern traditions of Jews from Yemen and other Arab countries. Within a relatively short period, the various ingredients blended together to create an Israeli folk musical tradition of mixed European and Middle Eastern style. In more recent years, Israeli music has been heavily influenced by European and American popular and rock music.

Today Jewish musical traditions continue to be developed, especially in liturgical music and the music of Israel. Styles of liturgical music change over time but generally retain certain traditional elements. Among Jews in the Western countries, there was a period in the nineteenth century when German Romantic music had a great influence on the music of the synagogue. Choral music with multipart harmonies in a highly Westernized style composed by Salomon Sulzer, Louis Lewandowski, and other German Jewish composers was widely used in the liturgy. In the early decades of the twentieth century, cantorial music with much coloratura display and emotional bravura was very popular in America and Eastern Europe. Concerts given by famous cantors were filled to overflowing, and some cantors used their cantorial pursuits as a stepping stone to operatic careers. In recent years, the popularity of cantorial and choral music in the synagogue has declined. More folksy styles have replaced the formal choirs and cantors in many places. Music that is catchy and singable has gained popularity, while long solo cantorial "arias" are out of style. Although serious musicians often complain that the music of the American synagogue has been taken over by pseudo-Hasidic and "summer camp" styles, they seem to be fighting a losing battle. The more popular style is "in" at present, although this style may change in the future and, undoubtedly, new styles will come into vogue.

Outside the synagogue, Jewish music is also cultivated in various circles. Though outside very Orthodox communities most Jews listen to non-Jewish music more often than to Jewish music, some enjoy listening to recordings of Yiddish music, Ladino music, or Israeli songs. At Jewish weddings and parties in the United States, varying amounts of specifically Jewish music are played—at least a stereotyped hora or "Hava Nagila"—before the crowd turns to some general rock style. Though Hebrew rock music is preferred by Israeli youth to the folk music of the pioneering days, many Israelis still enjoy singing and dancing to the Israeli folk tunes of earlier days. Attempts are underway to capture the varied Jewish musical traditions in sound recordings and musical notation. The Israel National Library, as well as other Israeli institutions, has collected a huge archive of musical examples. Though many of the old Jewish musical traditions are disappearing, some are being preserved and enjoyed by appreciative listeners at traditional celebrations and concerts and on recordings.

Appearance and Ancestry

"Funny, You Don't Look Jewish"

THE PHYSICAL AND GENETIC MAKEUP OF THE JEWS IS A SENSITIVE SUBJECT. A great deal of ink has been spilled on the issue, much of it inaccurate, stereotyped, or downright racist. The misuse of the concept of the "Jewish race" by anti-Semites, culminating in the wholesale slaughter perpetrated by the Nazis, has made the subject taboo to many people. Yet the topic itself has a legitimate side as well and is intimately related to the themes discussed elsewhere in this book. Throughout the book, we have seen that Jewish culture around the world has certain structural elements in common, but diverges so much in detail in different places as to be unrecognizable. We have often noticed a great gap between modern Jewish practices and those of ancient Judaism. This raises a similar question concerning the physical background of the Jews. To what extent can the Jews of today trace their genetic ancestry to the Jews of the Bible and the Talmud? Have they carried practices through family tradition down through the centuries by an unbroken chain, or are most of today's Jews, like many of their practices, of non-Jewish origin, but Judaized?

The Role of Ancestry in Traditional Judaism

Judaism has traditionally been much more than just a religious faith. It has been a national or ethnic religion; the concepts of *religion* and *peoplehood* are so intertwined in traditional Judaism that one cannot tell where one ends and the other begins. Jews conceived of themselves as the descendants of the biblical patriarchs. Their prayers constantly repeat phrases like "our God and God of our fathers," "who has done miracles for our ancestors," and "who has taken us out of Egypt"—all of them implying physical descent from the ancient Israelites. Even when early Christianity rejected Judaism and claimed to have superseded it, it still referred to the Jews as "Israel of the flesh" (and to itself as "Israel of the spirit").

Modern Zionism, too, is based in part on the assumption that modern Jewry is the physical descendant of ancient Jewry. The establishment of the State of Israel is therefore a reestablishment. The Jews are not "settling"; they are "returning" to their ancient homeland. For the religious among them, Israel is the land that God promised to their ancestors and is now giving to them.

Yet traditional Jewish views have never totally relied on physical ancestry. The legal definition of a Jew, according to tradition, was the child of a Jewish mother *or* a convert to Judaism. Either background would entitle one to be considered fully Jewish. The consensus of the rabbis was that a convert had the right to refer to God's having "done miracles for our ancestors." A convert was considered the descendant of Abraham and Sarah, the first Israelites. Descent could be symbolic as well as physical.

Racial Theories about the Jews

At the end of the nineteenth century and the beginning of the twentieth, the term *race* was very popular and was thrown around pretty loosely. Just as people (including quite a few Jews) spoke of a "Jewish race," they talked of an "Anglo-Saxon race," an "Italian race," or a "Slavic race." None of these "races" have a scientific basis. But to many individuals (especially bigoted ones) talking about race seemed modern, biological, and rational, and far superior to bigotry based on "mere emotion."

Ideas of the "Jewish race" differ in some ways from other uses of the word *race*. In most cases, groups have been considered a race because of specific, easily recognized physical features (light or dark skin; wavy, wooly, or straight hair; a particular kind of eyelid). Racism directed against such groups generally assumes that "all people who look that way" have a certain set of intellectual, moral, or cultural features (smart, stupid, sneaky, or good at business). In the case of anti-Jewish racism, the order is reversed. The existence of certain cultural, intellectual, or moral features attributable to Jews was long assumed before some anti-Semites began to say "and besides, they all look alike." The physical features of "looking Jewish" were "discovered" only relatively recently, and they were usually based on subtler or more ambiguous features than those in our standard ideas of race.

The stereotype of what Jews supposedly look like varies but often includes the hooked "Jewish nose." In countries where the majority population is mainly blond and blue-eyed, the stereotyped Jew is dark. The Nazis claimed, among other, things that Jews had flat feet, a nose shaped like the number 6, thick lips, and black curly hair—features that the majority of Jews don't have (Illustration 9.1). In their certainty of knowing what a Jew looked like, Nazi mobs sometimes mistakenly attacked Spaniards, Italians, and other dark-haired people.

In the nineteenth century, when physical anthropologists began to study the subgroups of the Caucasian race, they came up with three main subtypes: (1)

9.1 Nazi anti-Semitic cartoon of Jews leaving Germany, depicting them with stereotyped hooked noses shaped like the number 6.

Nordic: tall, blond, and blue-eyed, with a narrow head; (2) Alpine: shorter, with gray or green eyes, brownish hair, and a broad head; and (3) Mediterranean: a narrow head, dark eyes, and dark hair. The Nazis sometimes charted even more complex subdivisions, as exemplified by a Nazi school chart that showed six subtypes of Germans alone—Nordisch (Nordic), Dinarisch (Austrian), Fälisch (Westphalian), Westisch (Western), Ostisch (Eastern), and Ostbaltisch (east Baltic) (Illustration 9.2).

Racial theorists also made use of discoveries in linguistics, which showed that most major European languages were part of the same Indo-European (or Indo-Aryan) language family. The Indo-European languages included such seemingly different languages as German, English, French, Italian, Latin, Greek, Russian, Polish, Lithuanian, Armenian, Persian, and Sanskrit. Another group of languages with a totally separate ancestry were the Semitic languages, which included He-

Nordisch

Westisch

Fälisch

Dinarisch

Ostbaltisch

Ostisch

9.2 *Schreiber's racial scientific chart (a Nazi school chart), which depicts six different German racial types: Nordic, Western, Falian, Dinaric, East Baltic, and Eastern.*

brew, Aramaic, Arabic, and Ethiopic. Many nineteenth century thinkers assumed that these separate language groups were created by peoples of different ancestry—the Aryans and the Semites. For some, *Aryan* became a code word for *Nordic* and *Semite* a code word for *Jew*.

Both Jewish and non-Jewish physical anthropologists were fascinated with the investigation of the "Jewish racial type," and their research yielded some surprising results. The bulk of the European Jews (Ashkenazim) differed from the classic Middle Eastern Mediterranean type. They tended to be broad-headed rather than long-headed and included a noticeable proportion of individuals with light-colored hair and eyes. How could they be the pure-bred descendants of a Middle Eastern people? Some scholars "solved" this problem by arguing that there were actually two (or even three) Jewish races. Most wrote more favorably about the "Sephardic type" than about the Ashkenazim. The former were said to be "truly Semitic," "Oriental," or Mediterranean and were often described as having "fine features." By contrast, the Ashkenazim were often described as "coarser" than the "pure-bred" Sephardim and were viewed as a mixed race with an Oriental, West Asian, or Slavic admixture.

Physical Appearance and Jewish Ancestry

Despite the misuse of the study of Jewish physical ancestry in the past, there has been a recent revival of interest in the question. One reason for this is the widely differing appearances of the Jews arriving in Israel from various parts of the world. This makes Israel a "natural laboratory" for studying whether in fact there is any biological unity behind this seeming heterogeneity. Even more important, the tremendous strides made in genetics and the study of DNA in recent years have fueled the revival of research on the biology of the Jews. It is now possible to explore questions of ancestry on a much more fundamental and deeper level than merely outward appearances. Genetic tests give much more accurate results than were previously possible, and DNA studies will continue to be honed. Results obtained today will probably be revised in the future as knowledge in the field continues to explode.

The possibility of a common ancestry shared by Jews all over the world involves two related but separate questions. First, is there a common ancestry at all? Second, is this common ancestry a descent from the Israelites of the Bible or from some other people? (Some, for instance, have claimed that the Khazars of southeastern Russia are the ancestor of many of today's Jews.) The evidence about what the biblical Children of Israel looked like is sparse, but bits of evidence do exist. Besides some ancient sculpted bas-reliefs, there are many hints in the text of the Bible itself. All seem to indicate that the ancient Hebrews, like the Middle Easterners of our day, had Caucasian features and dark hair.

The biblical texts, which give us hints about the appearance of the ancient Israelites, are rarely explicit. Most need a good deal of interpretation. In the Song of Songs, for instance, the female speaker states, "I am black and comely….Do not stare at me because I am black, for the sun has darkened me" (Song of Songs 1:5-6). This reference seems to indicate that her dark color was caused by tanning rather than by racial ancestry. The male personage in the book is described as having "curls black as a raven" (Song of Songs 5:11). In Leviticus there are many descriptions of the strange skin disease called *tsara'at* (usually mistranslated as leprosy). The disease caused the skin to develop red or white lesions and sometimes made the skin hair turn white. Leviticus 13:29–37 describes a particular type of tsara'at in the hair or beard that caused the appearance of thin yellow hair. The appearance of black hair growing in the lesion was a sign that the disease was cured, an indicator that black was the normal hair color of practically all ancient Israelites. In other parts of the Bible there are references to several persons as being *admoni* (red); some have interpreted this to mean "red-haired," while others think it means "of ruddy complexion."

Even if we can assume that the biblical Israelites looked more or less alike, it is clear that this is not the case for Jews today. Ashkenazic Jews tend to be lighter in skin color, eye color, and hair color than Jews from the Middle East. Even among the latter there are great differences, with Yemenite Jews generally considerably darker than Jews from Iraq or Turkey. Ethiopian Jews generally have the same

9.3 Czechoslovakian Jews at the beginning of the twentieth century.

9.4 Moroccan Jewish merchants in traditional dress, Rabat, 1950.

dark skin and mixed Caucasian-black African features as their Christian neighbors. The medieval Jews of Kaifeng seem to have been physically indistinguishable from other Chinese people. But even within individual communities there is
often a wide variety of physical types, leading one to question the idea of a single
Jewish ancestry.

Looking at a sample of photographs of Jews from various parts of the world
gives us an idea both of the great variety of Jewish physical types and of the pit-
falls involved in making any judgments about Jewish ancestry based on appearance. Because of the wide variations in physical appearance even within the same
community, a single photograph of "an Iraqi Jew" would tell us very little. How
could one judge if the particular example is typical unless one has seen a large
number of members of the group? Even then, what the typical look is remains a
matter of opinion. For that reason, most of the illustrative material given here
shows groups of people rather than just one individual example (Illustrations
9.3-9.9).

9.5 Jewish girls in Baghdad in modern dress.

9.6 *Yemenite (Aden) Jewish couple in London in modern dress.*

9.7 *Wedding of a "white" Jewish woman and a "black" Jewish man in Cochin, India.*

Another pitfall in attempting to detect ethnic differences from physical appearance is our tendency to confuse cultural and biological characteristics. Someone may look like a "typical Yemenite Jew" more because of his hairstyle, dress, and bearing than because of his actual physical features. For this reason, whenever possible, this chapter presents pictures of members of a group both in traditional clothing and in modern dress. Naturally, the physical differences among groups of Jews in modern dress are often quite noticeable, but the differences seem less extreme than among groups in native costume.

Despite these caveats, the photos clearly show differences among Jewish groups in different parts of the world and similarities among Jews in the same community. Although individual cases always differ, we can see a continuum from lighter to darker eye, hair, and skin color when we move from Ashkenazic,

9.8 Ethiopian Jews still wearing traditional dress in Israel.

9.9 The same group of Ethiopian Jews after changing into modern dress

through European Sephardic, to North African and Iraqi, then Yemenite, and finally Ethiopian Jews. Differences in other features, such as the shape of the head, the waviness of the hair, and the shape of the nose, are also evident from group to group. Sometimes, however, ancestral differences, which were very important to local observers, seem hard for us to detect. The marriage of a Cochin "black Jewish" man to a Cochin "white Jewish" woman was a great communal scandal in southern India. Looking at the picture of the couple (Illustration 9.7), it is hard to see the racial differences very clearly, despite the long tradition banning intermarriage between the two groups.

To evaluate the significance of these pictures properly, we should not merely compare the photos of Jews in different countries but also compare them to photos of local non-Jews. Such a global comparison is beyond the scope of this book and would require a separate full-length work. We have not undertaken it here, both because of the large number of photos that would have been needed and because it would be even harder to find typical looks of the larger non-Jewish populations than it would be to find photos of typical Jews. We can evaluate the differences in Jewish physical appearance from country to country, but a comparison of their physical appearances to that of the rest of the population must await further studies.

Measuring Hair Color, Eye Color, and Skull Shape

Until recently, physical anthropologists who collected measurements of the features of various ethnic groups had to depend on visible physical features. Among the favorite features used for measuring and identifying races and "subraces" were height, skin color, hair color, eye color, and skull shape. More recently, anthropologists have been able to investigate less visible hereditary markers, such as blood types and the prevalence of specific hereditary diseases. In the last few years, highly precise and complex methods of DNA analysis have been applied to the study of human genetics. By studying the proportion of different variations of specific genes, geneticists are exploring in depth the differences among various ethnic groups.

Many scholars have collected data on the various physical traits of the Jews. Though exact numbers often differed, most of the work seemed to outline similar trends. Individual figures on hair and eye color sometimes differ because various researchers had differing judgments about what constitutes light and dark eyes or hair. In fact, there is a continuum of colorings rather than a clear differentiation among blond, brown, or black hair or among blue, green, gray, or brown eyes. When it comes to the "coloring" of the Jews, most studies have shown that Ashkenazic Jews differ from non-Ashkenazic Jews and also from their Northern European neighbors. Unlike the Jews of the Middle East, a considerable number of Ashkenazic Jews have light eyes and light hair, but this percentage is significantly lower than that of non-Jewish Europeans. In 1911, Maurice Fishberg collected data on Ashkenazic Jews in various countries and found that 7.2 to 25.5 percent of Ashkenazic Jews had fair hair and 33.0 to 53.7 percent had light eyes. In his 1874–1875 study of 10 million school children in Germany and neighboring countries, the German scientist Rudolf Virchow found that Jewish children had about a 50 percent lower incidence of blue eyes (19 vs. 43 percent) and blond hair (33 vs. 72 percent), than the sample as a whole. (Since children have a higher percentage of blond hair than adults, the figures for blond hair are much higher than those given by Fishberg. But the overall picture showing Ashkenazic Jews as darker than their neighbors, but still with a large percentage with fair hair and light eyes, is confirmed.) Statistics on non-Ashkenazic Jews show a much darker population, but one that varied from country to country. According to Fishberg, among Italian Jews and European Sephardim, 4.8 to 18.5 percent had fair hair and 18.7 to 30.9 present had light eyes. Among Jews in North Africa and the Caucasus, over 94 percent had dark hair and only about 15 percent had light eyes. One early investigator of Yemenite Jews found no one with light hair or light eyes among them (Map 9.1).

The measure of skull shape based on the ratio of the length and width of the head, or "cephalic index," was considered by nineteenth century and early twen-

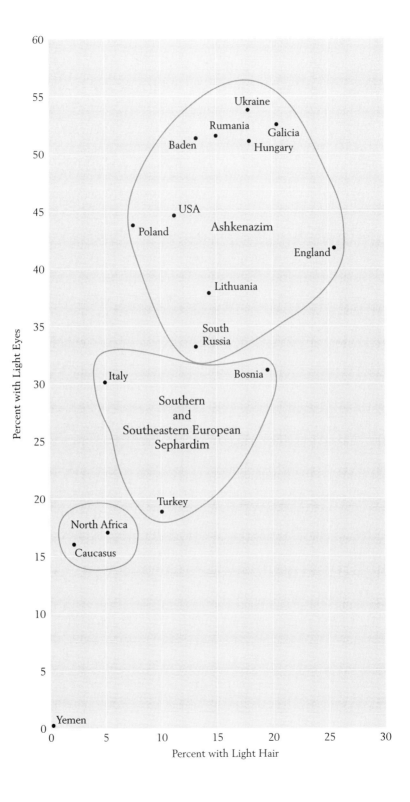

tieth century physical anthropologists to be an especially scientific method of classifying human beings. They used impressive-sounding Greek terms such as "dolichocephalic" for long-headed individuals and "brachycephalic" for those who were broad-headed. Physical anthropologists studying human populations found fairly systematic differences in the shape of the head from one region to another. Racial theorists, like the anti-Semitic Houston Stuart Chamberlain, even claimed that the "form of the head and structure of the brain exercise a quite decisive influence upon the form and structure of the thoughts."

Studies of the skull shape of Jews have not turned up a uniform Jewish racial type, but rather have shown great variations among the Jews. Ashkenazic Jews had a tendency toward broad-headedness and were generally a little more round-headed than the Gentile populations in Germany, Poland, and Lithuania. Very broad heads were the rule among Jews in the Caucasus, Central Asia, and Habban in South Yemen (whose Jews were among the most broad-headed populations in the world). On the other hand, Jews generally had narrow heads in Yemen (despite its proximity to Habban), Turkey, and North Africa from Morocco to Egypt. In most areas, the variation in the characteristics of Jews was more or less parallel to the variation among their non-Jewish neighbors. Where the non-Jews had round heads, so did the Jews, and where they were long-headed, the Jews usually were also (Maps 9.2–9.3). One clear exception is found among the Jews of Turkey, whose head shape resembles the narrow heads of the Spanish and Portuguese Christians from whose countries they emigrated more than the broad heads of the majority population of Turkey. The shape of the head, presumably a hereditary feature, does not seem to confirm the genetic unity of the Jewish people.

Two other aspects of traditional stereotypes of Jews were the "Jewish nose" and the "Jewish look." The cliché of the Jewish nose has not been confirmed by actual surveys. A study of Jews in New York City in the early twentieth century showed a majority with straight noses and only about one in seven with aquiline (hooked) noses. Aquiline noses are found among many non-Jewish peoples in the Middle East and Southern Europe and even among American Indians. Thus it fails as a reliable test for a Jewish racial type.

Map 9.2

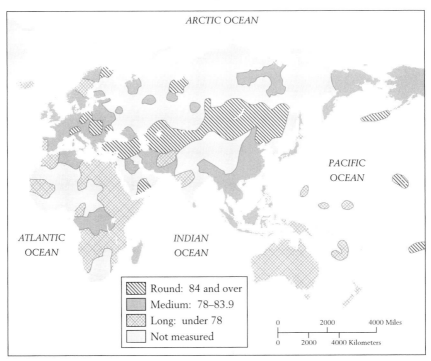

Sephalic index of the general population
(Sephalic index is calculated by dividing the width of the head by its length and multiplying by 100.)

The vaguer trait of "looking Jewish" is impossible to measure. Some of the aspects that were thought to make people look Jewish—were cultural, for instance, their distinctive clothing, beard, or headdresses. Others, like their supposed "melancholy eyes" or tendency to walk in a stooped manner, may have been a result of their status as a persecuted minority rather than an inherited feature. Under conditions of equality or independence, this look seems to have become less common.

Other supposedly hereditary physical features of the Jews, even those that are documented, are also likely to have resulted from environment rather than genetics. One finding of many researchers of the early twentieth century was that

Map 9.3

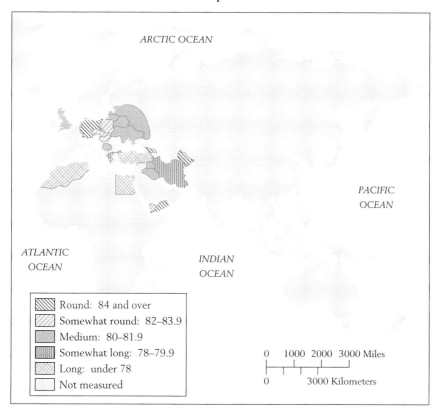

Cephalic index of Jewish populations

Jews were on average 1 or 2 centimeters shorter than their Gentile neighbors, especially in Eastern Europe, Iraq, and the Caucasus. Height is determined not only by heredity but also by environment. The short stature of Jews in traditional societies may simply have been the result of poor nutrition. It is well known that American-born children of foreign-born parents (both Jewish and non-Jewish) are frequently much taller than their parents. Another feature that was recorded in Eastern Europe among army recruits was body girth. On average, Jews tended to have narrower chests than non-Jews of similar size. This too is likely to be the result of environment, especially the more sedentary occupations of the Jews and their poorer nutrition.

Not all visible physical traits refute the idea of Jewish genetic uniformity as clearly as those mentioned up to now. A study of fingerprint patterns among various Israeli populations shows remarkable uniformity among Jews from Germany, Poland, Bulgaria, Turkey, Egypt, Morocco, Iraq, and Yemen. All had an index of whorls and loops (as opposed to arches) noticeably higher than those of European and American non-Jews but relatively close to those of eastern Mediterranean Arabs. This seems to indicate some Mediterranean heritage even among Ashkenazic Jews.

Genetic Tests

As genetic tests have become more sophisticated, the study of obvious physical features has given way to the evaluation of invisible and theoretically more accurate factors that can be analyzed only in the laboratory. Many of the earliest biological tests used by physical anthropologists were based on blood typing. Information on large numbers of individuals in different parts of the world exists concerning the three blood types, A, B and O (AB is a combination of the first two). Type B, for instance, is relatively rare in Western Europe (usually below 12 percent) and is much more common in Central Asia (up to 40 percent) and parts of Africa. Among American Indians it is almost nonexistent (Map 9.4). In general, type A is high in Europe and Asia Minor but far lower in much of Africa and Southern Asia.

If we look at a graph of A and B blood group distributions of various Jewish population groups and compare them with a graph of non-Jewish groups in roughly the same geographic areas, our first impression is one of confusion. The proportions of the blood groups among Jews seem to vary at least as much as they do in the general population. When we begin to group and compare similar groups, the picture becomes clearer. Both Jewish and non-Jewish groups in Europe, North Africa, and Western Asia tend to cluster around approximately the same center (19–31 percent A, 9–20 percent B). There are a number of groups

Map 9.4

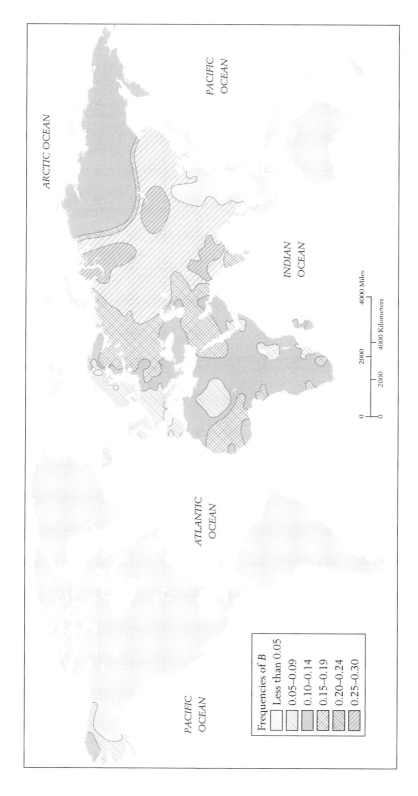

ARCTIC OCEAN

PACIFIC
OCEAN

INDIAN
OCEAN

ATLANTIC
OCEAN

PACIFIC
OCEAN

Frequencies of B

Less than 0.05
0.05–0.09
0.10–0.14
0.15–0.19
0.20–0.24
0.25–0.30

0   2000   2000   4000 Miles

0   2000   4000 Kilometers

Percentage of type B blood in the general population

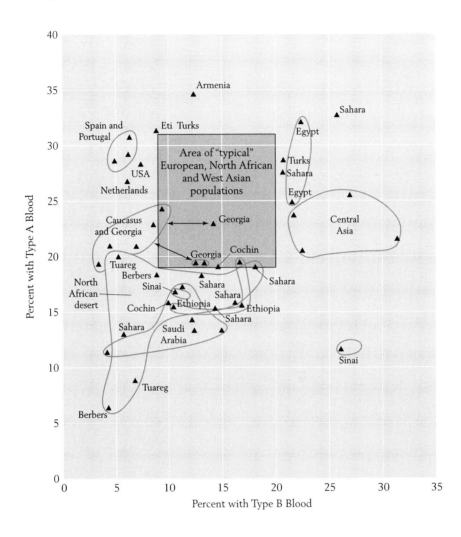

that diverge greatly from this center. These include non-Jewish groups such as the Berbers of North Africa, various groups in the Caucasus mountains, and inhabitants of Saudi Arabia, all of whom have low values of both A and B, and Central Asians, who have very high rates of B (Map 9.5). In the case of the Jews, several "exotic" groups diverge very far from all others, namely, the nonrabbinic Karaites, Bene Israel, and Samaritans and the rabbinic Jews of Cochin, Habban in

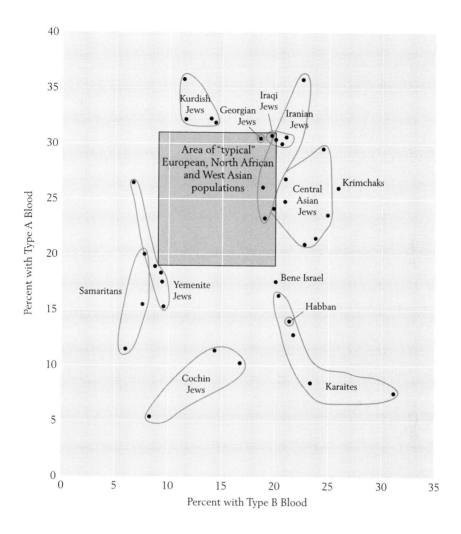

South Yemen, and the Crimean Krimchaks (Map 9.6). Divergent from the central Jewish group, but less so, are the Yemenite and Central Asian Jews. There seem to be considerable differences between most Asian Jewish groups (Iran, Iraq, Kurdistan, Central Asia) and the North African and European Sephardim (Map 9.7).

In most cases, Jewish and non-Jewish populations in the same place have more

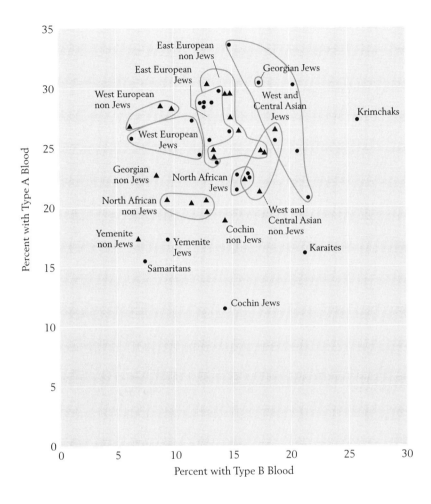

similar percentages of blood groups A, B, and O than do Jews in different parts of the world, but there are some important exceptions. The Georgian Jews are totally different from the bulk of other populations of the Caucasus and have much higher A and B values. Kurdish Jews have A values almost 10 points higher than their Muslim neighbors. Iranian and Iraqi (non-Kurdish) Jews differ from their neighbors as well, although to a smaller extent. In North Africa, Jewish B values are several points above those of Muslims, but otherwise the two are quite similar. The Ashkenazic Jews have a pattern resembling that of European Christians, with one noticeable but fairly small difference. Jews in Central and Eastern Europe are more similar to one another than to Christians in those areas. Jews tend to have values between those of Eastern and Western European Christians but closer to those of the former.

Unlike the A, B, and O patterns, genes in the Rh blood groups show that Ashkenazic Jews resemble Mediterranean groups rather than their Christian neighbors. The "Mediterranean chromosome" (CDe) differs little between Ashkenazic and North African Jews (52 percent compared to 53–56 percent) but is higher than among North European non-Jews (41–43 percent). Ashkenazic Jews are midway between North African Jews and Northern European Christians in their level of the "Northern European" chromosome (cDE) and the "African gene" (cDe). For the latter they are somewhat higher than European Christians, lower than North African Jews, and much lower than black Africans, whose values range from 45 to 90 percent. Yemenite and Kurdish Jews have much higher ratios of the African gene than Ashkenazic Jews. The Ashkenazim consistently show more Mediterranean traits than their non-Jewish neighbors. Tests for other blood components show some markers in which Jews are closer to their neighbors than to Jews in other countries and others (like the Rh chromosome) in which Ashkenazic Jews are more Mediterranean than their European neighbors.

Recent scholars have attempted to sort out the complex results of the various tests to assess the "genetic distance" among various groups. The surprising results of a study using nine classical genetic markers is that Ashkenazic Jews are most like Iraqi and Iranian Jews, who, in turn, resemble Iraqi and Iranian Muslims. All three of these Jewish groups are very different from Polish Christians. Jews and non-Jews from the Cochin area in India are somewhat different from the Iraqis, Iranians, and Ashkenazim but not as different as the Polish Christians, the Yemenites, the Ethiopian Jews, and the Bene Israel of Bombay. Each of these three latter Jewish groups resemble the non-Jews of their area more than anyone else.

Some new data on blood components show Ethiopian Jews midway between African blacks and the European-Asian population (including other Jews). Within the array of the Europeans and Asians, Jewish groups tend to cluster with other Mediterranean groups, midway between the Far Eastern and Western European populations. The patterns shown by these new data are not straightforward enough to confirm or deny the earlier data, which seemed to link Ashkenazim with the Mediterranean population. A look at many of the graphs of individual items shows strange groupings (Yemenite Jews and Chinese, Bulgarians and Indians, Swiss and Greeks) that do not seem to indicate any close genetic relationships. It will probably be some years before the heredity of the various ethnic groups is untangled.

While most genetic characteristics are inherited from both parents, certain types of genes are contributed exclusively by the mother (mitochondrial DNA) or by a father to his sons (Y-chromosome genes). So far, little clear evidence has been produced about Jewish genes in the maternal line, but a recent study of paternally inherited genes has produced some remarkable results. According to tradition, the status of Cohen (Jewish priest) can only be acquired by descent from a father who is a Cohen. In a study of Y-chromosome DNA, a group of scientists have found a statistically significant distinction between male Jews who claim the status of a Cohen and those who do not (Table 9.8). Only 1 out of 68 priests, in comparison with 22 out of 120 non-Cohen Israelites, have a positive YAP gene on the Y chromosome. This difference holds true for both Ashkenazic and non-Ashkenazic Jews. If these results are confirmed, they provide graphic confirmation of the validity of traditional family claims to priestly status. The most recent reports on these studies continue to show genetic similarities among the priestly group but indicate that Levites, traditionally considered intermediate between priests and ordinary Israelites, do not have a shared genetic base.

Genetic Diseases

Although most diseases have little or no hereditary transmission, some conditions are known to be carried by the genes. Studies of the distribution of these diseases have been another key used to unlock the genetic makeup of the Jews. Most of

	Cohen	Israelite
Negative YAP chromosome and:		
DYS19=B	37 (54.4%)	39 (32.5%)
DYS19=A	11 (16.2%)	11 (9.1%)
DYS19=D or E	8 (11.7%)	12 (10.0%)
DYS19=C	11 (16.2%)	36 (30.0%)
Positive YAP chromosome	1 (1.5%)	22 (18.4%)
(no matter what DYS19 is)		
TOTAL IN SAMPLE	N=68	N=120
Negative and DYS19=B or A	48 (70.6%)	50 (41.6%)
All others	20 (29.4%)	70 (58.4%)

these genetic conditions are rather rare. Some are inevitably fatal (like Niemann-Pick and Tay-Sachs diseases), while others cause severe symptoms but are not as lethal (like dysautonomia) and still others are barely noticeable to the patient.

There is no such thing as a hereditary disease found in all Jewish groups and not found elsewhere. Most "Jewish genetic diseases" are confined to a specific localized Jewish population. Some diseases are found almost exclusively in the Ashkenazic population; others are found chiefly among non-Ashkenazic Jews, though these are generally restricted to a few countries rather than spread out throughout the non-Ashkenazic Jewish world. Gaucher's disease, whose symptoms include an enlarged spleen, bone fractures, and bleeding problems, is a predominantly Ashkenazic disease also found among some non-Ashkenazic Jews and some non-Jews. Some diseases once thought to exist only among Jews have now been found to be widespread in certain other ethnic groups as well.

At one time, certain diseases of Ashkenazic Jewry seemed to scholars to be clearly localized in a particular area. Tay-Sachs disease and Niemann-Pick disease seemed most common among Jews in Lithuania, Belarus, and northern Poland, while Bloom's syndrome and familial dysautonomia were found more often in Jews from areas further south, in Galicia and Hungary. But further investigation showed that the various Ashkenazic disorders cannot be localized so definitely. In general, Ashkenazic diseases seem to be less confined to a specific area than are diseases in the non-Ashkenazic Jewish communities.

More recent research has disproved the assumption that Tay-Sachs disease is confined to Ashkenazic Jews. Instead, it shows that the disease exists among members of various ethnic groups on every continent, although Ashkenazic Jews are still the majority. The gene for Tay-Sachs disease seems to be present in about 1 in 30 Ashkenazic Jews, 1 in 30 French Canadians, 1 in 60 Moroccan Jews, and about 1 in 160 members of other groups. (The actual incidence of the disease is much lower since only babies who have the gene from both parents develop the disease.) It turns out that the ailment can be caused by many different mutations, and their distribution varies among different ethnic groups. There is no reason to believe that populations subject to the disease are genetically related.

The most common genetic diseases of non-Ashkenazic Jews are quite different from those of Ashkenazim. Most of these diseases are restricted to a specific geographic area in Asia or North Africa. Deficiency in the body chemical glucose-6-phosphate dehydrogenase (G6PD) is found among a number of Middle Eastern and Mediterranean peoples. Among its manifestations is a serious blood reaction to eating fava beans. The deficiency is high among male non-Jews in some Iranian populations, as well as in Saudi Arabia, Iraq, and Egypt. Among Jews it is most common in Kurdistan (where 61.6 percent have the deficiency), Iraq (24.8 percent), the Caucasus (28 percent), and Iran (15.1 percent). Among Ashkenazic Jews it is found at a very low rate (0.4 percent)

Familial Mediterranean fever is particularly widespread among North African Jews, with the highest gene frequency found in Libya. It is found less often among Iraqi, Turkish, and Egyptian Jews, is absent in Jews from Yemen and Iran, is very rare in Ashkenazic Jews, and is frequent among Armenian Christians. Thalassemia is a disease found among both Jews and non-Jews mainly around the Mediterranean and seems to be most common in Greece, Italy, and Cyprus. Among Jews, alpha-thalassemia is most common among Yemenite and Iraqi Jews (not Kurdish Jews), while beta-thalassemia is often found in Kurdish Jews (12–20 percent) and in many Israeli Arab villages.

The evidence of hereditary diseases among Jews cuts two ways. On the one hand, it is clear that certain diseases are much more common among Jews than among other populations. This could be seen as evidence in favor of common ancestry. On the other hand, none of the Jewish hereditary diseases are found among all Jewish groups; instead, all of them appear to be confined to specific geographic groups within Jewry. The Ashkenazim, in whom the geographic localization of the disease seems less precise than among non-Ashkenazic Jews, appear to be more uniform genetically than non-Ashkenazic Jews. This reinforces the impression given by data on blood groups.

Even when a group of Jews does share the genes for a particular disease, it is no proof of descent from ancient Israelites. The genes could have come from a relatively recent mutation. The mutation for idiopathic torsion dystonia among Ashkenazic Jews has been dated to some time between 1400 and 1750, a relatively late period in Jewish history.

The gene for a particular disease could spread in several different ways. One means of spreading, known as "genetic drift" and the "founder effect," is particularly common in small populations that do not intermarry with outsiders, especially if they expand rapidly. Purely by chance, the small number of original settlers in a particular area had atypical genes compared to the population as a whole from which they emerged. These genes would then be much more common in the group that descended from them than in the original group and would spread rapidly. This explains why such groups as the Amish (Pennsylvania Dutch), French Canadians, and Finns are known for their high rates of hereditary diseases.

The other mechanism is evolutionary advantage. Certain diseases or physical traits may bring with them increased chances of survival under specific circumstances (especially in carriers of diseases who themselves do not have the disease). The genes for G6PD deficiency and thalassemia seem to be associated with immunity to malaria. Therefore, in areas with heavy malarial infestation, like Kurdistan, carriers of these diseases have a better chance of surviving and reproducing than do those without the gene. This accounts for the frequent appearance of the gene in certain areas. It tells us relatively little about common ancestry and much more about environment.

Similar arguments have been made about certain physical differences from area to area. It has been argued, for instance, that in sunny climates, dark skin, eyes, and hair are a survival advantage compared to paler coloration. In contrast, light-colored individuals seem to have less trouble getting sufficient vitamin D in cold, cloudy climates than do darker people. The higher percentage of blue eyes among Ashkenazic Jews than among Jews in the Middle East may be less the result of different ancestry than of "natural selection" in different climates.

Some Jewish diseases may have a mixture of environmental and hereditary factors. This seems true of the uneven ethnic distribution of heart attacks, various types of cancer, diabetes, and colitis. Rates of heart disease seem to be higher among Jews in the United States than among other Caucasians and higher among Ashkenazim in Israel than among other Jews. In part this seems to be the result of differences in diet. Ashkenazic Jews have a diet higher in fat and lower in carbohydrates than that of Yemenites, for instance. In the Israeli-born generation, the differences are smaller. Diabetes, certain kinds of cancer, and colitis are also tied to diet and, in the case of colitis, to emotional stress as well. The children of immigrants often have different patterns of disease than do their parents because of changed lifestyles.

A number of conditions were once considered more common among Jews than among other groups. Among these are mental illness, retardation, hernia, hemorrhoids, nearsightedness, cystic fibrosis, and a number of rarer conditions. Some anti-Semites used these cases to "prove" the decadence of the Jewish race. Some of these assumptions came about either because Jews were the first patients seen with a particular disease or because they were more likely, for cultural reasons, to seek medical attention than others. In the conditions mentioned above, further investigation has shown that Jews are not especially susceptible. In others, the prevalence of the disease is caused by environmental or cultural conditions. The high level of Creutzfeld-Jacob disease (mad cow disease) among Libyan Jews turned out to be caused by eating sheep's brains, not by heredity.

How Jewish Genes Could Have Mixed with the Genes of Their Neighbors

Despite the reputation that Jews historically have had of keeping themselves separate from the peoples around them and rejecting intermarriage, there is considerable evidence that much "non-Jewish blood" has entered the Jewish people in various ways. Some of these ways are fairly well documented, while others, for obvious reasons (such as illicit sexual unions), are not.

Although traditional Judaism has not been a proselytizing religion for a long time, this was not always the case. In Greco-Roman times, for instance, large numbers of people were attracted to Judaism, read its scriptures translated into Greek, and practiced some Jewish rituals. Some of these "God fearers" took the next step and converted fully or had their children converted. Mass conversions to Judaism are recorded (1) in the time of the Hasmonean Jewish ruler John Hyrcanus, who forcibly converted the Edomites (about 100 years before the Christian Era), (2) in the fourth century CE southern Arabian kingdom of Himyar in the area of today's Yemen, and (3) among the Khazars. The Khazars are probably the best-known converted group because of the theories of their connection with the origins of Ashkenazic Jewry.

The attitude of Judaism to conversion changed with the coming to power of Christianity and Islam in the areas where the Jews lived. Although both religions originally spread because of the presence, influence, and proselytism of the Jews, neither tolerated any further conversions to Judaism. From then on, conversions of members of the majority religion to Judaism were severely punished and often exposed the Jewish community to grave danger. As a result, Jewish communities shied away from conversions and became more reluctant to accept converts. As those communities became populated almost exclusively by born Jews, they became more distrustful of those who wished to convert. Negative talmudic statements like "Converts are as difficult for the Jews as a scab" became popular adages. Despite this, there was a small but steady stream of conversion to Judaism even in the Middle Ages and the early modern period, though much smaller than the flow of converts in the opposite direction.

Besides conversion, which is a well-known factor, there are other elements that people have been less comfortable talking about. One of these is slavery. The Torah permitted the possession of both Jewish and non-Jewish slaves, though with certain restrictions. A male Gentile slave was to be circumcised, and all Gentile slaves were expected to observe the bulk of Jewish religious law. A slave who was freed became a full-fledged Israelite. The practice of purchase and partial conversion of non-Jewish slaves by Jews was generally forbidden by Muslim and Christian authorities at the same time as they outlawed conversion to Judaism. Nevertheless, it is likely that many ex-slaves entered the Jewish population in ancient times. It should be noted here that ancient slavery did not have the association with dark skin color that it had in American history. The bulk of the slaves were Caucasians; a large proportion of them came from the Slavic lands, not from Africa.

We know even less about other forms of genetic mixture than about the case of liberated slaves. We know that religious intermarriage was forbidden by Jewish, Muslim, and Christian authorities. The very existence of the prohibition may be evidence that such unions sometimes occurred. Illicit unions outside of marriage have generally left even less of a trace, though we know of individual cases, even in the Middle Ages, of Jews who had one non-Jewish parent. In some societies, like medieval Spain, the restrictions on nonmarital unions were ignored more frequently than in others. Rapes of Jewish women during pogroms or at other times have been frequently discussed. Though the number of such violent encounters is unknown, it is assumed that in most cases the offspring were brought up in the Jewish community.

Intermarriage on a large scale has become widespread in most countries of the Diaspora in the past 100 years. Previously, mixed marriages were either illegal or extremely rare. In our generation, close to a majority of all Jews in the Diaspora marry persons not born Jewish. In a minority of cases, the non-Jewish partner converts to Judaism; in the majority, neither partner converts. In any case, in the modern American Jewish community, unlike traditional communities, most Jews have at least some relatives by marriage who are not Jewish.

What all of these factors show is that the Jews have never been totally cut off from the gene pool of the outside world. In some periods, like the Greco-Roman era and recent years, the influx of non-Jews into the Jewish community has been relatively great; at other times, like the Middle Ages, such influx was comparatively rare. In most cases, we do not have even the vaguest idea of the magnitude of the conversion, interbreeding, or intermarriage. This makes it impossible to calculate the percentage of genetic mixture within the Jewish people based on historical sources. For this reason, we rely heavily on the evidence from physical appearance and genetic testing to answer the question.

Are We Any Closer to an Answer?

Despite tremendous advances in genetic analysis, the issue of Jewish genetic heredity remains unresolved. Some scholars believe the evdence indicate that the Jews are more like their non-Jewish neighbors than they are like each other, while others argue just as strongly that it shows the essential unity of much of the Jewish people. Some see Ashkenazic Jews as containing considerable European ancestry, while others see them as essentially Mediterranean. The picture is still muddy, although perhaps it is in the process of becoming clarified.

It would seem that there is evidence both for Jewish mixture with surrounding peoples and for genetic unity among the Jewish people. It may be a matter of ascertaining the proportion of common heredity versus imported genes in the various groups of Jews, rather than judging them as either all converts or all original Israelites.

The question is an interesting intellectual problem and is perfectly legitimate as long as racial characteristics are not used to determine authenticity. Whether the Yemenites are the most authentic descendants of biblical Jews or mainly converted southern Arabians does not matter in terms of the authenticity of their culture. All Jewish cultures are a mixture of imported and native traits; all are equally authentic insofar as they have integrated their folk cultures into a Jewish framework of meaning. The physical heredity of the Jews is an aspect of their cultural and religious unity and diversity, and should not be used as a criterion for judging "who is the most Jewish."

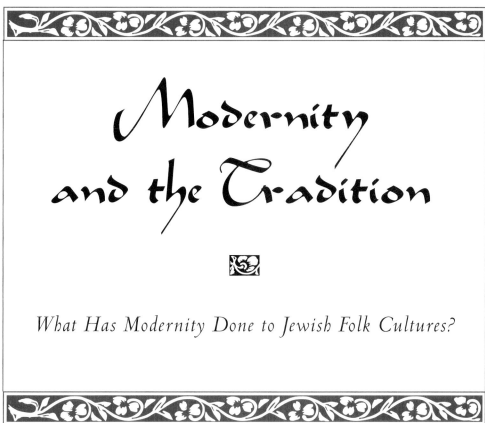

Modernity and the Tradition

What Has Modernity Done to Jewish Folk Cultures?

FOR A LONG PERIOD IN JEWISH HISTORY THERE WAS A FUNDAMENTAL SIMILARITY between the way of life prescribed in the religious law codes and the way most Jews actually lived. In communities where harmony between traditional law and actual Jewish life predominated, the processes described throughout this book prevailed. Folk traditions helped to fill in the blanks in the written prescriptions, and within a commonly shared framework, Jews around the world created varying local interpretations of the framework.

In modern times, this consonance between custom and law was challenged and then largely abandoned. Most Jews today do not observe even the basic outlines of Jewish traditional religious practice. Such former near universals as avoiding nonkosher foods; not cooking, smoking, and traveling on the Sabbath; and regular daily prayer for men three times a day have become the province of a small minority of Jewry. Most Jews observe Jewish traditions selectively, if at all. Therefore, whatever Jewish folk practices survive now exist in a completely different framework. Rather than being supplements or embellishments of a common framework of law, they have become either remnants of an earlier culture or independent signs of Jewishness unattached to any greater framework.

Modern times began at different dates in different parts of the world. The first important inroads of modernity were felt by the Jews of Western Europe in the second half of the eighteenth century and the first half of the nineteenth. Governments began to experiment with granting citizenship to the Jews and integrating them into the educational, cultural, and social life of the country. In most of Western Europe, namely France, Germany, Holland, and Italy, there was a remarkable increase in Jewish prosperity and in Jewish participation in the cultural life of society as a whole. The process of modernization was slower in Eastern Europe, where authoritarian governments and economic underdevelopment long delayed the integration of the Jews. But even in Eastern Europe, the decline of traditional religion and the rise of various modern Jewish ideologies like Zionism and Jewish socialism were noticeable by the end of the nineteenth century. In much of the Middle East, modernization came from outside influences, especially the influence of colonial powers like France and England. Some areas, like Algeria, Tunisia, and Morocco, were directly taken over by the Western powers. In others, like the Turkish Empire, Western influence was more indirect, through schools and cultural institutions sponsored by Western Jewry. In most Middle Eastern countries by the early twentieth century, the forces of Westernization were noticeable in education, dress, and language use (especially the influence of French), and some laxity in religious practice became noticeable. Even Yemen, where religious tradition remained virtually untouched, was not completely exempt from the influences of modernity in the twentieth century.

Mixing of Jewish Cultures

Regardless when modernity began to enter a community, the old patterns of universal Jewish observance and a separate Jewish folk culture began to weaken. But modernity has had another effect, in addition to turning Jewish religious observance into the exception rather than the rule. The earlier condition for the growth of folk traditions—the isolation of each group of Jews—no longer exists. In premodern times, each local group assumed that its folk tradition was "the" Jewish tradition, but today almost everyone is aware that Jews in other countries, or sometimes as close as next door, observe different traditions. Modernity has brought into contact folk traditions that were formerly separated by barriers to communication and travel.

Because the various traditions are now in contact with each other, they influence each other constantly. People are now able to mix formerly distinct traditions in a smorgasbord of their own. This is the Jewish parallel to the "global village" created by modern television, newspapers, and travel. The same person can listen to Yiddish music and Yemenite songs, eat blintzes and falafel, and attend synagogues following different religious rites.

This mixing of Jewish cultures has been intensified by the almost total shifting of Jewish settlement patterns in the past hundred and fifty years. The two largest Jewish communities in the world by far—the United States and Israel—consist almost entirely of individuals whose families have arrived within the last 100 years. Most of the old geographic centers of Jewish culture, shown in the maps in Chapter 2, have almost no Jewish residents today. In Eastern and Central Europe the Nazi Holocaust, and in the Middle East the emigration of the vast majority of Jews from the Muslim world to Israel, have left only the tiniest remnants of a Jewish community in the old areas of settlement.

In America, the vast majority of the Jewish population is of Ashkenazic (mainly East European) origin, with only small traces of Middle Eastern groups.

But even here there has been a mixture of geographically distinct groups. In Israel the mixing is much greater, with people from many different lands and cultures ending up living together in the same town, on the same street, or in the same apartment house. Contact is inevitable. Israelis used to say that compared to the American melting pot, Israel was a pressure cooker. A great deal of mixing of Jewish populations is also to be found in modern France and, to a lesser extent, in Latin America, especially Mexico, Brazil, and Argentina.

The radically different conditions of modern Jewish life have transformed Jewish folk traditions in a number of paradoxical ways. On the one hand, as religious observance has declined and as science has replaced many folk beliefs about healing and the spirit world, many old practices have died out or become mere vestiges of their former selves. But this has not happened to all folk beliefs by any means. It is quite common for folk traditions to get mixed and then spread to groups that did not formerly practice them. This pattern of convergence, which has been noticed in world culture as a whole, is far from total, however. In the face of the homogenization of world culture (and Jewish culture), there has also been a countervailing force—the revival of national and group identity. Practices that might otherwise have been abandoned have been revived as an assertion of identity. New types of ethnic identification have taken the place of older patterns.

Disappearance of Old Patterns and Creation of New Ones

The rapid changes in Jewish life in modern time have caused neither the disappearance of Jewish traditions nor their homogenization, though elements of both are surely evident. Just as common is the rise of new customs, new cultural practices, and a changed geographic pattern of customs and habits. The present state of Jewish traditions is as complex and dynamic as it ever was in the past.

Several contradictory patterns in Jewish cultural customs exist today. The old distinctiveness of Jewish cultural practice has disappeared. Distinctive costume patterns among most Jews have vanished, and fewer and fewer Jews today speak traditional Jewish vernacular languages like Yiddish, Djudezmo, and Judeo-Arabic. For most Jews, these languages have been replaced either by the official language of the general population, generally written in the same alphabet that non-Jews use, or, in Israel, by the revival of Hebrew as a spoken language. But even in these two areas, where the old Jewish patterns seem to have weakened the most, there are countervailing forces at work. Traditional Jewish costumes are still sometimes worn on special occasions, especially weddings and ethnic festivals. Whereas the first generation of Yemenite immigrants to Israel tried to wear Western wedding costumes, there has been a revival of the traditional woman's wedding costume, even among Yemenite Jews who have drifted away from much of Yemenite tradition (Illustration 10.1). Specifically Jewish styles of dress have

also been preserved to varying degrees by Orthodox Jews in various countries and are not necessarily restricted to specific occasions.

Something similar has happened with Jewish vernaculars. Although the vast majority of Jews no longer speak these languages, there has been a revival of interest in them in two separate circles. The first center of interest is among small groups of educated young people and in the universities. Yiddish, Djudezmo, and other Jewish vernaculars are being studied by academics, cultivated by small circles of devotees, and taught formally in schools and colleges. The groups involved in such revival efforts are small, but there are larger circles that look upon these efforts with satisfaction. Completely separate from these groups devoted to the preservation of the languages are the Hasidic groups and some right-wing yeshiva that have preserved Yiddish as a language of instruction and even as the language

10.1 A modern Yemenite bride wearing traditional costume for the henna ceremony in contemporary Israel.

of daily life in some of their communities. Only Yiddish has been preserved by Orthodox groups but not any of the other Jewish vernaculars.

More has happened, though, than the mere perpetuation of old patterns of clothing and language. New patterns have emerged that show substantial changes. In the Hasidic world, long black coats and fur hats for men and wigs for women are often much more luxurious than the old, shabby garments worn in Eastern Europe. Pious young women in America and Israel have introduced new items of stylishly modest clothing to their wardrobes, including the beret and "snood" (a bag-like cloth head covering used to conceal long, flowing hair) to cover the hair and have produced catalogues of modest clothing available in specialty shops or even by mail order or on the Internet.

In the revival of folk costumes for weddings, too, new patterns can be observed. The wedding costume of the capital of Yemen, San'a, is now used even by brides from other towns in Yemen, and it is worn for a shorter portion of the wedding ceremonies than had previously been common.

A similar pattern is noticeable with regard to language. The revival of Yiddish among the educated is generally artificial. The speakers have to search for occasions to use the language, which is really a mere supplement to their natural spoken language, usually English or Hebrew. Academics have coined a host of new Yiddish words to describe phenomena unknown to traditional Jewish societies like marshmallows, nuclear physics, and Freudian psychology. Even in Hasidic circles, there are some whose knowledge of Yiddish has become rather rudimentary and artificial.

These changes in language and costume indicate a pattern much more widespread in folk cultures around the world. Much of what was once a natural, unself-conscious form of expression, because it was the only way of life known to those who practiced it, has now become a conscious effort designed to demonstrate identity. This movement has been described in the United States as "symbolic ethnicity." The particular trait is no longer something that is done every day out of necessity; it is now consciously revived for special occasions to make a cultural point. Italian-Americans who are proud to be Italian may not be able to speak Italian, but they may still identify themselves as members of the group. The same is true among Jews as a group and among subgroups of Jews. Some examples of this phenomenon are the revival of the Mimouna post-Passover celebration among Moroccan Jews in Israel, the celebration of Chanukah as a major Jewish holiday in the United States, and the widespread interest in Eastern European klezmer music around the world. In each of these cases, traditional practices form the core of the modern occurrence, but the social context has been totally transformed, and the practice given a more public and sophisticated image.

The revival or preservation of folk practices in a modern context is the result of a changing and ambivalent attitude of many persons today toward "progress." Whereas a few generations ago many educated people fought against folk practices as backward and superstitious, a more respectful attitude has now become more common. Paradoxically, as folk life has become weaker because of the overwhelming success of modernity and presents less of a threat to modern culture, America after the 1960s has come to celebrate ethnicity. Many of the children and grandchildren of those who turned away from traditional ways of life feel a sense of nostalgia or loss about cultures that seem to have faded away, and have tried to revive what their parents fled. The revival of the past based on nostalgia and preservationism always differs from what that past had originally been. It is often sanitized and lacks the dirt, danger and conflict that had been part of the old.

A parallel to the American rediscovery of ethnicity has occurred in Israel. During the first decades of the State of Israel, government officials and educators worked hard to acculturate new immigrants. Through the policies of *shelilat hagola* (rejection of the Diaspora) and *mizug aliyot* (mixing of immigrant groups), Israel in the 1940s and 1950s endeavored to wean newcomers away from their traditional languages and cultures and toward the secular, Hebrew-speaking civilization they were trying to build in Israel. Former native traditions of dress, speech, and folk practices were discouraged as primitive. Israel desired to create a unified and relatively homogeneous Jewish population. Since the 1960s, however, there has been a reversal of cultural policy in Israel that parallels changes in the United States. At the same time that Hebrew has succeeded in replacing the old vernaculars, many Israelis have shown renewed interest in the heritage of their parents and grandparents. Jews of Middle Eastern origin no longer easily accept the superiority of Ashkenazic ways, and the government has shown a renewed respect for the traditions of the *Edot Hamizrach* (Eastern communities).

In the United States, many Jews have followed the trends of other ethnic groups trying to reconnect with their roots. This effort expresses itself in many ways, including renewed interest in family genealogy and nostalgia for the shtetl. Publications like *The Jewish Catalog* that gives guidance on how to practice various folk arts and customs, in addition to religious practices, receive wide circulation. But except for a fairly small minority of Jews who have turned to full-blown acceptance of tradition, the vast majority, even those who express nostalgia for and interest in the customs of the past, do so very selectively.

Technology and Jewish Music

Sometimes the very forces of technology that broke down the isolation of folk culture and paved the way for modernity can be used to perpetuate traditions in transformed ways. We can see examples in the field of music. The circulation of Jewish folk music from many different countries has been made possible by recordings. At the same time that recordings preserve cultural forms that might otherwise have disappeared, they transform them in several ways. The geographical separateness of the various traditions disappears. Ashkenazic Jews can learn Yemenite songs and dances, just as Jews of Middle Eastern origin can listen to klezmer music and Yiddish art songs. When they perform the music of a culture other than their own, musicians often transform the tempo, voice quality, and style of a piece to fit their own traditions, leading to new combinations and influences.

The international power of rock music has also affected Jewish musical traditions. A spate of rock-influenced Jewish religious music for weddings, communal singing, and celebrations has come into existence since the 1960s. This new music and its accompanying dances have become exceedingly popular in Orthodox circles and have replaced much of the earlier, less exciting folk music traditions. Records and concerts of the current stars of religious rock music, all of it sung by men or boys and most of it in Hebrew, find enthusiastic audiences. In Israel new folk traditions, based on both imported and native traditions, are very popular. The Romanian *hora* and the Arab *debka*, along with modified Yemenite traditions, have become part of a repertoire of Israeli dancing that enjoys popularity in many countries.

Jewish Cuisines in the Modern World

Jewish cuisines have also been both preserved and transformed by the modern world. Certain types of food, especially those rich in animal fats like gribenes (fried goose or chicken skins), have been replaced by more healthy products. Vegetables formerly made with a thick sauce are now cooked in water, vegetable oil has replaced chicken fat, and salads have become more popular. The transformation of food preparation has affected traditional recipes as well. Cooks today rarely prepare all of their ingredients from scratch. Many ethnic ingredients are readily available in stores in processed form. One can buy frozen blintzes, kreplach, and borekas almost as easily as frozen pizza or waffles. Ready-made bread, bagels, pastries, and cakes often substitute for homemade versions. Matzo ball soup is available in cans, precooked couscous grains can be bought in many supermarkets, and Middle Eastern casseroles are available in packaged form at kosher markets. Almost every kind of ethnic bread is now available commercially in places where there is enough demand, and certain Jewish products like bagels have gained such wide popularity that most people who eat them are not Jewish.

The same consumer who goes to the market to buy a Jewish ready-made food product is also likely to pick up items originally belonging to other cuisines. Many products of non-Jewish ethnic cultures are now readily available for individuals who adhere to the Jewish dietary laws. Kosher pizza shops and kosher Italian and Chinese restaurants can be found in most major Orthodox communities. In California, kosher Mexican food is popular. There are also strictly kosher restaurants in which Thai, Indian, Argentinean, and French cuisines are served. Some restaurants pride themselves on offering a selection of national cuisines. Many affluent and observant Jews who adhere strictly to the kosher laws no longer eat only traditional Jewish foods but instead prefer the foods of other cultures. The same applies to kosher wines. No longer are Jews who keep kosher restricted to the sweet, thick variety popular among Eastern European immigrants to the United States; instead they can choose among kosher French, Spanish, Italian, and California vintages.

For Jews who do not observe the restrictions of Kashruth, the range of foods is even greater. Certain ethnic cuisines seem especially popular among Jews. For reasons no one has ever satisfactorily explained, American Jews have been among the best customers of Chinese restaurants. Some have even suggested that you can tell an American Jewish neighborhood by its large number of Chinese restaurants. Sometimes, however, Jews who do not observe Kashruth feel an attraction to traditional cuisine. There are a large number of "Jewish" but nonkosher restaurants in the United States and elsewhere where matzo balls, corned beef sandwiches, kugel, and other traditional foods are served. Sometimes one can see a paradoxical scene in a Jewish neighborhood supermarket before the holidays. An obviously Orthodox customer will have a cart loaded down with California kosher wine, kosher quiche mix, kosher filo dough, and kosher soy sauce, while an obviously secular customer will be buying nonkosher chicken together with thick red wine, borsht, gefilte fish, and kasha. The nonkosher consumer may wax nostalgic about brisket, while the kosher consumer is excited about trying kosher sushi.

What is evident from all these examples is that Jewish folk practices have changed very rapidly in the past half century, far more rapidly than ever before. Jewish cultural habits are now practiced in very different contexts and mean something very different from what had been the case in traditional Jewish society. The type of internal differentiation in Jewish culture has also changed greatly. In traditional society, individual communities were very uniform in costume, language, eating habits, religious observance, and folk beliefs. Barriers to communication created cultural regions, which were clearly defined geographically. In modern society, both factors have changed. On the one hand, Jewish people living in the same geographical areas often exhibit great differences in their beliefs, practices, and habits. An Orthodox Jew and his secular neighbor will differ greatly in their daily lifestyle. At the same time, people in widely separated regions of the world can dress substantially alike, eat the same foods, listen to the same television programs, and communicate easily with each other.

Forces Influencing Modern Jewish Culture

Perhaps the best way to summarize the patterns of Jewish popular culture today is to see it as the product of three opposing forces. The first force, already discussed, is the elimination of regional differences, reducing the strength of tradition and making the Jewish world more uniform and less distinct from the surrounding cultures. The second force is the preservation of the older cultures and of identity with tradition. The third force is the transformation of the old geographic patterns into new patterns of geographic differentiation and new local cultures. The cultural configuration that is emerging will probably be influenced by all three forces. There is no way to predict what the configuration will look like in a generation or two.

In order to understand how these three forces work and interact, let us look at some examples of emerging Jewish culture. In the realm of language we can see all three forces at work. Homogenization is at work in two directions—the triumph of modern Israeli Hebrew over all Jewish vernaculars and the adoption of the language of the non-Jewish majority by most Diaspora Jews. Forces working to preserve older patterns exist but are relatively weak. The Israeli pronunciation of Hebrew has triumphed over all the regional traditions, at least in conversational Hebrew. When it comes to the Hebrew used for religious purposes (the liturgy, Torah study, and sermons), there has been some resistance. Although most non-Orthodox congregations, and some Orthodox ones, in the United

States have replaced the Ashkenazic pronunciation tradition with the Israeli one, certain Orthodox groups have been moving in the opposite direction. It is now viewed by some as more pious to use Ashkenazic pronunciation, sometimes even with a strong Eastern European accent, instead of Israeli Hebrew in the synagogue. Some younger Jews who were taught the Israeli pronunciation have taught themselves the Ashkenazic pronunciation in order to seem more authentic. Similarly, some young Yemenite Jews pride themselves on preserving the traditional Yemenite pronunciation in their synagogues and in teaching their musical tradition to their children. In general, this countervailing tendency is weaker than the trend toward homogenization, but it is often quite striking.

The creation of new traditional patterns is less obvious but also exists. One could argue that in very Orthodox circles in America, a new Jewish vernacular has developed based on English but full of Yiddishisms and Hebraisms: "He learned out from this that it's oser [forbidden] to use the hot water on Shabos." "Boruch hashem! [Thank God]. It was mamesh a ness [really a miracle] that I was rescued from the car accident." In the twentieth century, American Jewry also developed a version of Ashkenazic Hebrew pronunciation that differs from that in other countries. Even though this pronunciation is in retreat in the face of Israeli Hebrew, it is still widely heard in American synagogues.

There are many other examples of these phenomena in other aspects of Jewish life. In the United States and Israel, there has been a rise in the number of organizations designed to strengthen Sephardic identity and raise Sephardic pride, as well as attempts to revive ceremonies like the Moroccan Mimouna or the premarriage henna ceremony. The existence of "ethnic synagogues" is still quite noticeable in Israel and in the Diaspora. Although they have special appeal to the immigrant generation, the synagogues that preserve ethnic traditions have had considerable staying power over second-generation members of Yemenite, Moroccan, and other non-Ashkenazic backgrounds. On the other hand, the subgroups among Ashkenazic Jews (except among Hasidic groups) have pretty much disappeared. Synagogues preserving the German, Hungarian, Polish, and Lithuanian traditions have not survived far beyond the immigrant generation. The division between Ashkenazic and non-Ashkenazic traditions, however, has tended to

10.2 Passover seder on a secular Israeli kibbutz.

remain, perhaps because of the greater differences. Individuals may switch allegiance to the tradition of the majority in their locality, and intermarriage between Middle Eastern and European Jews may mix traditions, but cultural distinctions between the two major subdivisions of the Jewish people are still generally noticeable.

New regional traditions are also emerging based on the different mix of immigration to various countries. Despite many similarities, one can clearly differentiate between the Jewish popular cultures of Israel, France, England, Latin America, and the United States. Each area is in the process of developing a Jewish cultural scene distinct from the others. In Israel, there is a sharp division between the secular majority and the Orthodox minority. The culture of the secular majority is often viewed as Israeli rather than Jewish. Many Israelis never attend the synagogue, do not keep kosher, or observe the religious restrictions of the Sabbath. These same secular Jews, however, speak Hebrew, observe the Sabbath as a day of recreation and family outings, and often celebrate the Jewish holidays in nontraditional ways. On nonreligious kibbutzim, the Passover Seder often includes nontraditional elements based on agricultural and nationalist themes and may never mention the name of God, but it is certainly a form of Jewish observance (Illustration 10.2). In France, where North African Jews slightly outnumber the older Ashkenazic Jewish community, Algerian, Moroccan, and Tunisian customs have now become very noticeable. Couscous, merguez (sausage), and anisette are eaten and drunk by many French Jews and are widely popular among non-Jews as well. In Latin America, where the Jewish community is often a middle-class enclave in a sea of poverty-stricken Catholics, Jewish communal life often revolves around luxurious Jewish sports clubs rather than synagogues. In England most Jews are not very observant, but many of them remain loyal to the Orthodox synagogue and would not think of joining Reform or Liberal synagogues. The pattern of "parking around the corner from the Orthodox shul," which is on the road to extinction in the United States, is still very much the norm in England and in former Commonwealth countries such as South Africa. In American Jewry it seems natural to assume that Jews are either Orthodox, Conservative, or Reform, a division of the community unknown in most other countries with large Jewish populations.

These divisions in overall patterns are often reflected in specific practices as well. The increased participation of women in Jewish ritual has advanced much further in American Jewry than in most parts of the world. The existence of the bat mitzvah, counting women as part of the prayer quorum, calling women to the Torah, and the ordination of female rabbis have now become the rule in Reform, Reconstructionist, and Conservative synagogues in the United States (Illustration 10.3). Even in Orthodox circles, an increase in female roles has become a matter of discussion. Such phenomena as the women's Talmud class, women's prayer groups, and a modified form of the bat mitzvah have been introduced in modern Orthodox circles, though they are the subjects of great controversy and resistance. Such innovations are far less common even in Reform Judaism outside the United States, and they are virtually nonexistent among religious Jews in Israel. This is one of the reasons why the attempt by women to gain the right to lead services at the Western Wall in Jerusalem has failed to excite much of the Israeli public. Most Israelis who care about the status of women tend to find religion an irrelevant matter and do not understand why women, most of them American, are so interested in religious participation.

The national differences in culture are, of course, noticeable in much less weighty matters as well. Israeli and French Jewry has a much smaller Ashkenazic element than the Jewry of the United States does. This is evident in the kinds of

10.3 An unconventional modern twist on tradition. Women at Jewish Theological Seminary in New York wearing prayer shawls and phylacteries [tefillin], traditionally reserved for men.

Jewish foods and music popular in the various countries. Lox and bagels are typically American Jewish foods but are not particularly popular in Israel or other Diaspora Jewries. Subtle or not so subtle differences in cultural temperament are also noticeable. Israelis have different ideas about personal space than Americans do; one can see this easily in crowds and in the supermarket. The use of cellular phones in public places is much more socially acceptable in Israel than in the United States. The climate and surroundings have ensured that there is a greater Middle Eastern atmosphere in Israeli Jewish culture than among American Jews.

Local culture has made inroads into the popular culture of Jews even where one might not expect it. The subtle inroads of American culture into the lives of even Orthodox American Jews are often striking and surprising. The yarmulkas of many American Orthodox boys are decorated with baseball team logos, Disney characters, and American and Israeli flags. In non-Orthodox circles, new feminine versions of the yarmulka and the talit, in modified color schemes and styles, have developed. At American Orthodox weddings, along with modified and jazzed-up versions of traditional Jewish melodies, one is almost certain to hear the Greek-American dance *miserlou*. On college campuses, Orthodox young people in a humorous mood sing the grace after meals to the tune of the Notre Dame fight song. In Australia the popular tune "Waltzing Matilda" is used for the same purpose. Advanced yeshiva students in the United States often take a break from their studies to play basketball.

Even within a single country there are traces of new patterns of regional difference. A traditional Jewish wedding in New York City is preceded by an elaborate *smorgasbord* (using that Swedish word), while in other parts of the country, such as Baltimore or Chicago, the wedding begins with the marriage ceremony and few or no hors d'oeuvres beforehand. Equal participation in the liturgy for women gained much quicker acceptance in Conservative synagogues in the western United States than it did on the eastern seaboard. Many American Jews differentiate between the mentality of "New York Jews," described as brash, intellectual, and ethnic, and the more subtle style favored in other parts of the country.   Jews in the southeastern United States playfully wish each other "Shalom Y'all," while a congregation in Hawaii calls itself "Shaloha" (a combination of "Shalom" and "aloha"). In Israel, linguists are beginning to detect differences in vocabulary in the Hebrew of Jerusalem, Tel Aviv, and Haifa. In France, the Jewish community of Strasbourg, with its strong Western Ashkenazic roots, has a different ambience than the huge community of Paris or the more isolated, mainly Sephardic communities of southern France.

✦ ✦ ✦

Jewish popular culture is far from dead, but it is taking radically different new forms. Many old patterns are breaking down, and newer ones are being created. The formerly sharp boundary between Jewish culture and majority cultures is vaguer than ever before, and the influence of local non-Jewish cultures on Jews in various parts of the world has become greater than ever. Formerly separate Jewish folk cultures are now in contact and have influenced each other greatly. The new patterns coming into existence do not fit as neatly into a pattern of universal Jewish meaning and regional coloration as did the older patterns. The common bond of a shared authoritative system of Jewish law has been lost, probably never to be restored. Jews today are united less by their common religious beliefs and practices and more by a vague sense of mutual attachment and identification that is certainly more subtle and elastic than the old bond but may be an effective sub-

stitute. Our increased ability to travel long distances has enabled formerly separated Jewish communities to come into personal contact with each other. Shared
historical memories of past persecution, as well as pride in Jewish accomplish-
ments and in the State of Israel, are among the factors that have helped preserve a
sense of Jewishness, despite the declining importance of shared religious practice
as a binding force. The end result of all these changes will be new systems of Jewish culture that will differ greatly from those of the past. What these patterns will
look like in 100 years is very hard to predict. We can only say that cultural change,
which has always existed in Jewish life, will continue at a far more rapid pace than
anything known by previous generations, and that whatever form it takes, Jewish
civilization will continue to develop and flourish.

Suggestions for Further Reading

Acknowledgments

Emily Rose, *Portraits of Our Past: Jews of the German Countryside* (Philadelphia-New York: Jewish Publication Society, 2001).

Chapter 2   Regional Cultures

Although many Jewish history books discuss Jewish migrations in passing, there are none that I know of which deal specifically with Jewish migrations around the world. On the other hand there is a rich literature on Jewish communities in various countries, some of which deal with migration as well. The following is a small selection from the multitude of such books in English, which I found interesting and useful. Some of these volumes are mainly collections of visual materials, while others are popular or scholarly studies of the particular group.

A general survey of non-Ashkenazic Jewry written for a popular audience and stressing the "authenticity" and exoticism of the Jews of the "East" is Devora and Menahem Hacohen, *One People: The Story of the Eastern Jews* (New York: Sabra Books, 1969 (Second edition, Adama Books, 1982)).

More specialized studies dealing with specific countries or regions are: Norman A. Stillman, *The Jews of the Arab World in Modern Times*, 2 volumes (Philadelphia-New York: Jewish Publication Society, 1991); Shlomo Deshen and Walter Zenner, eds., *Jewish Societies in the Middle East: Community, Culture and Authority* (Washington, DC: University Press of America, 1982); Andre N. Chouraqui, *Between East and West: A History of the Jews of North Africa*. Translated by Michael M. Bernet (Philadelphia: Jewish Publication Society, 1968); Harvey E.

Goldberg, *Jewish Life in Muslim Libya: Rivals and Relatives* (Chicago and London: University of Chicago Press, 1990); Nissim Rejwan, *The Jews of Iraq: 3000 Years of History and Culture* (Boulder: Westview Press, 1985); Abraham L. Udovitch and Lucette Valensi, *The Last Arab Jews: The Communities of Jerba, Tunisia* (New York: Harwood Academic Press, 1984); Esther Muchawsky-Schnapper, *The Jews of Yemen: Highlights of the Israel Museum Collection* (Jerusalem: The Museum, 1994); Marc Angel, *The Jews of Rhodes: The History of a Sephardic Community* (New York: Sepher-Hermon Press, 1978).

On Italian Jewry, a classic but still valuable study is Cecil Roth, *A History of the Jews of Italy* (Philadelphia: Jewish Publication Society, 1946). Two very useful pictorial works dealing with Italian Jewish life are Vivian B. Mann, *Gardens and Ghettos: The Art of Jewish Life in Italy* (Berkely: University of California Press, 1989), and Ruth Geller, Henryk Geller, and Ard Geller, *Roma Ebraica/Jewish Rome: A Pictorial History of 2000 Years. (*Rome: Art International, 1970).

Quite a few interesting and informative works have been written recently on the Jewish communities in India. Among them, are Ruby Daniel and Barbara C. Johnson, *Ruby of Cochin: An Indian Jewish Woman Remembers* (Philadelphia: Jewish Publication Society, 1975); J.B. Segal, *A History of the Jews of Cochin* (London: Vallentine Mitchell, 1993); and Nathan Katz and Ellen S. Goldberg, *The Last Jews of Cochin: Jewish Identity in Hindu India* (Columbia: University of South Carolina Press, 1993).

Erich Brauer and Raphael Patai, *The Jews of Kurdistan (*Detroit, Wayne State University Press: 1993), is based on Brauer's fieldwork in the 1930s at a time when Kurdish Jewish culture was still vibrant in its homeland; Lawrence Loeb, *Outcast: Jewish Life in Southern Iran* (New York, 1977), is based on the author's fieldwork in Shiraz in the 1970s.

On the Jews of Ethiopia, David Kessler, *The Falashas: A Short History of the Ethiopian Jews* (London-Portland: Frank Cass, 1996), upholds the traditional view of the Jewish origins of the groups, while Steven Kaplan, *The Beta Israel (Falasha) in Ethiopia from Earliest Times to the Twentieth Century* (New York University Press, 1992) and James Quirin, *The Evolution of the Ethiopian Jews: A History of the Beta Israel (Falashas) to 1920* (Philadelphia, University of Pennsylvania Press, 1992) take the more controversial view that Ethiopian Judaism developed as a breakaway from Ethiopian Christianity.

William Charles White, *Chinese Jews: A Compilation of Matters Relating to the Jews of Kaifeng-Fu* (Toronto, University of Toronto Press, 1942) is a classic compilation of documents relating to this most exotic of Jewish communities.

There is a large literature of books memorializing specific European Jewish communities destroyed by the Nazis. One of the best and most recent is Yaffa Eliach, *There Once was a World. A 900 Year Chronicle of the Shtetl of Eishyshok* (Boston-New York-London-Toronto:

Little Brown and Company, 1998). A lavishly illustrated memorial to Jews in the Netherlands is Mozes Heiman Gans, *Memorbook. History of Dutch Jewry from the Renaissance to 1940 with 1100 Illustrations* (Baarn: Bosch and Keuning, 1977).

A good introductory survey of German Jewish history is Ruth Gay, *The Jews of Germany: A Historical Portrait* (New Haven: Yale University Press, 1992), which covers the subject from beginning to end. A much more detailed treatment covering the period since the seventeenth century is the four volume *German Jewish History in Modern Times*, edited by Michael A. Meyer (New York: Columbia University Press, 1997).

Several excellent pictorial histories on groups within Ashkenazic Jewry have been put together in recent decades. Among the best is Nachum Tim Gidal, *Die Juden in Deutschland von der Römerzeit bis zur Weimarer Republik* (Gutersloh: Bertelsmann Lexikon Verlag, 1988) which deals with Germany [although the descriptions are in German, the illustrations are still of interest to the English speaker]. For Eastern Europe the best available pictoral histories are Lucjan Dobroszycki and Barbara Kirshenblatt-Gimblett, *Image before my Eyes: A Photographic History of Jewish Life in Poland, 1864-1939* (New York: Schochen Books, 1977), and Zvi Gitelman, *A Century of Ambivalence, The Jews of Russia and the Soviet Union, 1881 to the Present* (New York: Schocken Books, 1988).

Many very valuable articles [in Hebrew] are found in the journal *Pe'amim [Studies in the Cultural Heritage of Oriental Jewry]* which has appeared from 1977 to the present.

Chapter 3 *Jewish Languages*

Probably the most detailed discussion of Jewish languages in general and of Yiddish in particular written in the English language is Max Weinreich, *History of the Yiddish Language* (Chicago: University of Chicago Press, 2 volumes, 1980). Especially relevant to the discussion in this book is his chapter 2 (pp. 45-174) entitled "Yiddish in the Framework of other Jewish languages." On Yiddish the following are particularly relevant: Marvin Herzog, *The Yiddish Language in Northern Poland* (Bloomington: Indiana University Press and The Hague, 1965); Dovid Katz, *The Origins of the Yiddish Language* (Oxford: Pergamon Press, 1985); and Dovid Katz, *The Dialects of the Yiddish Language* (Oxford: Pergamon Press, 1986). The journal *Field of Yiddish* contained scholarly articles on various aspects of the Yiddish language.

A great deal of interesting material is scattered throughout the pages of the journal *Jewish Language Review*, which appeared from 1981 to 1989 [in the latter year under the title *Jewish Linguistic Studies*]. A series of papers on the same field were published Herbert H. Paper, *Jewish Languages, Theme and Variations* (Cambridge, Mass.: Association for Jewish Studies, 1978).

David M. Bunis has written a number of scholarly works on the history of Djudezmo as well as an introductory book on reading this Judeo-Spanish language entitled *A Guide to Reading and Writing Judezmo* (Brooklyn: Adelantre, The Judezmo Society, 1975). A scholarly study of another Jewish vernacular is Joseph Blau, *The Emergence and Linguistic Background of Judaeo-Arabic; a study of the Origins of Middle Arabic* (Jerusalem: Ben Zvi Institute, 1981). Valuable articles on regional pronunciations of Hebrew are found in the *Encyclopedia Judaica* (1973) on "Pronunciations of Hebrew," and "Hebrew grammar."

Chapter 4   *Names*

A good general treatment on Jewish names is Benzion C. Kaganoff, *A Dictionary of Jewish Names and their History* (New York: Schochen Books, 1977). A general dictionary of Jewish family names around the world is Heinrich W. Guggenheim and Eva Guggenheim, *Jewish Family Names and Their Origins: An Etymological Dictionary* (Hoboken: KTAV Publishing House, 1992). Specialized but very reliable and useful are two books by Alexander Beider, *A Dictionary of Jewish Surnames from the Russian Empire* (Teaneck: Avotaynu, 1993), and *A Dictionary of Jewish Surnames from the Kingdom of Poland (*Teaneck: Avotaynu, 1996).

Chapter 5   *Religious Practice*

There is not a great deal of literature on variations in Jewish religious practices in English, though there is quite a lot in Hebrew. The best detailed survey of non-Ashkenazic customs in English is Herbert C. Dobrinsky, *A Treasury of Sephardic Laws and Customs* (New York: Yeshiva University Press, 1986).

On the architecture and layout of the synagogue, the classic work is still Rachel Wisch-nitzer, *The Architecture of the European Synagogue* (Philadelphia, Jewish Publication Society, 1964). A popular survey is Uri Kaploun, *The Synagogue* (New York-Paris: Leon Amiel Publisher, 1973).

Two scholarly studies of Jewish religious customs [both written in Hebrew] are Yitzhak (Eric) Zimmer, *Olam Keminhago Noheg: Perakim Betoldot Haminhagim* [Society and its Customs: Studies in the History and Metamorphosis of Jewish Customs], (Jerusalem: Zalman Shazar Institute, 1996) and Daniel Sperber's multi volume study *Minhage Yisrael: Mekorot vetoladot* [Jewish Customs: Sources and History], (Jerusalem: Mosad Harav Kuk, 1989-). At least 6 volumes of Sperber's studies have appeared. Unlike the present volume, the studies by Zimmer and Sperber are detailed explorations of the details of specific customs.

Some art books which deal with Jewish religious art of various countries are: Grace Cohen Grossman, *Jewish Art* (New York: Hugh Lauter Levin Associates, 1995); Bezalel Narkiss, *Hebrew Illuminated Manuscripts* (Jerusalem: Keter, 1969 [later edition: New York

1983]); and Gabrielle Sed-Rajna, et al., *Jewish Art*, Translated by Sara Friedman and Mira Reich (New York: Harry N. Abrams, Inc., 1997). More specialized treatments of specific aspects of the subject include Shalom Sabar, *Ketubbah: Jewish Marriage Contracts of the Hebrew Union College* (Philadelphia: Jewish Publication Society, 1990).

Many examples of Jewish ritual objects are to be found in such collected picture books as Barbara Kirshenblatt-Gimblett, *Fabric of Jewish Life* (New York: Jewish Museum, 1977) and Judah Loeb Bialer, *Jewish Life in Art and Tradition; Based on the Collection of the Wolfson Museum, Hechal Shlomo, Jerusalem* (London: Weidenfeld and Nicholson, 1976).

Chapter 6 Cuisine

An ambitious study of Jewish cooking traditions containing many fascinating details is John Cooper, *Eat and Be Satisfied. A Social History of Jewish Food* (Northvale, NJ: Jason Aronson, 1993). Most other studies of Jewish cooking in various parts of the world take the form of cookbooks. Among the most useful of these in English are:

Copeland Marks, *The Sephardic Kitchen: 600 Recipes Created in Exotic Sephardic Kitchens from Morocco to India* (New York: Donald I Fine Inc., 1992) and Robert Steinberg, *The Sephardic Kitchen: The Healthful Food and Rich Culture of the Mediterranean Jews* (New York: Harper Collins Publishers, 1992).

Chapter 7 Costume

Alfred Rubens, *History of Jewish Costume* (New York: Valentine Mitchell, 1967) has become the classic study of this subject. It is both richly illustrated and provides a running discussion on the various types of costume. For purposes of comparison of Jewish and non-Jewish costumes nothing matches the fascinating collection of photographs of Turkish costume assembled in 1873 [!] in Osman Hamdi Bey, *Les Costumes Populaires de la Turquie en 1873* (Constantinople: 1873). Some pictures which can be used to compare with Jewish costume in Eastern Europe are found in Orest Subtelny, *Ukraine: A History* (Toronto-Buffalo: University of Toronto Press, 1988), and in *The History of Ukrainian Costume from the Scythian Period to the Late 17th Century* (Melbourne: Bayda Books, 1986).

Chapter 8 Music

A good introduction to the history of Jewish music is the article on "Music" in *Encyclopedia Judaica* (1973). The classic and pioneering work by A.Z. Idelsohn, *Jewish Music in its Histor-*

ical Development (New York: Dover, 1929) still contains a huge amount of interesting material, even though later scholars often disagree with Idelsohn's attempts to prove the existence of an original core of Semitic-Oriental Jewish music. Even richer in material for those who can read musical notation is the ten-volume *Thesaurus of Hebrew Oriental Melodies*, which Idelsohn collected all around the world and published between 1922 and 1934. More up to date and more critical but also more limited in geographical scope are Eric Werner, *A Voice Still Heard: The Sacred Songs of the Ashkenazic Jews* (University Park: State University of Pennsylvania Press, 1976); and Hanoch Avenery, *The Ashkenazi Tradition of Biblical Chant between 1500 and 1900: Documentation and Musical Analysis* (Tel Aviv, 1978). For Sephardic music there is the huge collection of musical examples in Isaac Levy, *Liturgia Judeo-Espanola*, 11 volumes, 1965-80. A recent summary on Jewish musical traditions throughout the world is Amnon Shiloah, *Jewish Musical Traditions* (Detroit: Wayne State University Press, 1992). Much Jewish music is available on tapes and cassettes from numerous different sources.

Chapter 9 *Appearance and Ancestry*

The best overall summary of the question of Jewish physical ancestry is probably Raphael Patai and Jennifer Wing Patai, *The Myth of the Jewish Race* (New York: Scribners, 1975). Still containing much interesting detail despite its age is Maurice Fishberg, *The Jews: A Study of Race and Environment* (London-New York, Scribners: 1911). [For a fascinating discussion of how Jewish authors dealt with the tricky issue of "the Jewish race" in the early twentieth century see John Efron, *Defenders of the Race: Jewish Doctors and Race Science in Fin-de-Siecle Europe* (New Haven: Yale University Press, 1994)].

Some works that take up the question of Jewish ancestry in a scientific manner [and often reach very different conclusions from each other] are: A.E. Mourant, "Blood Groups of the Jews," *Jewish Journal of Sociology* (1959), 155-176; and Batsheva Bonné-Tamir and Avinoam Adam, *Genetic Diversity among Jews: Diseases and Markers at the DNA Level* (Oxford University Press: New York, 1992).

On the ancestry of Jewish priests [Cohanim] early results are published in Karl Skorecki et al., "Y Chromosomes of Jewish Priests," *Nature*, vol. 385 (2 January 1997), p. 32. This article is followed up by Neil Bradman and Mark G. Thomas, "Genetics: The Pursuit of Jewish History by Other Means," in *Judaism Today* 10 (Autumn 1998), 4-6.

Credits

2.1   Beth Hatefutsoth Photo Archive, Tel Aviv. Courtesy of Rivka Avshalomov, Israel.

2.2   Reproduced by courtesy of The U. Nahon Museum of Italian Jewish Art, Jerusalem.

5.1   Reproduced by courtesy of The U. Nahon Museum of Italian Jewish Art, Jerusalem.

5.2   Photo © The Israel Museum, Jerusalem/ David Harris.

5.3   Skirball Cultural Center, Museum Collection, 58.8. Photography by Lelo Carter.

5.4   Skirball Cultural Center, Museum Collection, 47.16. Photography by Lelo Carter.

5.5   Skirball Cultural Center, Museum Collection. Museum purchase with funds provided by The Maurice Amado Foundation at the behest of the Tarica Family. 57.6. Collection. Photography by Susan Einstein.

5.6   © Beth Hatefutsoth Photo Archive, Israel.

5.7   Skirball Cultural Center, Museum Collection, 56.491. Photography by Lelo Carter.

5.8   Skirball Cultural Center, Museum Collection, 56.5. Photography by Susan Einstein.

5.9   Aryeh Kaplan, *Tefillin, G-d, Man and Tefillin* (New York: National Council of Synagogue Youth, 1975). Used by permission of the National Conference of Synagogue Youth.

5.10 From Chaim Raphael, *A Feast of History*: *Passover through the Ages as a Key to Jewish Experience*. New York: Simon and Schuster, 1972.

5.11 From Joseph Toledano, *L'Esprit du Mellah*. Courtesy of Joseph Toledano, Jerusalem.

5.12 Photo: Joan Roth, New York. © Joan Roth, New York. Photo courtesy of Beth Hatefutsoth Photo Archive, Tel Aviv.

5.13 Photo: Joan Roth, New York. © Joan Roth, New York. Photo courtesy of Beth Hatefutsoth Photo Archive, Tel Aviv.

5.14 Skirball Cultural Center, Museum Collection, 2.59. Photography by LeloCarter.

5.15 By permission of Ruth Guggenheim, Zurich.

5.16 Photo © The Israel Museum, Jerusalem.

5.17 From *The Jewish Marriage Anthology* by Philip and Hanna Goodman (Philadelphia: The Jewish Publication Society, 1965, used by permission.

5.18 From *The Jewish Marriage Anthology* by Philip and Hanna Goodman (Philadelphia: The Jewish Publication Society, 1965). Used by permission.

5.19 Photo © The Israel Museum, Jerusalem.

5.20 Photo © The Israel Museum, Jerusalem.

5.21 © Beth Hatefutsoth Photo Archive, Israel.

5.22 © Beth Hatefutsoth Photo Archive, Israel. Courtesy of Shuta Bustanashvili.

6.1   From the Archives of the YIVO Institute for Jewish Research.

7.1   From *Tradition: Orthodox Jewish Life in America* by Mal Warshaw (Copyright © 1976 by Mal Warshaw). Reprinted by permission of Schocken Books, a division of Random House, Inc.

7.2   From David Landau, *Piety and Power: The World of Jewish Fundamentalism* (New York: Hill and Wang, 1993). Photo by Flash 90.

7.3   Photo by Carl Rathjens, courtesy of Beth Hatefutsoth Photo Archive, Israel. Copyright: Hamburg Museum of Ethnography.

7.4   From *Les Costumes Populaires de la Turquie en 1873* by Osman Hamdy Bey (Constantinople, Levant Times & Shipping Gazette, 1873)].

7.5   Drawing by Johann Jacob Schudt, *Jüdische Merckwürdigkeiten* (Frankfurt and Leipzig, 1714, from Ruth Gay, *The Jews of Germany* (New Haven: Yale University Press, 1992).

7.6   Courtesy of the Leo Baeck Institute, New York.

7.7   Illustration from the Dresden manuscript "Dresden Sachsenspiegel," Germany, 1220-1235. Courtesy of Sächsische Landesbibliothek, Dresden, Mscr. Dresd M32. Photo courtesy of Beth Hatefutsoth Photo Archive, Tel Aviv.

7.8   Courtesy of Aviva Muller-Lancet, Jerusalem.

7.9   From *Les Costumes Populaires de la Turquie en 1873* by Osman Hamdy Bey (Constantinople, Levant Times & Shipping Gazette, 1873).

7.10 By permission of Jean-Pierre Allali, Paris. Photo courtesy of Beth Hatefutsoth Photo Archive, Tel Aviv.

7.11 Beth Hatefutsoth Photo Archive, Tel Aviv. Courtesy of Sara Ben Tolila, Israel.

7.12 By permission of [X]. Photo courtesy of Beth Hatefutsoth Photo Archive, Tel Aviv.

7.13 From Alfred Rubens, *A History of Jewish Costume* (New York: Funk and Wagnalls, 1967).

7.14 From Alfred Rubens, *A History of Jewish Costume*, (New York: Funk and Wagnalls, 1967).

7.15 From Alfred Rubens, *A History of Jewish Costume* (New York: Funk and Wagnalls, 1967).

7.16 Courtesy of Dan Arnon, photographer, Petah Tikva, Israel.

7.17 Courtesy of Dan Arnon, photographer, Petah Tikva, Israel.

7.18 From the Archives of the YIVO Institute for Jewish Research.

7.19   Photo © The Israel Museum, Jerusalem

7.20   Credit: Beatrice Silverman Weinreich, New York.

7.21   From Alfred Rubens, *A History of Jewish Costume* (New York: Funk and Wagnalls, 1967).

7.22   From *Ukraine: A History* by Orest Subtelny (Toronto: University of Toronto Press, 1988). By permission of the author.

7.23   From *Behold a Great Image*, the Jewish Publication Society, 1978. Used by permission.

8.1   From Eric Werner, *A Voice Still Heard...The Sacred Songs of the Ashkenazic Jews* (Pennsylvania State University Press, 1976). By permission of Leo Baeck Institute, New York.

8.2   From A. W. Binder, *Biblical Chant* (New York: Philosophical Library,1959, p.20-21). By permission of the Philosophical Library, New York.

8.3   From *Jewish Music In its Historical Development* by A.Z. Idelsohn ©1929 by Henry Holt and Company Inc. Reprinted by permission of Henry Holt & Company, LLC.

8.4   From *Jewish Music in Its Historical Development* by A.Z. Idelsohn ©1929 by Henry Holt and Company Inc. Reprinted by permission of Henry Holt & Company, LLC.

8.5   From *Jewish Music in Its Historical Development* by A.Z. Idelsohn ©1929 by Henry Holt and Company Inc. Reprinted by permission of Henry Holt & Company, LLC.

8.6   From Eric Werner, *A Voice Still Heard...The Sacred Songs of the Ashkenazic Jews* (Pennsylvania State University Press, 1976). By permission of Leo Baeck Institute, New York.

8.7   From Leon Algazi, *Chants Sephardis* (London: World Sephardi Federation, 1958, p. 36). By permission of World Sephardi Federation, Jerusalem.

8.8   From Leon Algazi, *Chants Sephardis* (London: World Sephardi Federation, 1958, p.50). By permission of World Sephardi Federation, Jerusalem.

8.9   From the Archives of the YIVO Institute for Jewish Research.

9.1   From Elvira Bauer, *Trau keinem Fuchs auf grüner Heid und keinem Jud bei seinem Eid. Ein Bilderbuch für Gross und Klein.* [Don't trust any fox on the green meadow or any Jew on his oath. A picture book for young and old.] (Stürmer Verlag, 1936). Photo reproduction courtesy of Simon Wiesenthal Center, Los Angeles.

9.2   From the Becker Collection, Institute of Contemporary History and Wiener Library, London. By permission.

9.3   Courtesy of The Jewish Museum in Prague.

9.4   Photo © The Israel Museum, Jerusalem.

9.5   From *The Jewish Wedding in Bagdad and Its Filiations: Customs and Ceremonies, Documents and Songs, Costumes and Jewelry* by Itzhak Avishur, Volume 1 (Haifa: University of Haifa, 1990).

9.6   From *The Jews of Aden: A Community That Was* by Reuben Ahroni (Tel Aviv: Afikim, 1991).

9.7   From *The Last Jews of Cochin: Jewish Identity in Hindu India* by Nathan Katz and Ellen S. Goldberg (Columbia: University of South Carolina Press, 1993).

9.8   Photo: Doron Bacher, Israel. © Beth Hatefutsoth Photo Archive, Israel.

9.9   Photo: Doron Bacher, Israel. © Beth Hatefutsoth Photo Archive, Israel.

10.1   Used by permission of Herbert S. Lewis, Madison, Wisconsin.

10.2   From Chaim Raphael, *A Feast of History: Passover through the Ages as a Key to Jewish Experience*. New York: Simon and Schuster, 1972. [permission info to come]

10.3   Photographer: Frédéric Brenner. © Frédéric Brenner.

Recipes

Cholent: From *The Spice and Spirit of Kosher-Jewish Cooking*, Lubavitch Women's Organization, 1977.

Schalet: From Marie Elsässer, *Ausführliches Kochbuch für die einfache und feine jüdische Küche unter Berücksichtingung aller rituellen Vorschriften*. Frankfurt: Verlag von J. Kauffmann, 1911.

Gruenkernsuppe: From Marie Elsässer, *Ausführliches Kochbuch für die einfache und feine jüdische Küche unter Berücksichtingung aller rituellen Vorschriften*. Frankfurt: Verlag von J. Kauffmann, 1911.

S'kina: From *Sephardic Cooking* by Copeland Marks, copyright © 1992 by Copeland Marks. Used by permission of Donald I. Fine, an imprint of Penguin Putnam Inc.

T'fina: From *Sephardic Cooking* by Copeland Marks, copyright © 1992 by Copeland Marks. Used by permission of Donald I. Fine, an imprint of Penguin Putnam Inc.

T'beet: From *Sephardic Cooking* by Copeland Marks, copyright © 1992 by Copeland Marks. Used by permission of Donald I. Fine, an imprint of Penguin Putnam Inc.

Huevos haminados: From *Cooking the Sephardic Way*, Sephardic Sisterhood, Temple Tifereth Israel, 1971, p. 35. Recipe by Lianne Donnell of Rhodes. By permission of Sephardic Sisterhood, Temple Tifereth Israel.

Jerusalem Kugel: From *The Spice and Spirit of Kosher-Jewish Cooking*, Lubavitch Women's Organization, 1977.

Mina de cordero: From *Cooking the Sephardic Way*, Sephardic Sisterhood, Temple Tifereth Israel, 1971, p. 133. Recipe by Victoria Arditti Benezra of Izmir. By permission of Sephardic Sisterhood, Temple Tifereth Israel.

Matzeklöss: From Marie Elsässer, *Ausführliches Kochbuch für die einfache und feine jüdische Küche unter Berucksichtingung aller rituellen Vorschriften*. Frankfurt: Verlag von J. Kauffmann, 1911.

Passover Soup: From *Sephardic Cooking* by Copeland Marks, copyright © 1992 by Copeland Marks. Used by permission of Donald I. Fine, an imprint of Penguin Putnam Inc.

Hamin: From Marie Elsässer, *Ausführliches Kochbuch für die einfache und feine jüdische Küche unter Berücksichtingung aller rituellen Vorschriften*. Frankfurt: Verlag von J. Kauffmann, 1911.

Latkes: From *The Spice and Spirit of Kosher-Jewish Cooking*, Lubavitch Women's Organization, 1977.

Bimuelos: From *Cooking the Sephardic Way*, Sephardic Sisterhood, Temple Tifereth Israel, 1971, p. 123. Recipe by Lianne Donnell. By permission of Sephardic Sisterhood, Temple Tifereth Israel.

Cheese Blintzes: From *The Spice and Spirit of Kosher-Jewish Cooking*, Lubavitch Women's Organization, 1977.

Kasha Knishes: From *The Spice and Spirit of Kosher-Jewish Cooking*, Lubavitch Women's Organization, 1977.

Cheese Borekas: From *Sephardic Cooking* by Copeland Marks, copyright © 1992 by Copeland Marks. Used by permission of Donald I. Fine, an imprint of Penguin Putnam Inc.

Malawach: From *Sephardic Cooking* by Copeland Marks, copyright © 1992 by Copeland Marks. Used by permission of Donald I. Fine, an imprint of Penguin Putnam Inc.

Sambusak: From *Sephardic Cooking* by Copeland Marks, copyright © 1992 by Copeland Marks. Used by permission of Donald I. Fine, an imprint of Penguin Putnam Inc.

Carciofi alla guidia: From *Essentials of Classic Italian Cooking* by Marcella Hazan. © 1992 by Marcella Hazan. Reprinted by permission of Alfred A. Knopf, Inc.

Index